Brilliant Leadership

The need for restructuring and transforming business practices for the benefit of humanity and the environment is a major theme of this book. Interactivity and connectedness of people and things/data are transforming everything. Many organizations, even the traditional ones, have entered a process of transformation through innovation and rethinking their business models, which affects the way leaders communicate, lead, and co-create.

Brilliant leadership is a new intellectual framework to guide strategists, game changers, senior executives, and aspiring leaders. This new framework is based on our current work on leadership development and focuses on what it means to become a brilliant leader. Brilliant leaders have an authentic personality, the willingness to engage people/ teams, inspire others, facilitate (co-)innovation, commit to making significant contributions (humanity, environment, ethics), and be relevant. The framework is also consistent with the United Nations Sustainable Development Goals (SDG) of ensuring inclusive and equitable quality education, fostering innovation, and developing a lifelong learning mindset.

Each chapter of the book is more than a collection of ideas. It is a part of the new intellectual framework that describes "Brilliant Leadership." Each chapter includes a distinct contribution by experts and that, at the same time, is connected to other chapters through the book's organizing schema, paralleling how the different facets of leadership are inseparable from one another. Together, the chapters present a holistic view of what it means to become a brilliant leader in the transformative digital age. The framework demonstrates this connectivity through a theoretical framework (our model) and a plan (book chapters) of how to approach the specific research inquiry, the tenets of brilliant leadership.

What makes this new edition unique? The book is aimed at providing practical strategies and becoming a source of inspiration for what it means to have a new leadership mindset – a brilliant leader who understands how to communicate with empathy and authenticity, engage and inspire others, shift responsibility into shared commitment, and spark learning in a purpose-driven innovation culture.

Brilliant Leadership

Unlocking the Power of
Innovation-Communication

Edited by
Alan T. Belasen, Ph.D. and Nicole Pfeffermann, Ph.D.

A PRODUCTIVITY PRESS BOOK

First published 2025
by Routledge
605 Third Avenue, New York, NY 10158

and by Routledge
4 Park Square, Milton Park, Abingdon, Oxon, OX14 4RN

Routledge is an imprint of the Taylor & Francis Group, an informa business

Library of Congress Cataloging-in-Publication Data
Names: Belasen, Alan T., 1951- editor. | Pfeffermann, Nicole, editor.
Title: Brilliant leadership : unlocking the power of
innovation-communication / edited by Alan T. Belasen, Ph.D. and Nicole
Pfeffermann, Ph.D..
Description: New York, NY : Routledge, 2025. | Includes bibliographical
references and index. | Identifiers: LCCN 2024031008 (print) | LCCN 2024031009 (ebook) | ISBN
9781032800769 (hardback) | ISBN 9781032800752 (paperback) | ISBN
9781003495307 (ebook)
Subjects: LCSH: Leadership. | Creative ability in business. | Communication
in management.
Classification: LCC HD57.7 .B748974 2025 (print) | LCC HD57.7 (ebook) |
DDC 658.4/092--dc23/eng/20240719
LC record available at https://lccn.loc.gov/2024031008
LC ebook record available at https://lccn.loc.gov/2024031009

ISBN: 9781032800769 (hbk)
ISBN: 9781032800752 (pbk)
ISBN: 9781003495307 (ebk)

DOI: 10.4324/9781003495307

Typeset in Adobe Garamond
by Deanta Global Publishing Services, Chennai, India

This book is dedicated to new leaders, pioneers, and game changers who inspire innovation and (co)create an invaluable future for humanity. It is a dedication to embracing a human-centered leadership, to see the realm of what can be possible, to the discovery of the unknown, and to the awareness-driven impact that new leaders can make. Personal growth, development, and communication go hand in hand and keep innovation alive. They are at the heart of brilliant leadership.

Nicole Pfeffermann

To Amy Belasen Draheim, President and Founder of ABD Creative, for sparking innovation in the ever-changing hospitality industry by embracing new ways of thinking, marketing, and driving results for independent hotels and restaurants. Amy is a brilliant leader.

Alan T. Belasen

Contents

Foreword

It's common wisdom that you can't judge a book by its cover. But judging this book by its cover... it has the mark of a must-read. *Brilliant Leadership: Unlocking the Power of Innovation-Communication.* Can readers resist the temptation to take a look behind the cover?

Then, the real question is, did we need another book on leadership, even one with a captivating title?

Having read it, my answer is yes. Definitely yes.

In my 25 years of experience in leadership writing, teaching, and consulting – primarily in healthcare and arguably the most complex sector – it's been a thought-provoking occasion to read about robust theoretical frameworks for the new normality that the leadership of modern organizations is facing.

Technology, millennials, glocalization, diversity, and pluralism are among the salient factors that call for a change in the way leadership is framed and acted, particularly with regard to engaging people to "unleash the aspirational capital in organizational members." How desirable is this goal and yet how difficult is it to achieve? All the more important is the drive to pursue it.

This is what we expect from brilliant leadership. This is what readers will understand from reading this book, with its focus on the skill sets for acquiring the leadership style that can brilliantly "spark engagement and innovation."

Belasen and Pfeffermann have written, collected and edited series of great chapters that shed light on the organizational traps that hinder business performance and limit the potentialities of its human capital. Triangulations, toxic cycles, power misuse, gamesmanship, and reactivity, the five capital sins of organizations with poor leadership, are denoted by

- Lack of courage (and personal responsibility/accountability)
- Silo thinking (culture clash, heroism syndrome)
- Leader– follower relationship (no listening, judgmental posture, and retaliation)
- The magic circle (adverse selection of collaborators, evaluation bias)
- Reactive rather than proactive strategies (defense walls, last-minute changes)

An encyclopedia of horrors you might say. Which, unfortunately, notwithstanding 70 years of leadership research and teaching, are still common in most cases and contexts. Not just ineffective leadership but also one that is liable to fail in the new normality of up-and-coming cohorts of managers and employees within the ranks of millennials and Gen Zs. Extremely challenging to engage because they value meaningful motivation, these young people aim for goals that further meaningful work rather than monetary gain, question the hierarchical status quo, prefer working across multiple functions, place importance on relationships with superiors they can connect to as mentors, are open and adaptive to change and embrace it, have a passion for learning, are receptive to feedback and recognition, and value teamwork and social interaction in the workplace.

The authors offer advice for leaders wanting to stay clear of the five traps. Their frameworks on "skill set for overcoming the disempowering transactions" is brilliant, as is the in-depth discussion of the key factors – objectivity, engagement, maturity, connection, attunement – that should be heeded to avoid falling victim to the traps. Readers take heed.

In my experience and personal vocabulary, these factors are central to the leadership that distinguishes great chiefs from poor bosses.

1. *Lead from the front and walk the talk.* Courage and coherence are always the right mix.
2. *Curiosity instead of problemistic search.* Problemistic search is reactive behavior. If and only if the problem is perceived as such – i.e., awareness and urgency are recognized – then action can be taken. Conversely, we expect leaders to have a proactive posture. Issues need to be addressed before they become problems.
3. *Look through the window or look into the mirror.* A metaphor taken from the factory context: if performance is good, the merit should go to collaborators (look through the window), whereas if performance is unsatisfactory, the responsibility lies with the leader (look into the mirror). The basis for a workplace environment with high psychological safety.
4. *1 + 1 = 3.* The power of teamwork.
5. *Future-pulled rather than past-pushed.* Never play the retention of solutions. Retention of solutions refers to the natural tendency to search in one's own experience for solutions to problems. Organizations, like people, are largely driven by the past rather than pulled by the future. However, leaders are expected to be naturally inclined to explore innovation, benchmark against competitors, and infuse their organizations with the latest trends. That includes studying others and adopting positive and lateral thinking.

Exploring the issues from different angles, with surprising perspectives, with a robust research background, and with passion and rigor, the book will help readers become more aware of what it takes to be a leader who will step up to the challenges posed by the new normality of innovation-engagement.

Readers will find abundant opportunities for their own gap analysis of personal strengths and weaknesses that helps new leaders to become mindful of their weaknesses, initiate self-development efforts, and model the way for continuous improvement.

This is done by combining a reflective and innovative leadership style characterized by interdisciplinarity, out-of-the-box thinking, purpose-based and through mastering of conceptual frameworks and pragmatic skills underpinning the know-how to handle the paradoxes, and competing tensions and conflicts that physiologically impact on decision-making.

Only leaders who are self-aware and well equipped with what the authors describe as the new leadership mindset will be well positioned to meet conflicting expectations and aspirations in running their organization. They will come under public scrutiny as they contend with arduous trade-offs between stability and innovation, market success and social recognition, financial performance, and long-term growth.

Pluralism is taking place throughout modern organizations. All organizations are pluralistic to some degree. Pluralism has its origins in external and internal pressure on organizations. For instance, many external stakeholders apply severe pressures that affect an organization's strategy. Citizens through their associations seek and demand higher-quality services. Governments call attention to social needs. Industry associations monitor for compliance with norms and regulations. External pluralistic pressure can result in objectives that are contradictory with one another or unclear in purpose, generating ambiguity, thus ensuing barriers to strategic change initiatives or triggering strategic dilution or paralysis.

Here, again, is where the book provides readers with the tools to gain a better grasp of the challenges ahead for leaders and how such challenges can be analyzed through an adapted Competing Value Framework (CVF). The original CVF delineated complementary leadership mindsets and roles: on one side, the visioner and motivator, when acting as a transformational agent and relying on intangible-intrinsic sources of motivation to engage employees, while on the other side, the analyst and taskmaster, when acting as a transactional agent working through incentive systems, rules, and policies to achieve conformance from employees.

Research has clearly identified transformational leadership as the style best equipped for meeting current challenges, considering the ambiguity in decision-making and the expectations of the new cohort of employees (millennials and Gen Zs). More and more, transactional leadership is perceived as a function of management rather than its guide. The core difference resides in the fact that leading is a process of influencing goals and motivation, whereas managing is a process of delivering results, in essence, doing the right things versus doing things right. One is a leader because subordinates follow, not vice versa.

In this light, leadership is about the big picture, while management is about the details. Leaders engage in sensemaking, have vision and ambition, seek synthesis. Managers problem-solve through analysis. They focus on performance and execution. Leadership sets its sights on long-term horizons and strategic focus. Management has short-term goals and responsibility for day-to-day operations.

That is why leading with visionary capacity in the new normality demands the new mindset and skills that readers will find in this book. As the authors state,

> Brilliant leaders have the know-how to handle paradoxes and competing tensions. They invest in digital technology (structures, processes) to integrate the organization optimally while considering learning and development (employees, teams); they use strategic imagination to initiate disruptive innovation (markets, customers) while addressing the impact of their initiatives on customers, partners, and stakeholders (industries, competitors).

Leaders are able to understand the details that make the difference, to understand that "to be ready for AI means to become aware of the subtle differences in leading a digitalized business or building an AI-driven business."

A different new CVF leadership framework is then developed as the core structure of the book. It's built around four categories designed to capture leadership qualities and behaviors associated with strategy innovation, open innovation, cultural innovation, and business innovation, and the dynamic interplay between these factors. By focusing on these key areas of work, leaders can become brilliant leaders, grow their capability to effectively navigate disruptive times, and lead through complexity.

Each chapter of the book addresses these contents in detail and provides direction to improve the key qualities necessary to become a brilliant leader, a great innovator, and a communicator.

My spoiler alerts and praise end here.

My compliments go to Alan and Nicole for editing this volume and to the authors. They are to be commended for their insightful contributions.

To them, to this book, to all readers, *ad maiora*.

Federico Lega, PhD
Professor of Healthcare Management
University of Milan
Department of Biomedical Sciences for Health
Director CRC HEAD, Milan School of Management
Director MSc in Health Management (MASS)
Editor in Chief HSMR Sage
Board member EHMA

Acknowledgments

I would like to express my special thanks of gratitude to my co-editor Dr. Alan T. Belasen for his supportive, open-minded collaborative work. My thanks also go to all authors for taking the time to contribute a chapter. I would like to thank my loved ones for their support in writing the book. Lastly, I would like to thank all supporters and readers of my publications for motivating me to express my ideas and share another book with the world.

Nicole Pfeffermann

This book benefited from feedback and suggestions of many colleagues from numerous networks and affiliates including the *Management Education and Development, Gender and Diversity in Organizations, and Healthcare Management* divisions of the Academy of Management.

Special thanks go to my co-editor Dr. Nicole Pfeffermann, whose insights, ideas, and passion about how the new leadership paradigm should guide strategists, game changers, senior executives, and aspiring leaders helped shape the aims and scope of *Brilliant Leadership*. Many thanks to Dr. Federico Lega for his eloquent "Foreword" to the book and his confidence in how the book's framework helps chart the new theory and practice of brilliant leaders who cope with the complexity of the digital transformation through a purposeful, human-centric approach.

I would like to acknowledge the many contributors to this important book. Not only did they offer their depth of knowledge, but they also did believe in the importance and universal appeal of *Brilliant Leadership*. Their diverse perspectives and rich experiences helped make this book interdisciplinary and global, and drove the message that brilliant leaders inspire others, spark engagement and innovation, make significant contributions to humanity, the environment, and ethics in organizations, and are relevant.

Special thanks go to Kristine Mednansky, Acquisitions Editor, Taylor & Francis Group, who believed in the message and relevance of this book project. As with my previous books, Kris was instrumental in moving this book project through the various production phases.

My wife Susan provided the social and emotional support as well as the sounding board for many of the ideas in this book. Being surrounded by my five A's has always been rewarding and intellectually stimulating. Ari, PhD, an accomplished scholar and professor of economics at SIUE; Amy, an accomplished author, founder of ABD Creative Agency, podcast host, digital marketing expert, and a successful travel blogger; Anat, PhD, Ecology & Evolutionary Biology, NSF Postdoctoral Research Fellow in Biology, UT Austin Department of Integrative Biology; Amanda, a client service specialist in a global organization; and Abigail, MD, a hospitalist at Albany Medical Center. I am indebted to everyone.

Alan T. Belasen

Contributors

Alan T. Belasen holds a PhD from Rockefeller College, SUNY. For over 30 years, Belasen has been involved in executive education and development programs in the United States and abroad in startups, business enterprises, multinational companies, nonprofits, government agencies, academic institutions, and healthcare organizations. Belasen chaired the MBA Program at SUNY, Empire State College from 2004 to 2015 where he designed and supervised the implementation of the MBA in Management, MBA in Global Leadership, MBA in Healthcare Leadership, and MBA Pathway for Veterans.

Belasen has written over 150 journal articles, book chapters, and conference papers on topics such as executive education, self-managed teams, HR competencies, work motivation, women's leadership, communication innovation, corruption in business, trusted leadership, healthcare management, and leadership development.

Belasen's research papers appear in the *International Journal of Strategic Communication; The Journal of Healthcare Management; Journal of Racial and Ethnic Health Disparities; International Journal for Quality in Health Care; Gender in Management: an International Journal; The Journal of Health Administration Education; Leadership & Organization Development Journal; Journal of Human Resource Management; International Journal of Human Resources Development and Management; The Atlantic Journal of Communication; The International Journal of Leadership Studies, Journal of Economic Modeling; Journal of Management Development; Journal of Health Organization and Management; International Journal of Sport Marketing & Sponsorship; Journal for Advancing Business Education;* and the *Proceedings of the Academy of Management.*

Alan T. Belasen's books include the following:

Transforming Leadership, Improving Patient Experience: Communication Strategies for Driving Patient Satisfaction (Routledge, 2024); *Resilience in Healthcare Leadership: Practical Strategies and Self-Assessment Tools* (Routledge, 2022); *Dyad Leadership and Clinical Integration: Driving Change, Aligning Strategies* (HAP, 2019); *Women in Management: A Framework for Sustainable Work-life Integration* (Routledge, 2017); *Confronting Corruption in Business: Trusted Leadership, Civic Engagement* (Routledge,

2016); *Mastering Leadership: A Vital Resource for Healthcare Managers* (Jones & Bartlett Learning, 2015); *Developing Women Leaders in Corporate America: Balancing Competing Demands, Transcending Traditional Boundaries* (Praeger, 2012); *The Theory and Practice of Corporate Communication: A Competing Values Perspective* (Sage, 2008); and *Leading the Learning Organization: Communication and Competencies for Managing Change* (SUNY Press, 2000).

Belasen received the Outstanding Reviewer Award from the Academy of Management in 2000, 2001, 2010, 2011, 2016, 2017, 2018, 2019, 2022, and 2023. He is the recipient of the 2017 John L. Green Award for Excellence in Business Education, The International Accreditation Council for Business Education (IACBE); 2014–2015 SUNY Chancellors' Award for Scholarship and Creative Activities; and the 2003–2004 SUNY Empire State College'sTurbenAward for Excellence in Scholarship.

Lara Bertola holds a PhD in Organizational Psychology from ESCP Paris I Sorbonne, France, a PsyD in Clinical Psychology from the University of Turin, Italy, and an MA in Industrial Psychology from the same university. She is a certified psychotherapist and psychologist with a strong background in both clinical and industrial psychology. As an Assistant Professor in the Organizational Behavior and HR program at Rennes School of Business, Rennes, France, Bertola shapes curriculum, designs programs, and develops instructional materials. Bertola's professional contributions extend far beyond academia. As a scientific consultant, she actively engages in organizational projects, leading various national and international employee survey initiatives. Her insights and recommendations, based on her extensive expertise, are instrumental in guiding strategic decisions and fostering positive organizational outcomes.

Jaap Boonstra is Professor of Organizational Dynamics and Leadership at Esade Business School in Barcelona and Professor of Organizational Change at the Rotterdam School of Management of Erasmus University. Prior to that he worked as a professor of Organizational Change and Learning at the University of Amsterdam (The Netherlands) and as Dean of Sioo, Interuniversity Center for Organizational Change and Learning (The Netherlands). As a non-executive board member and an independent consultant, Jaap supports social organizations and global alliances in their development. Jaap was involved as an advisor in the development of the Global Alliance for Banking on Values. He has written many articles and several books on transformational change, innovation in organizations, organizational culture, and leadership. His most influential books are *Alliances for Sustainable Futures* (Edward Elgar, 2023), *Change as Collaborative Play* (Boom, 2019), *Cultural Change and Leadership in Organizations* (Wiley, 2013), *Intervening and Changing* (Wiley, 2007), and *Dynamics of Organizational Change and Learning* (Wiley, 2004).

Aurelie Cnop is Researcher and Guest Lecturer in Organizational Behavior at the London School of Economics and Political Science (LSE) and Imperial College London. With a background that includes over a decade of teaching Negotiation Skills, Managing People and Teams, and serving as the Academic Director of the Specialized Master's program in Digital Transformation and Leadership at ESCP Europe Business School, Cnop combines practical and theoretical expertise. She holds an MSc in Business Engineering from the University of Louvain and both an MSc and a PhD in Organizational Behavior from LSE. Her research explores the impact of employee contributions on leadership, team engagement, and well-being, particularly in high-pressure situations. With more than 15 years of experience in strategy consulting for global firms like Novartis Consumer Health, DHL, and Santander, she now advises UK governmental and digital sector organizations, aiming to enhance their strategic performance and leadership excellence.

Amy Eisenberg consults with hospital systems with the goal of helping practitioners manage patient interactions more effectively. With her team, Eisenberg also trains health professionals in effective end-of-life conversations, including guiding ethical choices and communicating empathically. Eisenberg's model was published in Academic Medicine, which was based on her pilot work at Jersey Shore Medical Center/Meridian Health System and the Atlantic Health System. She has written and produced two plays: *Anna's Story*, an adaptation of the Atlantic Health System short film of the same name, about the need for end-of-life decision-making, and *A Tear in the Universe*, illustrating the emotional experience of medical students. Eisenberg developed *It Couldn't Happen to Me*, a series of videos with a coordinated training program, sponsored by the American Medical Association, about the perils of prescription drug abuse.

Barry Eisenberg has 40 years of experience in healthcare management, consulting, and higher education. He established and directed a management development program at Memorial-Sloan Kettering Cancer Center in New York, and later served as Vice President of human resources and then as Vice President of administration/operations in a New Jersey-based hospital. In addition to directing SUNY Empire State University's MBA in Healthcare Leadership, Eisenberg consults with health care organizations on strategic planning, mergers and acquisitions, market expansion, and board of directors' development. Eisenberg is co-author of *Mastering Leadership: A Vital Resource for Healthcare Organizations and Transforming Leadership, Improving the Patient Experience: Communication Strategies for Driving Patient Satisfaction* as well as many articles and book chapters on healthcare management. He also maintains a blog with a wide distribution: https://barryeisenbergauthor.com/blog. Eisenberg serves on the boards of multiple nonprofit organizations dedicated to expanding access to scholarship, social justice, and promoting arts education.

Cherrelle Hall is a higher education practitioner and researcher, with more than a decade of experience in higher education. She is currently pursuing an EdD in educational leadership and change from SUNY Empire State University. Hall has published research on the Covid-19 pandemic's impact on student loans in the *Journal of Higher Education Policy and Leadership Studies*. Her research interests include leadership development in higher education for women of color; student financial literacy and college access for underrepresented student populations; diversity, equity, and inclusion in higher education institutions; minorities and gender in higher education; and higher education policy.

Tim Mazzarol is Emeritus Professor and Senior Honorary Research Fellow at the University of Western Australia where his research focuses on entrepreneurship, innovation, small business management, marketing, strategy, commercialization, and the co-operative and mutual enterprise business model. He is a Qualified Professional Researcher with the Australian Research Society, and the Coordinator of the Co-operative Enterprise Research Unit (CERU), at UWA. Tim is also the founder and Director of the Centre for Entrepreneurial Management and Innovation (CEMI), and a founder Director and Company Secretary of the Commercialization Studies Centre (CSC) Ltd., a not-for-profit public company dedicated to encouraging best practice in commercialization. He is the author of several books on entrepreneurship, small business management, and innovation. His research has been published internationally. He holds a PhD in Management and an MBA with distinction from Curtin University of Technology, and a Bachelor of Arts with Honors from Murdoch University, Western Australia.

Andrew Mountfield has over 25 years of experience in strategy and performance management across a wide range of industries and business functions and research in the field of strategy, leadership, and change. He has worked as a Manager in the pharmaceutical industry, as a Partner at PwC Consulting, and was country CEO of Horváth management consultants in Switzerland. He completed his research master's at HEC Paris and Oxford University and received his doctorate from Ashridge Business School. In addition, he has completed graduate degrees at the Cambridge Institute for Sustainability Leadership (CISL) and Bocconi SDA, Milan. Andrew is currently a senior research fellow at Saïd Business School, Oxford University, where he leads the Oxford Rethinking Performance Initiative, and is a guest lecturer at CISL. He is the editor of two volumes on strategy and performance management and is the lead author of three recent book chapters on sustainability strategy and implementation.

Mariana Ortega is an executive coach who possesses deep values of relationship building, inclusion, and human-centered leadership. She spent 20+ years leading corporate learning and development across various industries, including ed tech (Amplify

Education), entertainment (Sony Music), food and beverage (Godiva Chocolatier), and luxury goods (Ralph Lauren). Mariana holds an MA in Adult Learning from SUNY Empire State University and since 2019 has applied her skills as a certified coach, demonstrating multifaceted abilities that help leaders achieve greater innovation through a human-centered approach that secures and promotes psychological safety. In 2023 she started her private practice, Cultural Compass Coaching & Consulting, where she focuses on coaching first-generation professionals navigating complex career environments. Mariana coaches leaders at every level from organizations such as Comcast, Sony, National FFA, and others, using her insights to guide small, mid-size, and large organizations in strategizing leadership development to secure a robust succession pipeline.

Nicole Pfeffermann has in-depth expertise as a management consultant in digital business, strategy and innovation, and innovation communication and more than 15 years of professional experience in IT-driven innovation management in logistics, (high-) tech markets, and R&D transfer projects. She was Startup Coach and Senior Lecturer in digital business, information and knowledge management, and methodology and Co-editor of the international contributed volumes *Strategy and Communication for Innovation*, *New Leadership in Strategy and Communication*, and *New Leadership Communication—Inspire Your Horizon*, Springer, including book presentations in collaboration with Jacobs University Bremen, Deutsche Post DHL and University of Cambridge, IfM. She holds a Diploma in Business Economics and has an interdisciplinary PhD in Engineering (robotics/automation) at the University of Bremen.

Sophie Reboud is Professor of Entrepreneurship, Strategy and Management of Innovation at the Burgundy School of Business in Dijon, France, and an Honorary Research Fellow at the University of Western Australia. She has 20 years of experience as a researcher and consultant in the field of management and strategy of small firms. Originally trained as an agronomist, she served as a Research Engineer for École Nationale Supérieure des Mines de Paris for five years and completed her PhD there. Sophie's research interests are in the strategic management of innovation and creativity. This includes firms in the food sector and low-tech industries with specific focus on intellectual property and strategy in small firms.

Rosilyn Sanders has a PsyD in Organizational Leadership Psychology with a concentration in Consulting from William James College, Newton, MA, and an MA in Counseling. She is Prosci ADKAR certified Change Management Specialist, and has a Lean Six Sigma Yellow belt certification. Sanders is Assistant Professor in the Industrial Organizational Psychology program at Empire State University, NY, where she is responsible for creating curriculum, program design and development, and instructional design. In addition, Sanders is one of, if not the first, African American woman Organizational Leadership Consulting Psychologists from Arkansas. She is the founder and owner of Sanders Consulting & Associates, LLC, a local consulting agency providing professional development, coaching, and consultation to individuals, teams, and organizations. Sanders is an active member of Blacks in I-O Psychology, American Psychological Association, Division 13 Society of Consulting Psychology, and Alpha Kappa Alpha Sorority Incorporated.

Nicolas Sonder is a partner at PwC and PwC Legal and is responsible for the German legal practice on digital transformation for the public sector. He is the author of a monograph and more than 40 contributions on public business law and member of the government and public services leadership team. He has over 10 years of experience in leadership practices.

Leigh Thompson is the J. Jay Gerber Distinguished Professor of Dispute Resolution and Organizations at the Kellogg School of Management, Northwestern University. An acclaimed researcher, author, and speaker, Thompson's research focuses on negotiation, creativity, and teamwork. Thompson's books include *Negotiating the Sweet Spot: The Art of Leaving Nothing on the Table*, *Creative Conspiracy: The New Rules of Breakthrough Collaboration*, *Making the Team*, *The Mind and Heart of the Negotiator*, *The Truth about Negotiations* and *Stop Spending, Start Managing*. Thompson directs several executive education programs, including Negotiation Mastery Class, Leading High-Impact Teams, High Performance Negotiation Skills, Constructive Collaboration, and Negotiating in a Virtual World. Thompson created several publicly available teaching videos: *Negotiation 101*, *Teamwork 101*, *High Performance Collaboration: Leadership, Teamwork, and Negotiation* (MOOC series with Coursera), as well as, *Is Your Team Slacking? Managing Virtual Teams*, *High-Performance Negotiation Skills for Women*, and *How Brainwriting can Neutralize the Loudmouth*s.

Lisa Unangst is Assistant Professor of higher education leadership at Empire State University. Her research interests include higher education access and experience among displaced learners, as well as comparative and cross-national constructions of "diversity" in higher education. She is Associate Editor of Higher Education Research and Development. Unangst has published in *Comparative Education Review*, the *Journal of Higher Education Policy and Management*, and *Higher Education Policy*, among other outlets. She served as Lead Editor of the 2020 Brill-Sense publication *Refugees and Higher Education: Trans-national Perspectives on Access, Equity, and Internationalization* and is author of the forthcoming Routledge title *Immigrants and Refugees at German Universities: Diversity, Internationalization, and Anticolonial Considerations*.

Chapter 1

What Makes a Brilliant Leader? The New Leadership Mindset

Alan T. Belasen and Nicole Pfeffermann

The need for restructuring and transforming business practices and the influence of leadership for the benefit of humanity and the environment is a major theme of this book. Interactivity and connectedness of people and things/data are transforming everything. Many organizations, even the traditional ones, have entered a process of transformation through innovation and rethinking their business models, which affects the way leaders communicate, lead, and co-create.

New artificial intelligence AI ambitions are also of increasing interest for game changers, strategists, executives, and business and organizational leaders. The shift to real-time internet, human-like robotics, and wearable devices also have a tremendous effect on business strategy and leadership. As a result, innovation-communication is key to those who discover new business opportunities, align their value chain, and develop partner-centric, and AI-driven business models.

This chapter provides an introduction and an updated perspective on new leadership, with a skillset and mindset approach to guide new leaders and present a new framework: Brilliant Leadership. Why is this important? Because leadership has changed. New leadership focuses on the linkage between innovation and communication by empowering and inspiring individuals and teams, raising (brand) awareness, and stimulating conversations with the aim of creating higher values and shaping corporate culture. The development from strategy to innovation is key for thriving and succeeding in the digital-transformative age. It is not about playing a particular role as a leader. It is about having a deep commitment to authenticity, strong self-awareness, and showing up as a leader by being intentional with actions and choices.

DOI: 10.4324/9781003495307-1

According to Deschamps (2020), executives are not just witnessing the change of everything, but they are aware of these new circumstances and focus on the right profiles in their C-suite. New leaders know how to unleash the aspirational capital in organizational members and spark engagement and innovation through communication relationships (Moriarty, 2023) and the creation of communication spaces for inclusive innovation (Alayza & Gonzalez, 2023) so that employees from all backgrounds and with different talents, insights, skills, and abilities feel respected and are fully recognized (Fortin & Fry, 2023; Sonder, 2023).

Leadership communication has shifted from a classical, hierarchical-informative style to a new authentic and inspiring communication style that is also interactive and purpose-driven (Cnop, 2023; Darnell & Parish, 2023). New leaders have the responsibility to lead with respect and integrity, communicate with clarity and purpose, win over stakeholders, and influence markets. Hence, communication is a critical success factor for new leaders to bring forward new ideas, be understood in exchanges with responsive partners, co-create new contexts, and transform their systems (Pfeffermann, 2023). It is closely related to communication intelligence and innovation to increase interactions that are clear, open, and compelling (Woodward & Shaffakat, 2020).

The next sections center on two major themes to develop a better understanding of the need for a new leadership framework: (1) rethinking how communication affects behavior and (2) focusing on innovation, a new understanding of strategy and value chain.

Rethinking How Communication Affects Behavior: The New Leadership Skillset

Change is nowadays everywhere. But do leaders have the right approach and mindset to create new realities and help businesses innovate and step into their respective growth zones? The most critical success factor is the way leaders influence individuals' behaviors, beliefs, and values; listen to others without judgment, and update their knowledge schemes as a cognitive navigation system for personal and business growth (Pfeffermann, 2023). In this dynamic information-interaction process, new leaders play a vital role in guiding organizational members through the maze of five typical disempowering transactions and communication blueprints (Figure 1.1).

Triangulation

Triangulation plays a significant role in our daily professional life, and we are often caught up in triangles with other people and issues not knowing how to resist or deal with it. As a result, we ignore, enable, or engage in it without understanding the long-term negative consequences for ourselves or others. Objectivity is nearly impossible

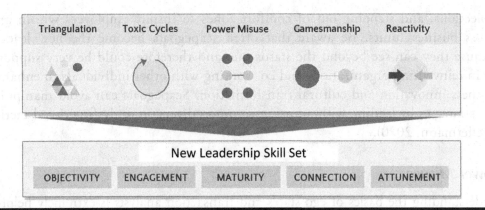

Figure 1.1 Skill Set for Overcoming the Disempowering Transactions

because of the heritage of triangulated relating and thinking patterns that have been manifested over the years.

It is very important for new leaders to understand triangulation and with whom to triangulate to successfully lead transitions and turn ideas from the creative world into impactful businesses. For example, the anxiety of stepping into the unknown and creating new pathways is often delegated to others instead of having the moral courage to move forward with the new direction and reality.

Triangulation is a short-term mechanism that forces leaders to fall back on their automated response system, or comfort zone, during crises or unknown situations rather than being authentic in identifying smart choices for acute problems (Belasen & Frank, 2008). It is a cognitive shortcut for feeling relieved and going forward in life without observing and facing conflicts and building stable, trustful, and mutual relationships.

Toxic Cycles

Why do we expose ourselves to toxic cycles? It is a subconscious self-survival strategy to engage and interact with people and stay connected to ideas and situations. However, it may trigger manipulative, narcissistic, (self-)destructive, and mentally controlling behavior (Belasen, 2016). From a relational system perspective, the concept 'golden child and scapegoat' plays a vital role in understanding toxic transactions and cycles of dysfunctional engagement, such as silo-thinking and the scapegoat role of toxic leaders or the idealization of entrepreneurship and devaluation of organizational members and teams. It is a dysfunctional relating style that leads to separation, competition, and being stuck in the same old cycles instead of stepping into the firm's growth zone and co-innovate at all business levels.

In empowered cultures, scapegoats recognize the negative outcomes of toxic leadership by holding leaders accountable, blocking emotional abuse and negative projections, and stepping out of comfort zones to inspire employees within and across business units. Be aware that often scapegoats become the new leaders because they can see beyond the status quo and therefore could be very supportive in reinventing organizations and co-working with other individuals to enhance business innovation and cultural transformation. Scapegoats can avoid manipulative strategies by leading without using common diversion or dysfunctional tactics (Pfeffermann, 2020).

Power Misuse

Understanding the basics of ego states and transaction analysis is extremely helpful in clarifying misunderstandings in conversations, nurturing relationships, and feeling responsible for how to relate to others in lateral and hierarchical structures. If the workplace feels like kindergarten and draining your ability to deal with a controlling boss, it is a signal that individuals around interact from a child-to-parent state.

On the contrary, in the adult state, individuals experience open communication, come up with fresh ideas, co-create new solutions in a multisensory way, and respond to others without judgment or fear of retaliation. In this mature state, humans experience mutual relationships in the flow and respect each other without the need to build up defensive walls, devalue others, or play power-control games. It is the self-skill set that allows leaders to live up to their full potential, successfully grow ideas in their own communication space, and appreciate values, such as authenticity, equality, curiosity, and integrity.

Gamesmanship

We need to be seen, understood, known, and heard in relationships and be connected to others, which means we allow others to see who we are and let down our walls and become emotionally available. Understanding the continuum of closeness/togetherness and separateness as a relating skill is important for effective interactions, finding balance, and reducing emotional discomfort in critical situations. If this relational skill set is not fully developed, it can lead to emotional detachment, enmeshment, and gamesmanship because often people prefer to 'buddy' with like-minded individuals and groups and build defensive walls to feel protected and comfortable leading to repetition of similar behaviors.

Leaders with new mindsets create safe environments for organizational members by making themselves emotionally available and by guiding and facilitating interactions. The effectiveness of coaching and mentoring can be measured by the ability to mirror the individual with positive intentions, by understanding the rhythm of interacting, and by truly seeing the individual in terms of responding to gesture, action, and language.

Reactivity

Any reactivity—emotional and behavioral reaction to a situation and conversation—involves an energy exchange and emotional attachment. Why is it important for business relationships? In focus groups, meetups, and other business situations, individuals share their ideas, interact, and get access to new information, as well as figure out new relationships and the consequences of negotiations.

Reactivity is often the result of the negative effects of emotional abuse and walking on eggshells in dysfunctional environments. Consequently, developing the skill of curiosity and attunement is key to reinforcing positive attachments in collaborative settings and business partnerships. For instance, intentionally asking quality questions and showing serious interest in learning more about an individual's world and emotional experience could open the door for a trusting relationship. The good news is that we can learn and expand our skill set to build healthy and trusting relationships. The new leadership skill set described below helps to strengthen the personal growth capability:

- **Objectivity**: Ability to build self-differentiated, mutual relationships with consistent relating and evolving interactions and being authentic to deal with conflicts, resolve problems, and manage transitions
- **Engagement**:Ability to understand the effects of toxic cycles of emotional abuse,the role of the concept 'golden child and scapegoat' in dynamic systems, and how to appreciate and acknowledge human talents and ideas
- **Maturity**: Ability to respect each other and appreciate mindfulness, awareness, and equality in relationships and interact with others without judgment
- **Connection**: Ability to handle our own emotional disappointments and neglect and feeling unseen, unknown, unheard, and misunderstood in relationships, and how to better connect with individuals, self-connect, and have a feeling of belonging
- **Attunement**: Ability to offer a space to align and join individuals to grow their ideas and find their emotional stability and personal power for new pathways and transitions

Focusing on Innovation: A New Understanding of Strategy and Value Chain

Innovation is a critical factor for a company's success. It stands for progress and evolution at both data-driven information and system level (e.g., applications). The traditional and e-value chain models—focused on industrialization and regulation—are no longer adequate for the new business model, strategy, development, and innovation.

For many companies, a new value chain approach is also a new leadership imperative. It means to be prepared for innovation and new AI ambitions and, at the same time, consider the new linkage between innovation and communication. It is important for a new leader to better understand the relationship between technology, strategy, and innovation-communication. Reskilling may include creative AI thinking, AI business strategy and implementation, designing customer experiences, building stakeholder relationships, and developing app interfaces. Hence, we need to recognize the importance of interaction designs and how we can create business value through communication for innovation. It makes a difference in leading a future-ready or transitioning company.

Although it is a widely accepted principle that innovations can be an essential driver for a company's growth, the impact of innovations on a company's value is not guaranteed. Communication of innovations and innovation management—as a determinant to affect diffusion and market commercialization—are both crucial for the success of a company. For instance, the classical value chain shows the fragmentation of communication activities for innovations. Communication of innovations is both a secondary activity in corporate communication, technology development, and innovation management and a primary activity in marketing. Thus, there is a need for a new communication value chain approach.

In addition, strategic business innovation includes value chain transformation and sound integration of the e-value chain that captures critical dynamic capabilities to address rapidly changing environments. Resources and capabilities tend to improve a company's competitive advantage and lead to a strategy that is unique and difficult to imitate.

Value chain transformation is like any other transformation: It needs time to shift from one reality to another and alter business practices including current mindsets and skills. For instance, the integration of a new e-value chain is challenging in terms of building a digital mindset and creating new added values, such as the structuration value, collaboration value, and/or selection value. In the second step, digital tools and processes are needed to transform a business. To be ready for AI means to become aware of the subtle differences in leading a digitalized business or building an AI-driven business. The value chain is thereby no longer focusing on discrete information but rather it focuses on the importance of interdependence and the value of connections and on the dynamic capability of innovation-communication as a prerequisite for innovation (Pfeffermann, 2023).

What is strategy innovation and why is it crucial for leaders? In a classical view, strategy is understood as a planning and execution process, including strategic positioning based on customer values that articulates how a company can win in a specific environment. This is a process by which a company centers on customer values and new opportunities that spark innovation and create a company's future. Strategy is renewing itself. The strategy has become part of innovation to make better choices for the business model. Strategy innovation is a new task for leaders who have the desire to build an open incubator group to harness the power of imagination that inspires and creates beyond what is (Reeves & Fuller, 2021).

Innovation-communication enables strategy innovation and creates an environment where innovators engage and inspire others to co-create and expand the communicating minds (Belasen & Rufer, 2013). Innovation-communication is no longer just a field of corporate communication or an extension of PR. It is part of leadership communication that enables the development of new leadership qualities, such as being service-oriented (ethics, humanity, environment), connection-focused (moving people, building trust), and relevance-driven (mission, vision, influence).

Moving Toward Brilliant Leadership

Being a new leader requires the development of a new skill set and a new attitude toward innovation-communication. While we covered many of the tendencies of new leaders in this chapter, including communicative behavior, qualities, and values, we continue by focusing on the new leadership mindset "innovation-communication" and particularly on three stages of "Awareness" (Figure 1.2). The "Action" part in Figure 1.2 will be addressed in Chapter 10. In this chapter, we center on self-awareness by using

New Leadership Communication [Interactivity]
  - Engagement (dialog, listening, asking right questions)
  - Expression (visionary ideas, strategic issues, purpose)
  - Relationship (openness, deep conversations, meaning)

New Leadership Qualities [Attitude]
  - Service-oriented (ethics, humanity, environment)
  - Connection-based (warmth, empathy)
  - Relevance-driven (visionary, powerful)

New Leadership Values [Standard]
  - Respect
  - Integrity (being your word, sincerity)
  - Responsibility (showing up, being accountable)

New Leadership Stages [Awareness]
  - reflective leadership style (learning & development)
  - innovative leadership style (interdisciplinary, engineering)
  - synthesizing leadership style (contradictions)

New Leadership Themes [Action]
  - Human intelligence vs. AI (counterfactual thinking)
  - From purpose to impact (e-value chain integration)
  - Digital workplace and ecosystem (collaboration, resilience)

Figure 1.2   The New Leadership Mindset

the Competing Values Framework (Belasen & Frank, 2010; Cameron et al., 2014) and highlighting the pathway of new leaders toward brilliant leadership.

As presented in Figure 1.2, a new leader is a good communicator for innovation. There are three main components that are important and needed to advance in your career as a new leader: engagement, expression, and relationship. Some skills, such as listening actively, speaking with heart and mind, and using the right words to engage and connect, represent a foundation for leaders in general. In particular, for new leaders, it is the new mindset that helps to go in the right direction and harness the power of innovation-communication. What does this mean? To focus on engagement means to interact with others with the intention to spark innovation and create a desired future for the company, such as, by engaging key stakeholders proactively through communication spaces (e.g. innovation workshops, creative playrooms and platforms) to exchange ideas with innovative thinkers and open-minded co-creators.

As a new leader, it is also essential to express visionary ideas and strategic issues, and to articulate the "Why" (purpose) of an organization. In this context, empathy and kindness are two traits that continue to become increasingly important in leadership communication. In addition, new leaders care about building connections and developing relationships to enhance corporate innovation. They understand the purpose of innovation-communication is to stimulate conversations about change, raise awareness about the future, and build a culture of empowerment focusing on humanity, moral and ethical values, and the environment.

Leadership profile awareness is a recognition of these tendencies and their impact on peers and followers. Gap analysis of personal strengths and weaknesses helps new leaders to become mindful of their weaknesses, initiate self-development efforts, and model the way for continuous improvement (see Chapter 10). Self-awareness increases personal control and professional growth, which helps leaders to remedy weaknesses, leverage strengths, and guide individuals and teams to pursue the best possible outcomes for their organizations.

Reflective leadership style: In this stage, effective communication means to reflect (not respond/react) and learn to value quality, emotional intelligence, relational communication, and relevance. It involves organizations where leaders and teams operate collaboratively and consider reflective innovation dialogs.

Innovative leadership style: The second stage relates to interdisciplinary thinking and leaders who are able and willing to think out-of-the-box in new ways and understand diverse viewpoints and different frameworks and methodologies. Effective communication is about clarity and transparency, reaching beyond boundaries, and having the ability to initiate and implement innovation.

Synthesizing leadership style: It is the art of bringing separate parts together to create something new and select crucial information in ways that make sense to self and others. This stage combines the synthesizing mind with the communicating mind. Leaders effectively communicate ideas and intentions by unlocking the power of innovation-communication. Innovation-communication focuses on awareness and trust through honest messaging, integrity, and respect.

These three leadership styles define the core attributes of the new leadership mindset, paving the way for the "Action" part, including assessment and development, described in Chapter 10. The next sections introduce the Competing Values Framework (CVF) and the conceptual boundaries of brilliant leadership.

Competing Values Framework—The Conceptual Boundaries of Brilliant Leadership

The model configuration of the four categories in the Brilliant Leadership model (Figure 1.3) is an adaptation of the Competing Values Framework (Cameron et al., 2014), a theoretical framework with construct validity well established in the literature (Belasen & Frank, 2008; Hartnell et al., 2011).

Inherent in the CVF is the assumption that performance outcomes are ultimately defined (and judged) by a set of competing values and that leaders consistently confront tough choices that are deeply embedded in organizational beliefs. For example, managers are expected to ensure stability within the organization and yet are also faced with a need to encourage change and innovation in response to market dynamics. The framework postulates that leaders with high cognitive complexity also enjoy behavioral flexibility that allows them to enact multiple behaviors that produce better outcomes in terms of business performance and stakeholder effectiveness.

The CVF (Figure 1.3) highlights complementary leadership mindsets and communication approaches (Belasen & Frank, 2010) within the context of a strong leadership culture (Cameron et al., 2014; Hart et al., 1993)—Visioner and Motivator (transformational); Analyzer and Taskmaster (transactional).

Transformational leadership inspires followers to do more than they originally intended to do by presenting them with a compelling vision and by encouraging them to transcend their own interests for those of the group or work unit. Transactional leaders, on the other hand, rely upon the economic value of a transaction (i.e., exchange of performance for reward) to motivate employees to achieve desired outcomes. Unlike transformational leaders who rely on intangible sources of motivation to energize employees, transactional leaders focus on structuring the incentive system using rules and policies to achieve conformance. The two types of leadership, transformational and transactional, therefore, seek to accomplish organizational goals by motivating employees on a continuum that ranges from extrinsic to intrinsic values.

The brilliant leadership framework in Figure 1.4, in line with the Competing Values Framework, consists of four categories designed to capture leadership qualities and behaviors associated with strategy innovation, open innovation, cultural innovation, and business innovation.

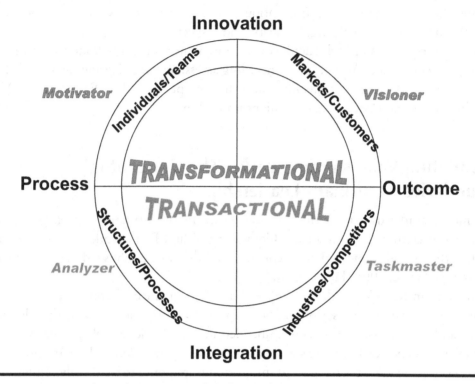

Figure 1.3   Competing Values Framework (Adapted from Cameron, et al., 2014)

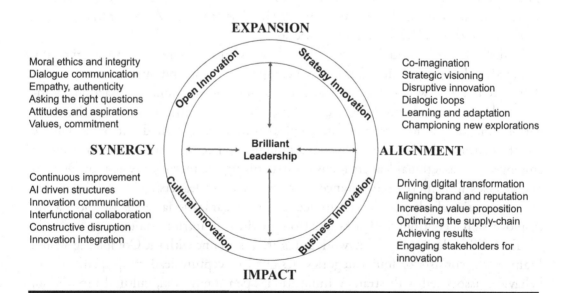

Figure 1.4   The Conceptual Boundaries and Scope of Brilliant Leadership

Strategy innovation is associated with the visioner's scope of responsibilities, creativity, and communication skills to bring about change. Brilliant leaders focus on co-imagination, strategic visioning, disruptive innovation, dialogic loops, learning and adaptation, and championing new explorations.

Open innovation aligns with the motivator, mutual respect, and truthfulness. Brilliant leaders emphasize moral ethics and integrity, dialogue communication, empathy, authenticity, asking the right questions, positive attitudes and aspirations, acceptance, and commitment to core values.

Cultural innovation is manifested in the analyzer's span of attention and the need to maintain internal consistency and accountability. Brilliant leaders center on continuous improvement efforts, alignment of AI-driven structures, innovation-communication, interfunctional collaboration, facilitating constructive disruption, and engaging in innovation integration.

Business innovation is reflective of the taskmaster and achieving performance outcomes. Brilliant leaders pay attention to driving digital transformation, aligning brand and reputation, increasing value proposition, optimizing the supply chain, achieving results, and engaging stakeholders for innovation.

Brilliant leaders have the know-how to handle paradoxes and competing tensions. They invest in digital technology (structures, processes) to integrate the organization optimally while considering learning and development (employees, teams); they use strategic imagination to initiate disruptive innovation (markets, customers) while addressing the impact of their initiatives on customers, partners, and stakeholders (industries, competitors). The conceptual framework in Figure 1.4 captures these competing tensions and paradoxes and uses a panoramic lens to reinforce the significance of the dynamic interplay between these factors. This is where brilliant leaders unleash their inner capacity to effectively navigate disruptive times and lead through complexity.

Brilliant leadership is a new conceptual framework to guide strategists, game changers, senior executives, and aspiring leaders. Brilliant leaders have an authentic personality, have the willingness to engage and inspire organizational members and stakeholders, facilitate co-innovation, and commit to making significant contributions to humanity, environment, and workplace ethics, and are relevant. The framework is also consistent with the United Nations Sustainable Development Goals (SDG) of ensuring inclusive and equitable quality education, fostering innovation, and developing a lifelong learning mindset.

Structure of the Book

The integrative framework described in this book demonstrates the interaction effects between internal and external triggers for action. The primary four sections of the book parallel the framework quadrants. Each part contains two chapters with distinct and complementary ideas that reflect the conceptual boundaries of the framework. Together, the parts and chapters represent a holistic view of how and why brilliant leaders communicate and act. The integrative framework is shown in Section 5, Chapter 10. As described in chapter 10, it can also be used diagnostically for leadership assessment and development that strengthens the new leadership mindset.

Section 1: Open Innovation

How Leaders Facilitate Co-Creation and Spark Innovation

Chapter 2: The Convergence of Empathy and Authenticity in Brilliant Leadership

This chapter addresses a critical question: What does empathy look like in a brilliant leader? Empathy has traditionally been defined as one individual's understanding of and respect for another's experience and, by extension, responding with compassion. It may be construed as the other person's perception—the feeling of being understood. In the context of an organization, does an empathetic leader automatically achieve the designation of "brilliant?" While empathy may be necessary for leadership effectiveness, it is not a sufficient condition for brilliance. Drawing on examples from fields like education, healthcare, and others, this chapter advances a model of empathy in brilliant leadership that focuses on three considerations. First, in the province of authentic leadership, empathy is best viewed not as an isolated quality or skill but as part of a balanced composite of traits, some of which may be necessary to temper unwarranted dependence on emotion as a factor in executive decision-making. This would be necessary to avoid falling prey to the paradox of empathy in which an excess converts it from a strength into a weakness.

Second, brilliant leadership is not possible unless stakeholders hold strong perceptions of leadership authenticity. Authentic leaders communicate with logic, clarity, honesty, and purpose—important tenets of brilliant leadership. Third, brilliant leaders demonstrate skills for creating and sustaining a culture of empathy in which each employee's empathy potential may be realized. In addition to serving as role models, brilliant leaders nurture a work environment such that employees feel respectful and trustful, ensure that their personal values align with those of the organization, justifiably believe leadership operates with integrity, participate in strategy development, view collaboration as an important vehicle for goal accomplishment, and place the interests on those served by the organization as a top priority.

Brilliant leaders weave expectations for empathic behavior into recruitment, performance, promotion, and communication standards, recognizing that a culture of empathy cannot materialize without leadership's role modeling along with a credo of dignity and inclusiveness.

Keywords: empathy, collaboration, culture, trust, inclusion, authentic leadership, organizational culture

Chapter 3: Promoting Innovation and Creativity through Human-Centered Leadership

Chapter 3 focuses on how leaders in human-centric workplaces promote innovation and creativity by influencing individuals and teams through a culture of shared value. One of the greater impacts of the global COVID-19 pandemic was how it significantly altered workforce expectations for organizational leadership.

Post-pandemic perspectives of what constitutes effective leadership were rapidly redefined from the traditional, authoritarian command-and-control model that was the default leadership style of the 20th century. These new expectations are calling for executives to integrate human-centric values into their leadership approach. This shift serves as the basis for this chapter to deconstruct what this looks like in practice, the ways in which it shapes company culture and community, and how it connects with influencing organizational innovation and creativity.

Across various studies, results show that leaders who demonstrate and celebrate human-centric values through behaviors that support psychological safety have measurably greater success in boosting team creativity and innovation. The authors share research and insights for contemplating how demonstrating and establishing a culture of psychological safety, a core value of human-centered leadership, generates accelerated learning, increased and better ideation, and transformative outcomes that challenge the status quo. The chapter also examines models and characteristics of human-centered leadership that fit comfortably within the transformational motivator mindset category of the brilliant leadership framework to connect how human-centric behaviors support senior executives' efforts to drive open innovation.

The chapter concludes with how leaders can implement the values highlighted above in daily business. The transfer from the dogmatic approach to a routine-based value-driven daily leadership behavior remains a main challenge. Hence, the role of the organization in assessing those behaviors and developing skills for daily leadership practices is explored. Practical examples of how leaders can leverage their new skills to begin building aspirational work environments that encourage continuous learning, diverse perspectives, and innovative problem-solving are provided.

Keywords: leadership values, creativity and innovation, human-centered leadership, daily business transfer, aspirational work environments

Section 2: Strategy Innovation

Beyond Boundaries—How Leaders Create a Purpose-Driven Innovation

Chapter 4: Co-Creation, Strategic Visioning, and Iterative Loops

This chapter focuses on the challenges brilliant leaders face to skillfully balance constraints and creativity. Brilliant leaders co-create a transformational vision that inspires and aligns stakeholders and that projects a future of success. They have the right balance between functional knowledge to execute the digital transformation and relational skills to promote ownership and shared accountability that empower individuals and teams through delegation and autonomy. These digital leaders traverse innovation while embodying qualities such as empathy, resilience, and agility needed to create purpose-driven innovation. They nurture creativity and adaptability—an approach that integrates innovation with human-centric values to navigate technological disruption.

According to the World Economic Forum, the top 5 skills for the year 2025 include analytical thinking, innovation, problem-solving, critical thinking, creativity, originality, and initiative. By leveraging digital technologies, organizations can innovate, achieve strategic objectives, and surmount obstacles encountered during the process of digital transformation through the implementation of structural changes. The transformations not only yield favorable outcomes for the organization but also allow leaders to acquire fresh skills that shape strategic thinking and that guide individuals and teams through complex tasks. Leaders need a better way to empower their teams during times of transformation, build trust, minimize ambiguity, and exploit new opportunities.

Keywords: divergent thinking, dialogic loops, co-creation, shared leadership, ambidexterity, trustworthiness, strategic visioning

Chapter 5: Transforming Business: Coping with Paradoxes in Purpose-Driven Innovation

This chapter focuses on values-driven alliances in which several parties work together to make a positive social, economic, and environmental impact. Because of the societal mission and the scope of values-driven alliances, collaboration is complex and full of paradoxes. Dealing with these paradoxes involves forming, building, developing, and evolving stages of these alliances. This chapter describes the practice of the Global Alliance for Banking on Values in the four stages of the life cycle of alliances and how this alliance has dealt with the paradoxes in creating and managing the alliance.

The chapter provides insights into the dynamics of innovative values-driven alliances and how leaders and professionals deal with paradoxes in the alliances' life cycle and in their communication and decision-making processes. The values, motives, and competencies of brilliant leaders are explored and discussed. The Global Alliance for Banking on Values is used as a case study to inspire scholars and practitioners to deal with the paradoxes that arise in creating purpose-driven alliances and managing innovative alliances with the aim of supporting societal transformation.

In addition to understanding the dynamics of alliances and the essential qualities of values-driven leaders, this chapter provides inspiration for people who want to contribute to a better world, working together with others. Leaders, professionals, and change masters are invited to reflect on their own capabilities in creating and managing values-based alliances and on the values, motives, and competencies of their own leadership in collaborative transformation to create a better and more sustainable world.

Keywords: values-driven alliances, values-driven leaders, brilliant leadership, interorganizational collaboration, life cycle of alliances, managing paradoxes, sustainability.

Section 3: Cultural Innovation

How Leaders Shape a Culture of Innovation through Collaborative Technologies, Risk Tolerance, and Empowerment

Chapter 6: Co-Creating Purposeful Change: From the Individual to the Organization

This chapter delves into the transformative effects of the COVID-19 pandemic on workplace dynamics, emphasizing the rise of the "Great Resignation," where employees are leaving their jobs in search of better work-life balance, flexibility, and fulfillment. This shift has prompted a deeper exploration into what employees value in their work environment and the increasing importance of intrinsic rewards over extrinsic ones, such as salary and bonuses. The authors analyze how dissatisfaction with traditional workplace norms and a lack of meaningful engagement is driving employees to prioritize job satisfaction, which encompasses autonomy, purpose, and a healthy work-life balance. This transformation is supported by various psychological theories including Self-Determination Theory and Maslow's Hierarchy of Needs, which suggest that fulfilling higher-order psychological needs is essential for agency, employee engagement, and organizational success.

The chapter further explores the role of leadership in addressing the often-overlooked potential of employees who choose to stay with their organizations—often seen as the backbone of stability and resilience during turbulent times—and how their deep organizational knowledge and loyalty provide a counterbalance to the disruption of high turnover. Recognizing that different generations of employees prioritize their own interests and values in different ways it is noted that leadership rarely addresses these alternative patterns of agency systematically. As the Leadership for Agency Framework is developed, the authors integrate it with the Brilliant Leadership framework, to propose specific strategies for organizations to adapt to these evolving expectations. Benefits include fostering an environment that values strategic innovation, open communication, cultural adaptability, and business acumen that ensure successful employee engagement and multigenerational agency in the post-pandemic era.

Keywords: motivation, engagement, culture, purposeful change, alignment

Chapter 7: Techno-Survive vs Techno-Thrive: The AI-Responsive Leadership Framework

The advent of generative AI marked a paradigm shift in leadership and for many, a "shock" to the leadership mindset. The chapter explores how leaders' emotional, cognitive, and behavioral responsiveness regarding generative AI affects team morale, decision-making, and organizational performance. The chapter examines the conditions for leaders to either excel (thrive) or struggle (wither) amidst the novel leadership challenges that AI poses. The focus is not on the technical or computational intricacies of AI but rather on how the adoption and inclusion of generative AI affect the emotions, cognitions, and behaviors of leaders and their teams, particularly with respect to decision- making. By examining and understanding the human experience of relationships with AI, leaders can better navigate its integration, thereby enhancing team performance, communication efficacy, and organizational effectiveness.

The AI-Responsive Leadership Framework (ARLF) identifies and organizes how leaders' responsiveness to and relationship with AI affects their own leadership style and effectiveness as well as that of others. The ARLF framework considers three critical dimensions: leaders' emotions and feelings regarding AI, particularly with respect to morality and ethics, as well as anxiety versus curiosity; their cognitions and decision-making regarding AI; and their behaviors and actions.

Keywords: generative AI, leadership effectiveness, emotion, cognition, behavior, ARLF framework

Section 4: Business Innovation

How Leaders Embrace Digital Transformation for Better Outcomes

Chapter 8: Driving Digital Transformation, Aligning Brand and Reputation

The rapidly changing global business environment influenced by globalization has compelled organizations to undergo digital transformation, which presents both opportunities and challenges. This chapter delves into the various aspects of digital transformation, highlighting that it encompasses more than just technological changes—it also involves cultural, workforce, and strategic shifts.

Digital transformation entails the integration of advanced technologies, merging physical and digital systems, innovative business models, and the creation of new products and services. It is a continuous and extensive process that impacts customer relationships, internal processes, and value generation. The interaction between people and technology becomes crucial in reshaping organizational structures, business models, and leadership practices.

To effectively navigate digital transformation, organizations must align their strategies with overarching goals and explore how digital transformation strategies can emerge through a bottom-up approach, beginning with new strategic initiatives and progressing toward higher levels. Additionally, leadership plays a central role in guiding organizations through these dynamic changes, with an emphasis on enhancing workforce skills and fostering innovation.

The key idea is that digital transformation is not limited to organizations that were not initially digital but also applies to those that are already involved in digitization. It raises questions about whether the process began long before the introduction of digital technology or if it occurred by integrating modern technology into existing automated processes. Digital transformation is depicted as an evolving phenomenon characterized by the adoption and utilization of emerging technologies.

As organizations grapple with the changes brought about by digital transformation, investing in leadership skills, and aligning strategies with goals become crucial for effectively navigating the complexities of the digital era. Given the evolving nature of digital transformation, continuous research efforts and a proactive approach to implementing innovation are essential to remain current with emerging trends and challenges.

Keywords: globalization, digital transformation, leadership, organizations

Chapter 9: Increasing Value Proposition, Engaging Stakeholders for Innovation

Innovation and its successful commercialization require the creation of compelling customer value propositions (CVPs), which form the foundation of effective business models. However, the value of any CVP must come from its acceptance by the target customer rather than the innovator. This chapter focuses on customer perception of value as a trade-off of perceived benefits against perceived sacrifices, a process that is complex and open to influencing and shaping by the innovator via communication with customers and key stakeholders.

These stakeholders include important customers, key suppliers, and complementary actors within the innovator's strategic alliance network. The value creation process involves successful management of knowledge acquired via communication exchanges both within and outside the innovator firm. Drawing upon the academic literature relating to successful commercialization within innovative small firms (ISFs), and multiple case studies of such firms, this chapter examines the interrelationship between the creation of compelling CVPs and their associated business models, and the role of stakeholder engagement and knowledge-based, interactive communication and organizational learning. Lessons for successful CVP generation and commercialization are also provided.

Keywords: customer value proposition, strategic alliance network, absorptive capacity, dynamic capabilities, business model.

Section 5: Harnessing the Power of Brilliant Leadership

Chapter 10: Inspiring the Next Generation of Leaders

This is the concluding chapter. It recaps the relevant and applicable innovation-communication expectations, attributes, and skills that brilliant leaders use to influence followers, mobilize support for the vision, and inspire change. The span of attention of brilliant leaders includes intellectual curiosity, updated knowledge, authenticity, and empathy that enable the exercise of ethical choices that consider the impact on stakeholders and the community.

The chapter also focuses on profile awareness as a powerful medium that allows leaders to understand their strengths and weaknesses, what motivates them, and how they make decisions. Self-assessment tools are designed to help increase self-awareness or understanding of one's strengths and weaknesses, behavioral patterns, and motivations. Executives can use these instruments to self-assess gaps in their behaviors and develop plans for self-development and continuous improvement to sustain their leadership brilliance in transforming organizations.

Keywords: assessment and development, trustworthiness, transformation, gap analysis

Conclusion

What makes this new framework of brilliant leadership unique? In this book, we provide practical strategies and become a source of inspiration for what it means to have a new leadership mindset—a brilliant leader who understands how to communicate with empathy and authenticity, engage and inspire others, shift responsibility into shared commitment, and spark learning in a purpose-driven innovation culture.

Each chapter in the book is more than a collection of ideas. It is a part of the new intellectual framework that describes "Brilliant Leadership." Each chapter provides a unique contribution that is distinct and, at the same time, connected to other chapters through the book's organizing schema, paralleling how the different facets of brilliant leadership are inseparable from one another.

Together, the chapters represent a holistic view of what it means by brilliant leadership. The framework demonstrates this connectivity through a conceptual framework (Figure 1.4) and a plan (book chapters) of how to approach the specific research inquiry, the tenets of brilliant leadership. This connectivity is also reflected in the core assumptions of the CVF (Figure 1.3) that portray master leaders as having strong cognitive complexity.

Cognitive complexity expands their intellectual curiosity and learning capacity, ability to sense needs, adapt their responses, and use their repertoire of knowledge, empathy, and innovative thinking to exercise ethical reasoning and make smart choices that are strategic and relevant and that consider the impact on stakeholders and their surroundings (Belasen, 2022). For example, leaders cannot invest in digital technology (structures, processes) to integrate the organization optimally without considering learning and development (employees, teams). They cannot introduce disruptive innovation without considering its impact on customers, partners, stakeholders employees, and so on.

In addition to enriching your learning about what makes a brilliant leader, the book chapters, which are authored by experts from diverse backgrounds, provide rich and broader perspectives for fostering a leadership innovation mindset.

Key benefits from gaining knowledge from this book include:

- The book is presented as a knowledge source for aspiring leaders and professionals wishing to expand applications of innovation-communication from a strategic perspective.
- Practical strategies and assessment tools for bridging gaps in leadership skills, knowledge, and abilities based on the Competing Values Framework and the new leadership mindset are illustrated with analysis and examples.
- Brilliant *Leadership* provides a new theoretical/intellectual lens for inspiring employee engagement and for driving disruptive innovation in a dynamic environment.
- Brilliant leaders can tap into "Why" and have the "Know-How" to influence a growth culture that drives results; leverages knowledge transfer through collaborative technologies; reframes new experiences and ideas through strategic imagination; and harnesses the transformative power of innovation-communication that matters.
- *Brilliant Leadership* guides strategists, aspiring leaders, decision-makers, and game changers on how to communicate for successful implementation of innovation.

References

Alayza, B., & González, D. (2023). Adaptive planning for inclusive innovation; Creating communication spaces for adapting digital government. In N. Pfeffermann & M. Schaller (Eds.), *New leadership communication—inspire your Horizon* (1st ed., pp. 301–322). Springer.

Belasen, A. T. (2016). Deception and failure: Mitigating leader-centric behaviors. In A. Belasen & R. Toma (Eds.), *Confronting corruption in business: Trusted leadership, civic engagement* (pp. 183–216). Routledge.

Belasen, A. T. (2022). *Resilience in healthcare leadership: Practical strategies and self-assessment tools*. Routledge.

Belasen, A. T., & Frank, N. M. (2008). Competing values leadership: Quadrant roles and personality traits. *Leadership and Organizational Development Journal, 29*(2), 127–143.

Belasen, A. T., & Frank, N. M. (2010). A peek through the lens of the competing values framework: What managers communicate and how. *The Atlantic Journal of Communication, 18*, 280–296.

Belasen, A. T., & Rufer, R. (2013). Innovation communication for effective inter-professional collaboration: A stakeholder perspective. In N. Pfeffermann, T. Minshall, & L. Mortara (Eds.), *Strategy and communication for innovation* (2nd ed., pp. 227–240). Springer.

Cameron, K. S. Quinn, R. E. Degraff, J., & Thakor, A.V. (2014). *Competing values leadership* (2nd ed.). Edward Elgar Publishing.

Cnop. A. (2023). Why should leaders prioritize purpose? In N. Pfeffermann & M. Schaller (Eds.), *New leadership communication—inspire yourHorizon* (1st ed., pp. 27–38). Springer.

Darnell, M. R., & Parish, N. B. (2023). Respect, dialogue, and innovation: Creating new ideas and solutions by committing to an ethical culture. In N. Pfeffermann & M. Schaller (Eds.), *New leadership communication—inspire your Horizon* (1st ed., pp. 127–136). Springer.

Deschamps, J. P. (2020). Do you have the right profiles in your C-suite for an effective Transformation. In N. Pfeffermann (Ed.) *New leadership in strategy and communication* (1st ed., pp. 37–46). Springer.

Fortin, M. D., & Frey, K. A. (2023). Essential communication skills for emerging leaders. In N. Pfeffermann & M. Schaller (Eds.), *New leadership communication—inspire your Horizon* (1st ed., pp. 65–76). Springer.

Hart, S. L., & Quinn, R. E. (1993). Roles executives play - CEOs, behavioral complexity, and firm performance. *Human Relations*, *46*(5), 543–574. https://doi.org/10.1177/001872679304600501

Hartnell, C. A., Ou, A. Y., & Kinicki, A. (2011). Organizational culture and organizational effectiveness: A meta-analytic investigation of the competing values framework's theoretical suppositions. *The Journal of Applied Psychology*, *96*(4), 677–694. https://doi.org/10.1037/a0021987

Moriarty, B. T. (2023). Unleashing aspirational capital: Sparking innovation and engagement through communication. In N. Pfeffermann & M. Schaller (Eds.), *New leadership communication—inspire your Horizon* (1st ed., pp. 201–210). Springer.

Pfeffermann, N. (2020). Introduction. In N. Pfeffermann (Ed.), *New leadership in strategy and communication* (1st ed., pp. 1–14). Springer.

Pfeffermann, N. (2023). Introduction: Leadership tasks, thinking and essentials for effective leadership communication. In N. Pfeffermann & M. Schaller (Eds.), *New leadership communication—inspire your Horizon* (1st ed., pp. 1–26). Springer.

Reeves, M., & Fuller, J. (2021). *The imagination machine*. Harvard Business Review Press.

Sonder, N. (2023). New leadership—Essential leadership skills for interactive daily business. In N. Pfeffermann & M. Schaller (Eds.), *New leadership communication—inspire your Horizon* (1st ed., pp. 53–64). Springer.

Woodward, I. C., & Shaffakat, S. (2020). Innovation, leadership, and communication intelligence. In N. Pfeffermann (Ed.), *New leadership in strategy and communication* (1st ed., pp. 145–164). Springer.

OPEN INNOVATION 1

Chapter 2

The Convergence of Empathy and Authenticity in Brilliant Leadership

Barry Eisenberg, Cherrelle Hall, Lisa Unangst and Amy Eisenberg

Empathy as a construct, a skill, and even a measure of personality orientation is associated with fields as varied as psychology (Lundy, 2007), addiction studies (Preller et al., 2014), comparative education (Evans & Unangst, 2020), theology (Doehring, 2018), and women's studies (Bhopal, 2013), and in parallel is a core component of leadership. This chapter situates empathy as an essential element of brilliant leadership. It also probes the need for empathy to engage with authenticity, reflexivity, relationality, and balance.

One way to begin thinking about empathy in, for, and through leadership is to explore how business leaders are trained in empathy by business administration programs, as well as how those same programs celebrate empathy. For example, a Harvard Business School online class titled *Design Thinking and Innovation* situates the concept within course content as follows: students will "practice empathy in applying a human-centered approach to design techniques, such as user research, user experience, prototyping, and journey mapping" (Harvard Business School Online, n.d.). An alumni profile produced by the MIT Sloan School highlights an entrepreneur whose empathetic sensitivity underlies a commitment to develop affordable housing (Husband, 2021), while the Tuck School of Business' Diversity, Equity, and Inclusion office introduces its work by stating a commitment to develop students' leadership *wisdom*, characterized by "inclusivity and empathy to understand and work effectively with others," improving not only prospects for organizational success but also "the world we live in" (n.d.).

DOI: 10.4324/9781003495307-3

In short, empathy is valued: it is framed by these institutions as reflecting maturity of judgment and aligned with entrepreneurial excellence as well as innovation. Moreover, empathy is inextricably linked to authenticity, and we posit that the latter is a necessary condition for the former.

The purpose of this chapter is to define empathy in the context of leadership, evaluate its interrelationship with authenticity, identify the importance of contextualizing empathy in a balanced role composite, and describe how leadership excellence goes beyond role modeling empathy by creating an organizational culture of empathy. In so doing, we will consider empathy across institutions and across leadership roles. We underscore that just as there are many different types of brilliant leaders, so too are there myriad *empathies* embedded within distinct national and organizational contexts. This chapter, then, is an invitation to consider both the necessity of empathy in the business world and its complexities.

Empathy and Authenticity: Definitional Context

Empathy has traditionally been defined as one individual's understanding of and respect for another's experience and, by extension, responding with compassion. In this light, empathy may be construed as the other person's perception, that is, the feeling of being understood. Thus, it is not surprising that the following traits would be associated with empathy: active listening, authenticity, perspective awareness as well as self-awareness, and emotional flexibility (Dennison, 2023).

As we will demonstrate, those who lead organizations tend to be more successful when they embody those traits. But brilliant leaders go beyond role modeling by striving to ensure that empathetic values are embedded in the organizational culture.

Empathy may seem to come more easily to some than to others. And yet, it would be a mistake to conclude that the only way to define empathy is as a fixed trait. If treated as such, much like height or eye color, it would not be feasible for one to develop in this area. Accordingly, we may also look at empathy as a mode of conduct. Building on the work of Van der Graaf et al. (2016), Lyu et al. (2022) distinguish between "trait empathy," which implies a relatively inherent stable amount of empathy, while "state empathy" is defined as "the transient affective reaction elicited in concrete situations." The latter definition would imply that contextual conditions influence the extent to which one responds with appropriateness, both cognitively and affectively, to another's mental, emotional, and even physical state. In this regard, empathy is more fluid and is influenced by a range of sociocultural and other factors.

The purpose of this chapter is not to resolve definitional distinctions, particularly since fields such as social science and neuroscience continue to explore where on the trait↔behavior continuum empathy properly lies. The position advanced here, rather, is that empathy, when applied to leadership is most advantageously viewed as encompassing both transcending trait-based explanations because of the value in creating organizational cultures hospitable to the practice of empathy and transcending behavior-based interpretations because of the importance in acknowledging that empathetic expression is a more natural mode of social engagement for some.

Moreover, we posit that one can strengthen their empathetic expression through learning, practicing, modeling behavior, and self-talk (Dunlop, 2023). Organizational leaders can raise both their awareness of the importance of compassion and their tendency to communicate compassion through such exercises as journaling or being coached (Shapira & Mongrain, 2010). Activities such as being asked to imagine the backgrounds of others in order to gain insight into their current emotional experience, receiving instruction on how to frame questions to explore another's motive, and learning conversational tactics that place an emphasis on probing can heighten the probability of empathetic communication (Rogers, 2020).

Central to the notion of brilliant leadership is the critical linkage between empathy and authenticity. While leaders may act on the premise that sensitivity to employee concerns is helpful in achieving organizational goals, brilliant leaders believe that empathy has value in its own right. In this regard, empathy is less a means to an end (e.g., profiting) but rather is consistent with Kant's notion of "Character," which underscores truthfulness as a core element of virtue (Klocking, 2018). From a stakeholder perspective, particularly employees, brilliant leaders would be seen as behaving in ways that reveal a genuineness of motives. Guided by the deontologically-based philosophical guidepost, "We should do our duty for no other reason than because it's the right thing to do" (The Ethics Centre, 2016), the brilliant leader's empathetic conduct is derived less from strategic or tactical interests than it is from one's personal sense of integrity. That, then, is a defining feature of authenticity, that it frames empathy as values-driven rather than outcome-driven.

Employees are quite sensitive to authenticity. As discussed throughout this chapter, there are a host of signs they may look for to determine if such authenticity is present. Take just one, openness to criticism. Is such a leadership practice effective? As Parmar (2015a) observes, LinkedIn, which received the highest score for corporate empathy on the Lady Geek Empathy Index (theempathybusiness, n.d.), continuously demonstrates receptivity to ideas and, of greater pertinence to the matter at hand, seeks and forthrightly addresses negative feedback. The benefit extends beyond the creation of a healthier corporate culture; it also produces a healthier bottom line. Parmar (2015b) reports that "The top 10 companies in the Global Empathy Index 2015 increased in value more than twice as much as the bottom 10 and generated 50% more earnings. Average earnings among the top 10 were up 6% this year, while the average earnings of the bottom 10 dropped 9%."

Thus, leadership authenticity may be viewed as a pillar of organizational success, at least for success that occurs on a sustained basis. Authenticity undergirds a culture of trust, transparency, and reciprocal engagement. Employees who work in high-trust companies enjoy their jobs 60% more, are 70% more aligned with their companies' purpose, feel 66% closer to their colleagues, and engage with one another more respectfully than those in companies assessed as low-trust (Zak, 2017).

In the presence of authentic leadership, employees are also more inclined to take risks, for example, to present an idea without fear of criticism. Risk-taking is a function of vulnerability, of revealing or disclosing an aspect of oneself that might be regarded as a weakness or an area to be developed. Growth emerges from such practice, at least when leadership grounds organizational culture in the importance of learning. In such organizations, leaders value vulnerability because it constitutes a springboard for organizational actualization. "Authentic leaders embrace vulnerability because they understand its power to foster trust, connection, and growth within themselves and their teams" (Perkins, 2023). Crucially, authentic leaders can determine the appropriate context and timing of vulnerability, creating the necessary balance between being open and making a connection with others while also maintaining professional boundaries.

Brilliant leaders, therefore, exercise concern for their employees in ways that are perceived as empathetically sincere, strengthening employees' disposition toward team-related engagement, civility, and collegiality.

Empathy: A Balanced Skill Composite

Relationships among an organization's strategy, culture, and structure are influenced by many factors. Take just one, the relationship between stability and change. The tug-of-war between them is among the most challenging for any company to navigate, requiring skillful leadership characterized by an aptitude for mobilizing and sustaining the support of stakeholders, particularly employees. Leaders whose manner of social engagement reflects empathetic concern for others will have an advantage, as that individual will exhibit sensitivity to employees' needs for predictability while mobilizing them to support change and play a role in bringing it about.

On the one hand, there is a tendency to stay with what works, so it is understandable – though not necessarily excusable, especially if you are a shareholder – that there will be resistance to change even when it may be considered essential.

On the other hand, taking change too far can prove alienating to stakeholders and destabilizing to the organization. Consider the Coca-Cola fiasco when the company was forced to retreat from reformulating its flagship soda in 1985, or The Gap, which had to take a similar measure following the introduction of a new logo in 2010. These companies took change beyond the comfort level of their consumers. On the other end of the spectrum, some years ago, it was argued that Apple, a company associated with cutting-edge innovation, was not exercising sufficient inventiveness (Poletti, 2016).

Thus, the absence of change can violate expectations for some companies as much as excessive change might for others.

The notion of how much to change and under what circumstances to do so is, of course, among the most consequential of leadership responsibilities. And, as noted, it is not without risk. That is why leaders who are proficient at analyzing, forecasting the need for, and executing change are highly sought (not to mention well-compensated). In certain industries, e.g., telecommunications and information technology, change tends to occur more frequently than in, say, the insurance industry. Consumers expect change and are psychologically predisposed to anticipate it from their telecommunications providers and information technology companies. The failure to update product lines can promote the view that the company is not keeping pace. Accordingly, it is here that we see the need for balance, as such companies would be advised to demonstrate that they are dependable, reliable, and relevant, and to maintain a focus on consumers' needs along with service and product quality. Such characteristics constitute a counterweight to change with their emphasis on durability and continuity.

Other industries focus more on stability than change. Consider the imagery of the logos or taglines of insurance companies; e.g., Prudential has the Rock (what is more stable and enduring than a giant and iconic rock?), and State Farm touts that "like a good neighbor, State Farm is there," a phrase connoting reliability, stability, trust, and familiarity. In short, companies in different industries are bound to change at different paces and for different reasons. What might be too rapid or extreme in one industry could be considered too slow and insufficient in another.

Finding the right ratio for stability and change within the broader context of environmental conditions, consumer needs and tastes, industry trends, and the organization's identity constitutes a considerable test for leadership. This principle applies to organizations of any size.

The healthcare industry offers a good example of how stability and change can be either effectively integrated or unsettling to employees. Historically, healthcare organizations have been operationally organized around vital functions that require the repetitive performance of tasks, many of which demand adherence to strict protocols to satisfy regulatory demands, for example, with respect to medication administration, caregiving procedures, and medical record reporting. In such organizations, change may be perceived by employees as disruptive and, by extension, a potential threat. However, over the past several years, adaptability to shifting environmental conditions has become as important a priority for healthcare organizations as has stability. Organizational reconfigurations have accelerated, most especially through mergers of hospitals and acquisitions of medical practices, ambulatory and rehabilitation facilities, imaging centers, and even retail pharmacies and insurance companies.

While organizational leaders in healthcare must attend to the vicissitudes of the ever-evolving market, policy, technological, and economic conditions, employees must attend to the operational necessities that require reasonable levels of stability. In short, in today's healthcare world, leaders must have some entrepreneurial talent while staff operate in a largely stable operational world. We posit that the execution of brilliant leadership is dependent on a balanced skill set, one which accounts for, as well as transcends and integrates, the potentially disparate needs of stability and adaptability, efficiency and quality, current and future. Moreover, it is the empathetic leader who is best positioned to bridge those seeming divides. But the key to empathy, much like with permanence and change, is balance.

The Competing Values Framework (CVF) discussed in Chapter 1 offers insight into the importance of leadership in navigating the permanence-change schism through balance. Originated by Quinn and Rohrbaugh in 1983, "the CVF highlights the contradictory nature inherent in organizational environments and the complexity of choices faced by managers when responding to competing tensions" (Belasen et al. 2015).

Managers at different organizational levels may emphasize a particular skill orientation based on the responsibilities specific to their role. For example, first-line supervisors in industrial environments may be required to devote much time and energy to coordinating and monitoring the activity of frontline workers. This focus on ensuring the maintenance of the system, rather than reorienting it, is depicted in the lower-left quadrant of the CVF with its emphasis on structure and process.

That supervisor's manager would likely have responsibility and accountability for department output, requiring skills in the domain of productivity oversight and reporting, roles that are still in the transactional, lower-right quadrant. It is important to note that in a well-functioning organization, both the supervisor and manager would display human-relations skills, including empathy, a point discussed more fully below.

As managers rise through progressively higher levels of organizational responsibility, their roles naturally expand across more dimensions of the CVF. Senior managers, and particularly chief executives, hold responsibility and are accountable for maintaining operational steadiness while formulating goals and corresponding strategies necessary to ensure viability and successful competitive positioning. The day-to-day work of the organization must be accomplished, but vision setting is of equal importance and, in many instances, is of even greater significance. Strategy is the bridge for linking mission and vision. The brilliant leader engages employees in constructing that bridge so that even while they attend to the requirements of the moment, they are encouraged to participate in envisioning the future and planning for it.

Absent empathy on the part of leadership, the tools for achieving employee engagement tend to be more confined to extrinsic rewards, such as compensation and benefits, and by achieving desired performance by administering pressure with the attending consequence of punishment in the event performance is subpar. The brilliant leader employs motivation as the tool of choice. And while it is certainly necessary to remain competitive in the arena of extrinsic rewards, the empathetic leader need not invest exclusively in them to ensure employee satisfaction.

The benefits of empathetic leadership are noteworthy. By seeking to understand the perspectives of others, the leader becomes sensitized to their feelings and can show regard for their emotional experiences. As such, empathy encompasses cognitive (understanding), affective, and behavioral dimensions of leadership experience (König, et al., 2020). As discussed, while authenticity-based empathy is ethically substantive in that it is not undertaken exclusively to achieve an ulterior purpose, such behavior does produce favorable tangible outcomes.

Particular benefits accrue to organizations in which employees report their leadership to be empathetic: (1) employees reveal a greater willingness to engage collaboratively and an enhanced willingness to overcome differences to do so (Duhigg, 2016); (2) employees report that they experience less stress, including during periods of institutional discomfort, which may be brought about, for example, by financial pressures or competition intensification (Scott, et al., 2010); and (3) employees experience higher levels of morale when leadership exhibits compassion (Dutton et al., 2014).

Taken together, these three benefits tend to create an atmosphere in which "employee performance optimization" is more likely to materialize (Kusumaningrum, et al., 2020). Such optimization is revealed in metrics such as productivity enhancement (volume and quality of output), higher employee retention, lower absenteeism, and increased levels of creativity (for example, participation in idea generation and strategic planning). Again, authenticity is essential as employees interpret leadership motives through behavior; when employees perceive that leaders' values are in sync with their own, empathy is viewed not as lip service but as a reflection of leadership integrity.

Nevertheless, empathy, like many leadership qualities, can be a double-edged sword. When it becomes too dominant a feature of a leader's performance repertoire, organizational performance may be compromised (König, et al., 2020). If the empathetic antennae are too sharp, the leader may be excessively predisposed to discovering signs of emotional distress in the organization, distracting them from other priorities that influence the well-being of the organization. Overreliance on empathy may cause a leader to elevate a relatively mild warning sign related to the emotional wherewithal of employees into a crisis. Or the amount of attention devoted to a potential warning sign could detract from attending to other matters related to the functional effectiveness of the organization.

With respect to the CVF roles, overreliance on empathy would be depicted by a dominance in the upper-left quadrant with more limited than necessary role presence in the other quadrants. In short, overreliance would disrupt the skill balance that leaders must possess to achieve a healthy disposition for the organization and high levels of employee satisfaction. Moreover, too concentrated an attunement on emotions may result in an excessive effort to maintain stability as opposed to implementing potentially necessary change. That is, such excessiveness could impede the leader from pursuing transformational goals.

Thus, overreliance on empathy paradoxically converts what would ordinarily be a strength into a set of blinders that can obscure other institutional imperatives. Most considerably, the balance across the CVF roles and skills may be compromised if the leader fails to contextualize empathy in relation to the full range of leadership obligations. When this occurs, empathy becomes more of a trap than an asset. In the long run, by way of extending the paradox metaphor, if the organization suffers, so would the very employees whose emotional well-being was prioritized by the empathetic leader.

The fallout from overreliance on empathy can extend into the realm of the personal and psychological. By embracing the distress of others too acutely, the leader or manager is more likely to feel stress, potentially leading to burnout (Bower, 2022). The mental acuity necessary for sound judgment and evidence-based decision-making, not to mention the need to catch warning signs in a timely fashion (König, et al, 2020) may not be the only casualty – so might the psychosocial health of the leader or manager.

The CEO who possesses a high empathy trait is likely to have more access to two important types of information. First, because that leader's receptors are more attuned to the emotions circulating throughout the organization, that leader will have insight into whether employees experience satisfaction and why, and, by extension, the triggers that are likely to be emotionally destabilizing. Second, and by virtue of the trust and openness of communication that empathy spurs, the leader has more access to information about the company. Because employees are more willing to engage openly, the information that reaches the leader is less likely to be sanitized or modified. In such cases, the leader is able to exercise judgment based on more reliable information.

But when the balance is off, when empathy is excessively pronounced, the outsized concern for those experiencing distress may dominate the channel for incoming information. If they elevate the distress to a level unwarranted by actual circumstances, the leader may become predisposed to "cry wolf."

What is the "right" amount of empathy? Too little can create an organizational culture devoid of trust and the ability to motivate and inspire stakeholders. Too much can detract from moving the organization forward. The person who can find the right balance across the complex skill set associated with leading an organization is well on the way to earning the designation of brilliant.

Brilliant Leadership and a Culture of Empathy

In *The HP Way*, David Packard (2006) describes an early professional experience at GE when the company undertook significant efforts to control theft, which included securing computers and related equipment and installing monitoring systems. The result: theft went up. Packard believes the explanation is simple: while the action was designed to reduce theft, the symbolism unmistakably communicated to employees that they were not to be trusted. And what occurs when employees believe management doesn't trust them? They are likely to feel disrespected and disengaged, and if the lack of trust festers, they may become cynical.

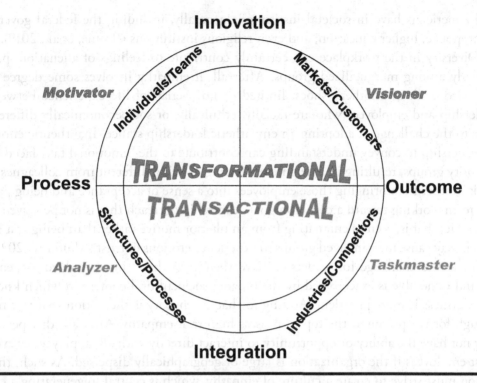

Figure 2.1   Competing Values Framework (Adapted from Cameron, et al., 2014).

One of the most precious commodities an organization has is trust. In the workplace, as in life, trust is established when people believe that those with whom they interact have their best interests at heart, have faith in their decisions, are honest and truthful, and believe that there is a safety net should some failure occur. When employees trust leadership, much can be accomplished. When they do not, success is likely to be that much more elusive.

Building and sustaining trust is not easy, especially in today's climate. In recent years, Americans are more apt to regard societal institutions skeptically, more prone than in previous generations to question whether the motives of those in charge are above board and grounded in their best interests. Consider that in 1972, 45% of survey respondents agreed with the statement "most people can be trusted" (Smith et al., 2016). By 2018, only 30% agreed with the statement. And by 2022, almost 60% of those surveyed internationally indicated that their "default" is to distrust other people (Edelman, 2023).

It is also not surprising for the spillover effect to influence attitudes in the workplace. Today, employees have a heightened predisposition to question the probity of their leaders. According to a recent survey of over 1,000 employees, "52% of respondents feel their company's efforts to be empathetic towards employees are dishonest" (Valadon, 2023). Such findings should come as no surprise given the diminishing faith that Americans have in societal institutions generally, including the federal government, police, higher education, and even religious institutions (Rainie, et al., 2019).

Diversity in the workplace can certainly contribute to feelings of alienation, particularly among marginalized groups. After all, if empathy involves some degree of ability to walk in another's shoes, limited or no overlap of life experience between leadership and employees who are racially, ethnically, or socioeconomically different adds to the challenge of adopting an empathetic leadership stance. Inauthentic efforts by leadership to convey understanding can contribute to the "emotional tax" faced by minority groups, resulting in a heightened feeling of being different from colleagues at work. Rather than bringing those employees into a sense of acceptance and being part of a team working toward a common goal, leadership outreach that is not perceived as authentic, that is, seen as emanating from an ulterior motive rather than being values-based, may cause marginalized groups to experience erosions of trust (Akubuiro, 2021).

Thus, the challenge for leaders to have their empathetic intent judged as genuine and honorable is exacerbated by the broader sociocultural context in which knee-jerk wariness is more prevalent. Adding to that complexity is the notion that it is not enough for the person at the top to possess high-trait empathy. After all, that person may not have the ability or opportunity to interact directly with all employees or even most employees if the organization is large or geographically dispersed. As such, that person must strive to create a culture of empathy, which is central to generating a climate of trust. And, while that has become more of an uphill battle, it is not impossible.

Research on compliance gaining indicates that credibility has three primary constituent parts, all interrelated: expertise, trustworthiness, and goodwill (Gass & Seiter, 2022). With respect to leadership, expertise can take multiple forms. In addition to content expertise in a field relevant to the organization's work, perceptions of a leader's expertise relate to the quality of judgment and decision-making, strategy development, cultivating consequential alliances, and advocacy for the organization.

The dimensions of trustworthiness and goodwill interlace quite considerably. Trustworthiness is a function of perceptions of leadership's personal integrity, which entails beliefs about the leader's character and the extent to which the person appears to be morally grounded, that is, authentic, as discussed throughout this chapter. Goodwill relates to the extent to which the leader "cares about me" and has "my interests at heart." Taken together, trustworthiness is a measure of the degree to which the leader is to be believed – taken at their word – while goodwill is a measure of what McCrosky and Teven (1999) term "perceived caring."

The risk of a leader acting in a manner that appears to be caring, that is, is deemed performative but is not perceived as trustworthy, is substantial. And yet, it is far from uncommon, as reflected in the survey referenced above indicating that over half the respondents believed their CEOs' empathetic overtures were not sincere. Building and sustaining a culture of empathy, one in which employees' predisposition to see the work environment through a lens unclouded by suspicion, takes a significant effort. And creating such a culture means working with and through others.

Leaders interested in building and sustaining a culture of empathy, that is, going beyond their personal role modeling and infusing the organizational atmosphere with a genuine sense that employees matter, would be encouraged to pursue activities that (1) recognize cynicism is triggered more easily than trust, (2) cultivate transparency and inclusion, (3) instill interdisciplinary practice, (4) view empathy and accountability as in sync, (5) promote the principle that the consequence of error should be learning, not the administration of punitive measures, (6) practice the language of empathy and build it into relevant organizational policy, and (7) honor the reciprocal nature of humility.

Trust vs. Cynicism. When cynicism takes root in an organizational culture, it can prove exceedingly, if not impossibly, challenging to undo. And given the current propensity for skepticism to color how employees view their organization's leadership, managing the cynicism-trust divide has emerged as a fundamental challenge for today's leaders.

CEO turnover hasn't helped. For example, the more frequent the turnover in the executive suite, the less time is available to cultivate and nurture empathetic norms in the psycho-social work milieu. While there was some downturn in overall CEO turnover during the pandemic, in 2022, turnover returned to the pre-pandemic levels of roughly 12% on a global basis and is predicted to increase by up to 7% in the coming couple of years (Tonello, et al., 2021). Leadership turnover varies by industry, of course, with healthcare and consumer companies leading the way in CEO turnover with 11% of CEOs leaving and being replaced in 2023 (SpencerStuart, 2024). Interestingly, it is in those very industries in which employees are asked to display empathetic vitality to their consumers that stability at the top is shakiest.

Whereas cynicism is relatively easily triggered, trust takes time to develop. It requires getting to know people, achieving some measure of familiarity, and seeing evidence of active listening and feeling heard. While that may seem intuitively sensible, the evidence suggests otherwise. In fact, many CEOs fail to recognize the importance of empathy in the workplace, viewing their revelation of emotions as inconsistent with their image of a leadership persona. A recent survey indicated that 68% of CEOs believed that showing empathy would render them not respected by their employees (Kurter, 2021). Absent active efforts to institute empathy as a prevailing characteristic of institutional culture, cynicism may fill the void.

Thus, a first and, arguably, the most critical precondition in building or strengthening a culture of empathy is recognizing its importance. The survey data indicate that this is antithetical to the widely held belief on the part of chief executives that emotional expression and respect are mutually exclusive. Shifting the mindset to the more demonstrably proven benefits of an integrated association of empathy and respect is basic to instilling an organization-wide ethic of empathy.

Transparency. Empathy, by definition, is not possible to emerge as a staple of organizational culture without transparency. But transparency is complex. Organizational leaders contend with varying and even competing pressures that influence how they view and define transparency and how they believe it is best exercised.

One of our authors consulted with a hospital system a few years ago that was engaged in acquisition negotiations. Senior leadership chose not to share its plans with middle management and staff for fear that the deal could fall through if the information became public during sensitive stages in the negotiation talks. At the same time, many of the hospital system's middle managers had seen positions like theirs become jeopardized when economies of scale opportunities created by acquisitions came to fruition. They wanted to believe that their leadership cared about them.

When leadership finally did announce the plan, ten days prior to the contract signing, many middle managers were disheartened and angry. They believed they were entitled to hear such potentially consequential news far earlier and that they should have been informed not just about the acquisition but also about what the acquisition might mean in terms of their positions. They came to believe that the lack of transparency signaled that leadership cared more about the acquisition prospects than about their livelihoods.

Leadership, on the other hand, believed that it was indeed forthcoming, as evidenced by their contention that the announcement was made as soon as assurances were in place that the merger deal was solidified. In this case, each group viewed transparency quite differently. Each group believed it was not understood and that the other side was short on empathy.

The larger issue, as our author came to understand, was that a foundation of transparency and empathy had not been in place. Senior management and middle management were separated by perceptions. Each looked at the timeframe of the announcement, not to mention the lack of consultation with middle management about the merger plan, and saw something quite different: for senior management, it reaffirmed their unwarranted belief that middle management would be satisfied with their handling of the issue; for middle management, it signaled a lack of concern about their welfare. It made them feel their interests were not paramount in the minds of senior management, and that senior management did not know what it was like to walk in their shoes. For middle managers, this failure to be heard was, at heart, a matter of trust.

The solution in this case would not have been to jeopardize the merger deal by announcing it prematurely. Had the news been leaked, even inadvertently, it could have derailed the merger since other hospitals had been vying quite competitively to become part of the hospital system. But had a culture of empathy been in place, middle managers would have been more understanding of the need to keep the deal under wraps. Transparency, thus, may be viewed as a perception contextualized by climate. If employees and other stakeholders believe that openness is a valued dimension of the work-life experience, and if such openness is part of a commitment to a culture of empathy – and, in this case, if employees had a history of believing that senior management always had their interests in mind – they will be far more understanding and forgiving when circumstances arise in which it would be necessary to suspend transparency for the greater good.

Interdisciplinarity. Promoting an interdisciplinary or cross-functional collaborative model in the workplace is a vital ingredient in fostering a culture of empathy. Assembling people from different functional areas to work on an issue sensitizes all to varying perspectives, heightening the understanding of each about the nature and importance of the contribution of the others. Of course, this is contingent on effective team leadership – a skilled facilitator who not only keeps the group focused on goals but ensures that each member is empowered to express their view and that differences are managed respectfully. When this occurs, the group is more accepting of the proposition that the greater good should prevail over parochialism, which tends to be characterized by beliefs about the superiority of one's point of view. It shifts the focus to "other-centric" by fostering a superego mentality in which ethical correctness is contingent on knowing and valuing the work of colleagues.

The interdisciplinary element is essential, not just for enhancing the empathetic inclination of team participants but because different perspectives can lead to novel solutions. Even Albert Einstein, who is often thought of as toiling away in isolation in a lab, depended on cross-functional teams quite extensively. Referred to as "muckers," Einstein brought together not only technical specialists but social scientists and lay people to contribute to and test out ideas (Boogaard, 2023). Exposure to diverse perspectives facilitates openness; for example, jurors' receptiveness to others' points of view and empathetic predisposition increased as their diversity strengthened (Somers, 2006).

Organizations that fail to create opportunities for cross-organizational exposure are more prone to silo cultures, fostering less creative solution development and a tendency for provincialism and groupthink to supersede respect as prevailing cultural norms. It may very well be that this sort of tribalism is likely to emerge in organizations in which leaders fail to institute an empathetic culture. Celebrating diversity means that all will feel heard, particularly those whose voices are at the outer margins of organizational influence. The brilliant leader ensures that such an institutional dynamic will be the cultural heart of the organization.

Empathy and accountability. Leaders who dismiss the importance of empathy often suggest that it leads to or equates with leniency. If a defining feature of empathy is forgiveness under any and all circumstances, or if, as argued earlier in this chapter, a leader relies too heavily on emotions as a managing framework, then indeed, leniency may be the outcome. While empathy implies an understanding of another person and a felt appreciation of and sensitivity to that person's experience, it is also grounded in respect for that person. On the one hand, accountability may be viewed as in conflict with empathy, as captured by the dilemma of how can a manager be expected to have an employee answer for poor conduct given the challenges that person has experienced?

Or, on the other hand, and as with brilliant leadership, accountability and empathy are unified, integrated in a higher order recognition that employees desire a clear understanding of boundaries, want to be acknowledged for a job well done, are motivated by positive recognition, and, indeed, desire to feel understood. When responsibility and accountability are synced, employees embrace accountability.

A principal outcome of error should be learning. It has long been debated whether and when to employ punitive measures to address behavior in the workplace. While certain behaviors may merit punitive responses, for example, ethical breaches, organizations increasingly find that policies emphasizing learning as a consequence of a performance lapse are more apt to lead to (1) greater willingness on the part of employees to report a personal failure or mistake, (2) a stronger inclination from supervisors to report errors committed by their employees, (3) enhanced motivation on the part of the employee to improve, (4) improved productivity and performance quality on the part of the employee, and (5) a greater likelihood the employee will remain with the organization (Belasen, et al., 2024).

Consider this scenario: Joe, a stock room employee in a hotel restaurant, fails to refrigerate three cartons of perishable items. Joe has been employed there for only two months and now is panicking that the food will have spoiled. Three options come to his mind. One, quickly refrigerate the food and hope (or pray) that it won't spoil. Two, blame the incident on the vendor delivery service, suggesting that the boxes were left in an unseen area. Three, confess.

In making his decision, Joe recalls that a member of the waitstaff spilled soup on a patron last week and was distressed. The manager quickly assembled a team to clean the area, graciously apologized to the customer and, of course, arranged for her clothes to be cleaned at the expense of the hotel while providing three meals at no cost.

Joe saw the manager bring the co-worker into his office. He thought that she would be severely chastised, if not outright fired. Fifteen minutes later, she emerged and explained to Joe that the manager first inquired how the mishap occurred. She explained that in her haste to serve the food, she did not assemble the meals on the tray in a properly balanced fashion. She then said that the manager informed her he had those same challenges when he started out years ago, that he occasionally avoided taking proper care because he was anxious about getting the food out on time. She found this comforting. The manager also arranged for a seasoned member of the waitstaff to coach her on tray balancing.

Joe chose option 3, confession. The manager asked why he neglected to refrigerate the food as soon as it arrived. Joe explained that in attending to multiple priorities, he simply overlooked it, a partial result of being new to the job. The manager expressed understanding and indicated that the pressure might be relieved if Joe had a checklist. Seeking to empower Joe, and confirm his trust in him, the manager asked Joe to develop the checklist, advising him to consult co-workers in the process, and the two would review it in a few days.

Joe was fortunate to work in an organization where a mistake is viewed as a learning experience. And at the core of this organizational culture is empathy. Joe felt that the manager understood his predicament. Over the next few months, it became apparent that the manager was not alone in exercising empathy. The leadership team of the hotel treated the manager just the same way the manager treated the restaurant staff. Joe was not surprised to learn that so many of the employees had long tenure with the hotel.

Widening the lens, research indicates that nonpunitive policies lead to improvements in safety and quality. This is especially important in organizations designated as High Reliability Organizations, or HROs. In such industries, which include airlines and healthcare, considerable investment must be made to prevent errors since the cost of a single untoward event can be exceedingly high. In those industries, nonpunitive emphases in performance management policies have been shown to lead to improvements in quality, safety, employee and customer satisfaction, and in empowering employees to take the lead in identifying potential risks (Belasen, et al., 2024; The Leapfrog Group, n.d.).

The language and policy of empathy. Empathy is unlikely to emanate and flow throughout an organization organically. The brilliant leader practices empathetic communication, which is a necessary but insufficient condition for instilling empathy. The brilliant leader also ensures that active listening is not just taught and encouraged but becomes institutionalized in recruitment and hiring standards, job descriptions, performance evaluation activities, and criteria for promotion. That leader also cultivates compassion by linking the mission of the organization to underlying values that emphasize the social good associated with the organization's work. Employee motivation is linked to the belief that the organization's values and their personal values have significant overlap.

Reciprocity of humility. A culture of empathy demands a particular type of risk-taking, the risk of being vulnerable, as discussed above. After all, it entails disclosing. And disclosing is a function of feeling safe, of the belief that the person listening is genuinely concerned. For a leader, this means acknowledging that they don't have all the answers and that they rely on the support of those throughout the organization. This is not a declaration of timidity. Paradoxically, the most emotionally mature leaders are the most willing to seek counsel. Of course, they are also decisive, willing to make tough decisions following a judicious evaluation of risk and benefit. In a paradoxical way, such vulnerability becomes a strength, because more trusting and more respectful behavior leads to a greater likelihood of others following suit.

Conclusion

One of our authors recently met with the leadership team of a hospital system to consult on system expansion. Upon arriving at the entrance to the main hospital in the system, where the meeting was taking place, our author saw a patient struggling to gain her balance as she was exiting a car. Our author offered to assist, and the patient asked if a wheelchair could be requested from a nearby security guard. The security guard responded, "It's not my job. And the patient valet is on a break. Try the information desk inside."

While the patient leaned against an exterior wall, the author entered the hospital and asked a representative at the information desk for a wheelchair. The representative replied, "It's not my job. Check with the security guard outside."

The author informed the representative that the guard recommended speaking with the information desk. The representative, exasperated, shrugged, and declared that she was too busy to take on a responsibility that wasn't hers. The author found a nearby wheelchair, escorted the patient to the registration area in the hospital, and then returned the wheelchair to the spot where it was found.

The executive suite, located on the top floor of the building, was beautifully appointed with plush carpet and photos, evidently staged, adorning the corridor walls depicting employees looking happy as they went about their business – like serving food to a patient and helping a patient onto a physical therapy table. There was even a photo of a pleasant security guard pushing a patient in a wheelchair, as both smiled. The irony was palpable.

Inside the mahogany-lined boardroom, the author explained to the hospital's leadership team the incident with the wheelchair. The CEO and board chair seemed baffled by the apparent indifference of the employees to the well-being of that patient. The author asked if security staff and information desk employees were included in presentations about hospital plans.

"Not generally," the CEO replied. "Their jobs are relatively straightforward, so the need for that is not great. Plus, we'd have to pay for replacements while they attended, which is a cost that's difficult to justify."

While the employees' behavior is far from excusable, their dispiritedness and disconnectedness to the interest of putting the patient first are quite revealing. The CEO views those employees as having narrow roles, seeing them as virtually commodified entities with limited impact on institutional goals. He does not view them as people with a deep desire to believe the organization cares about them. That lack of caring, in turn, is evident in the choices those employees make about where their duties begin and end. They clearly opted to draw boundaries around their work that may have fit the minimum standards of the job description but certainly failed to live up to the spirit of empathy.

And therein lies an important lesson of this chapter: authenticity and empathy are not universally practiced. The hospital system CEO was not antagonistic toward employees, and probably even believed that he did his best to ensure that the organizational culture was positive. But believing that one is doing their very best in that regard and actually doing it are not the same. The employees in the hospital did not have to explicitly state that they didn't feel as though they mattered. Their conduct spoke volumes. And the problem was not confined to their feelings. It detracted from their productivity, from their willingness to contribute their energy and talent to ensure that the organization was fully hospitable to those who come for care.

That patient has a choice as well, whether to use that facility or another the next time she needs medical care. There was little about the employees' conduct that would make it a certainty that she would use that hospital for future needs. As such, the CEO's contention of their limited impact on organizational goals was a miscalculation.

In this chapter, we discussed empathy and its fundamental relationship to authenticity. The research presented throughout this chapter suggests that for many executives, these constructs are not adequately valued and that many employees view empathetic overtures from leadership with skepticism. This points to the complex nature of empathy in the work environment. Empathy takes effort, hard work, and commitment. Building trust takes time, skill, and persistence.

Employees know authenticity when they see it, and they know empathy when they feel it. The brilliant leader understands this. And the brilliant leader understands that the prospects for organizational success rise when empathy is embedded in the organizational culture. But above all, the brilliant leader, ever values-driven, is bound to exercise empathy because it is the right thing to do.

References

Akubuiro, B. (2021, October 4). The catch 22 of authenticity for minority leaders. *Forbes.* https://www.forbes.com/sites/forbescommunicationscouncil/2021/10/04/the-catch-22 -of-authenticity-for-minority-leaders/

Belasen, A., Eisenberg, B., & Borgos, J. (2024). *Transforming leadership, improving patient experience: Communication strategies for driving patient satisfaction.* Routledge.

Belasen, A., Eisenberg, B., & Huppertz, J. (2015). *Mastering leadership: A vital resource for health care organizations.* Jones and Bartlett Learning.

Bhopal, K. (2013). Identity, empathy and 'otherness': Asian women, education and dowries in the UK. In Mirza, H. & Joseph, C. (Eds.). *Black and postcolonial feminisms in new times* (pp. 27–39). Routledge.

Boogaard, K. (2023). 3 examples of cross-functional collaboration that fueled innovation. *Miro.* https://miro.com/blog/cross-functional-collaboration-examples/

Bower, T. (2022, February 8). Too much empathy is damaging: 3 ways to get the balance right. *Forbes.* https://www.forbes.com/sites/tracybrower/2022/08/07/too-much-empathy -is-damaging-3-ways-to-get-the-balance-right/?sh=4ceb732971bc

Dennison, K. (2023, February 24). The importance of empathy in leadership: How to lead with compassion and understanding in 2023. *Forbes.* https://www.forbes.com/sites/ karadennison/2023/02/24/the-importance-of-empathy-in-leadership-how-to-lead-with -compassion-and-understanding-in-2023/

Doehring, C. (2018). Teaching theological empathy to distance learners of intercultural spiritual care. *Pastoral Psychology, 67*(5), 461–474.

Duhigg, C. (2016). What Google learned from its quest to build the perfect team. *The New York Times.* https://www.nytimes.com/2016/02/28/magazine/what-google-learned-from -its-quest-to-build-the-perfect-team.html

Dunlop, R. (2023*). Leading my change from within: An exploration of self-talk, self-compassion, self-awareness, and leadership.* Royal Roads University (Canada) ProQuest Dissertations Publishing, 30524111. https://www.proquest.com/openview/3f0aa0d0be4a93a6e38 0e43fefbbc4bb/1?pq-origsite=gscholar&cbl=18750&diss=y

Dutton, J., Workman, K., & Hardin, A. (2014). Compassion at work. *Annual Review of Organizational Psychology and Organizational Behavior, 1*(1), 277–304. https://www .annualreviews.org/doi/full/10.1146/annurev-orgpsych-031413-091221

Edelman Trust Barometer. (2023). *2023 Edelman trust barometer special report: Trust at work.* https://www.edelman.com/sites/g/files/aatuss191/files/2023-08/2023-Edelman-Trust -Barometer-Special-Report-Trust-Work.pdf

Evans, K., & Unangst, L. (2020). The K-12 to university pipeline in the US context: Implications for refugee students. In L. Unangst, H. Ergin, A. Khajarian, T. DeLaquil, & H. de Wit. (Eds.), *Refugees and higher education: Trans-national perspectives on access, equity, and internationalization* (pp. 295–312). Brill Sense. https://doi.org/10.1163/9789004435841

Gass, R., & Seiter, J. (2022). *Persuasion: Social influence and compliance gaining* (7th ed.). Routledge.

Harvard Business School Online. (n.d.). https://online.hbs.edu/?c1=GAW_SE_NW&source =US_BRND_GEN&cr2=search__-__nw__-__us__-__branded__-__audience&kw =harvard_business_school_online_exm&cr5=668868044151&cr7=c&gad_source=1 &gclid=CjwKCAjwh4-wBhB3EiwAeJsppGh0OwmW6ZM0IO1tBUEzjqqrYnqPP8ytcs JXlJEcxejTgkoihoBg7BoCiDEQAvD_BwE

Husband, A. (2021, November 15). Using empathy and entrepreneurship to improve affordable housing. *MIT Sloan School of Management.* https://mitsloan.mit.edu/alumni/using -empathy-and-entrepreneurship-to-improve-affordable-housing

Klocking, P. (2018). Immanuel Kant on authenticity. *Stack Exchange.* https://philosophy .stackexchange.com/questions/39313/immanuel-kant-on-authenticity#:~:text=Authent icity%20in%20Kant%20is%20closely,general)%20is%20basically%20equivalent%20 there

König, A., Graf-Vlachy, L., Bundy, J., & Little, L. (2020). A blessing and a curse: How CEOs' trait empathy affects their management of organizational crises. *Academy of Management Review, 45*(1). https://journals.aom.org/doi/epub/10.5465/amr.2017.0387

Kurter, H. (2021, June 27). High turnover? Here are 3 things CEOs do that sabotage their workplace culture. *Forbes.* https://www.forbes.com/sites/heidilynnekurter/2021/06/27 /high-turnover-here-are-3-things-ceos-do-that-sabotage-their-workplace-culture/?sh =587252dc288f

Kusumaningrum, G., Haryono, S., & Handari, R. (2020). Employee performance optimization through transformational leadership, procedural justice, and training: The role of self-efficacy. *Journal of Asian Finance, Economics and Business, 7*(12), 995–1004. http:// koreascience.or.kr/article/JAKO202034651879506.pdf

Lundy, B. L. (2007). Service learning in life-span developmental psychology: Higher exam scores and increased empathy. *Teaching of Psychology, 34*(1), 23–27.

Lyu. D., Liu, Q., Pan, Y. Wang, A., & Pei, G. (2022). The different role of trait empathy and state social exclusion empathy on subsequent feelings about gambling outcome: Evidence from event-related potentials and time-frequency decompositions. *Neuropsychologia, 176,* 5. https://www.sciencedirect.com/science/article/abs/pii/S0028393222002287#:~:text =Trait%20empathy%20is%20a%20general,et%20al.%2C%202016

McCroskey, J., & Teven, J. (1999). Goodwill: A reexamination of the construct and its measurement. *Communication Monographs, 66*(1), 90–103.

Packard, D. (2006). *The HP Way. Harper Collins.*

Parmar, B. (2015a, March 5). Empathy is not for wimps, it is for survival. *Financial Times.* https://www.proquest.com/docview/1669695613?accountid=8067&parentSessionId =zNQj1dK1bur1lclsmIwxQMSCczoc0JwgqYDQ7iyjXAQ%3D&pq-origsite=primo &sourcetype=Newspapers

Parmar, B. (2015b, November 27). The most (and least) empathetic companies. *Harvard Business Review.* https://hbr.org/2015/11/2015-empathy-index#:~:text=The%20top %2010%20companies%20in,index%20can%20be%20found%20here

Perkins, K. M. (2023, May 27). Authenticity: The key to great leadership and how to embrace it. *Forbes,* para. 11. https://www.forbes.com/sites/kathymillerperkins/2023/05/27/ authenticity-the-key-to-great-leadership-and-how-to-embrace-it/

Poletti, T. (2016, October 31). Apple's underwhelming Mac event was lacking in innovation. *Market Watch.* https://www.marketwatch.com/story/apples-underwhelming-mac-event -was-lacking-in-innovation-2016-10-27

Preller, K. H., Hulka, L. M., Vonmoos, M., Jenni, D., Baumgartner, M. R., Seifritz, E., & Quednow, B. B. (2014). Impaired emotional empathy and related social network deficits in cocaine users. *Addiction Biology, 19*(3), 452–466.

Quinn, R. E., & Rohrbaugh, J. (1983). A competing values approach to organizational effec- tiveness. *Public Productivity Review, 5*(2), 122–140. https://doi.org/10.2307/3380029

Rainie, L., Keeter, S., & Perrin, A. (2019). *Trust and distrust in America.* Pew Research Center. file:///C:/Users/barei/Downloads/pew-research-center_trust-distrust-in-america-report _2019-07-22-1%20(1).pdf

Rogers, K. (2020, June 24). Empathy is both a trait and a skill. Here's how to strengthen it. *CNN.* Retrieved from https://www.cnn.com/2020/06/24/health/develop-empathy-skills -wellness/index.html

Scott, B., Colquitt, J., Paddock, E., & Judge, T. (2010). A daily investigation of the role of manager empathy on employee well-being. *Organizational Behavior and Human Decision Processes, 113*(2), 127–140. https://doi.org/10.1016/j.obhdp.2010.08.001

Somers, S. (2006). On racial diversity and group decision making: Identifying multiple effects of racial composition on jury deliberations. *Journal of Personality and Social Psychology, 90*(4), 597– 612.

SpencerStuart. (2023). *CEO transitions.* https://www.spencerstuart.com/-/media/2024/02/ ceotransitions/2023_ceo_transitions.pdf

Shapira, L. B., & Mongrain, M. (2010). The benefits of self-compassion and optimism exer- cises for individuals vulnerable to depression. *The Journal of Positive Psychology, 5*(5), 377–389. https://doi.org/10.1080/17439760.2010.516763

Smith, T. W., Hout, M., & Marsden, P. V. (2016). *General social survey, 1972-2016.* Inter- University Consortium for Political and Social Research, National Opinion Research Center. https://www.icpsr.umich.edu/web/ICPSR/studies/36797

The Ethics Centre. (2016). *Ethics explainer: Deontology.* https://ethics.org.au/ethics-explainer -deontology/

theempathybusiness. (n.d.). https://theempathybusiness.com/

The Leapfrog Group. (n.d.). *About us. https://www.hospitalsafetygrade.org/theempathybusiness* https://theempathybusiness.com/

Tonello, M., Schloetzer, J., & McKenna, F. (2021). *CEO succession practices in the Russell 3000 and S&P 500: 2021 edition.* The Conference Board. https://www.conference-board.org/ topics/ceo-succession-practices/ceo-succession-practices-2021

Tuck Business School. (n.d.). https://www.tuck.dartmouth.edu/mba/life-at-tuck/diversity

Valadon, O. (2023, October 17). What we get wrong about empathic leadership. *Harvard Business Review.* https://hbr.org/2023/10/what-we-get-wrong-about-empathic-leadership

Van der Graaff, J., Meeus, W., de Wied, M ., van Boxtel, A., van Lier, P., Koot, H., & Branje, S. (2016). Motor, affective and cognitive empathy in adolescence: Interrelations between facial electromyography and self-reported trait and state measures. *Cognition and Emotion, 30*(4), 745–761. https://doi.org/10.1080/02699931.2015.1027665

Zak, P. J. (2017, January 1–February). The neuroscience of trust. *Harvard Business Review,* 84–90. https://hbr.org/2017/01/the-neuroscience-of-trust

Chapter 3

Promoting Innovation and Creativity through Human-Centered Leadership

Mariana Ortega and Nicolas Sonder

History will reflect on the early 2020s as a period of significant disruption for the global workforce. The COVID-19 pandemic put most of the world's population into lockdown, triggering massive supply chain disruptions and other serious challenges. As the pandemic stretched on, remote work was proven to be a productively viable alternative for many. This spurred the Great Resignation, which soon turned into the Great Reshuffle, opening the door for millions of employees to competitively pursue new job opportunities offering permanent remote-based roles, better pay, and progressive work cultures that prioritize psychological safety. After decades of top-down organizational structure and decision-making, the pandemic emboldened workers, empowered by a profound reassessment of personal values, to demand an overdue change in executive leadership approach. All of this put significant pressure on business leaders to re-examine and adjust.

Today, the global post-pandemic recovery, a new generation entering the job market, and the rapid rise of AI are conflating to produce the most radical shifts in the organizational landscape in more than 50 years. Global human management company ADP's annual report "People at Work 2023" shares insight on how the US labor market is still feeling the pandemic's aftereffects. The headline of its research by Richardson and Antonello (2023) is a clear confirmation that leadership styles must continue to flex and evolve to retain an engaged and effective workforce: "As workers continue to demand and expect to be given more, the onus is on employers to come up with innovative ways to satisfy their needs in a way that makes sense" (p. 6).

DOI: 10.4324/9781003495307-4

In that most recent data, Richardson and Antonello (2023) found that while pay and compensation has become a central focus, flexible working arrangements and an inclusive, psychologically safe work environment remain crucial top priorities for workers. This is evident in the metrics: despite an aggressive push from CEOs to bring employees back to the office five days a week, the mandate still only applies to less than 40% of the corporate workforce – a full 60% are working in full-time remote or hybrid roles (Richardson & Antonello, p. 45). Additionally, they reported that 75% of workers surveyed said diversity, equity, and inclusion (DEI) education and activities are still prominent in their organizations, "closely followed by mentoring [programs]" (p. 46).

Workplace culture and behaviors remain primary drivers for change in traditional leadership styles. Beddows et al. (2022) found that, more than ever, leaders "are openly thinking and talking about fundamental values that underpin human thriving and sustainability: authenticity, purpose, meaning, trust, compassion, physical and psychological safety, traumatic growth, diversity and inclusion, resilience, and well-being" (p. 54). They also assert that a human-centered leadership style, promoting authenticity and people-oriented values combined with a healthy respect for systemic agility, is the new aspirational standard (Beddows et al., 2022).

Yet in their efforts to navigate organizations through a persistent VUCA climate – volatile, uncertain, complex, and ambiguous – most CEOs have almost exclusively focused on chasing profits and gaining a competitive advantage by increasing the speed and output of innovation. This race can create toxic work cultures, especially in high-oversight environments where a dominating, task-focused leadership style is the default management technique, but for the most adaptable leaders, these insights represent an opportunity to try on a more agile and contemporary leadership approach.

What's emerging in both research and practice is a recurring theme: creativity and innovation thrive in organizational cultures that prioritize psychological safety as a core value equal in importance to operational excellence. Leaders who are integrating a human-centered leadership (HCL) style are finding that demonstrating and promoting psychological safety as a core leadership value, while upholding accountability for performance and results, measurably improves the velocity, quality, and quantity of innovative outputs. The best creative ideas struggle to surface in environments where fear, intimidation, or exclusionary behaviors are regularly exercised, consciously or unconsciously.

Leaders who are more comfortable with a task-oriented approach tend to initially balk at or dismiss this concept. The common prevailing perception is that to be an effective human-centric leader, firm decisiveness and operational excellence must take a backseat; one can lead with the head or the heart, but not with both simultaneously. Beliefs such as *transparency compromises positional authority, admitting fault or error suggests weakness, empathy and accountability are at cross-purposes,* etc. are examples of fixed mindset thinking. The concept of fixed versus growth mindsets was introduced by Carol Dweck (2016), the former being defined by the overarching belief that one's capacity and capability for basic traits are inherent and immutable; in other words, each person is born with a certain amount of talent, intelligence, and potential for aptitude, and once it's been exhausted or has reached capacity, there's no more cognitive space left for further growth or improvement. Fixed mindsets put individuals at a disadvantage in generating strategic or innovative solutions.

By contrast, human-centric leaders commit to continually embracing a growth mindset, defined as holding the predominant belief that meaningful improvement is achievable through earnest commitment and perseverance (Dweck, 2016). This approach tends to nurture a greater capacity for creative thinking, as well as inspiring it in others. Yet a growth mindset is not enough – it also requires authentic intention and grit to activate shifting one's leadership approach from transactional and high-control to transformative and human-centric.

The Path to 21st-Century Leadership

To better understand the dynamics of modern leadership, it's helpful to consider it in context of how leadership styles have evolved from the Information Age to the present day. The post-WWII economic boom introduced what would become the predominant leadership style of the 20th century. The authoritarian command-and-control management approach emerged from the militaristic principles the high-ranking American officers and generals used to defeat Axis powers overseas during WWII. Once the war ended, military leaders were commonly offered business leadership positions at private companies upon their return Stateside. Predictably, they defaulted to the kind of leadership that had worked in the war and with which they were most familiar: intense supervision, total commanding authority, and strict control of all important decisions. As such, this exhaustive top-down management approach became the de facto model for what competent leadership "should" look like and was quickly adopted as the aspirational standard for leaders in organizational hierarchies.

The Rise of Command-and-Control

It's fair to note that the command-and-control style exists on a continuum of intensity. It can present as militaristic or micromanaging, but it's generally rooted in inflexibility. That said, it's also true that command-and-control is an effective method of leadership when applied in its proper context; specifically, in high-risk/high-complexity situations scenario where highly detailed direction, precise timing, and flawless execution are crucial to ensure survival. This is brilliant for the battlefield and, for business, it's best reserved for singular high-stakes scenarios with potentially devastating consequences. It's when command-and-control is applied to the management of everyday operations that it tends to become problematic. Seeds of worker resentment, dissent, and attrition are planted when individual thinking and autonomy are continuously subject to constant demands for compliance.

This highlights another issue: command-and-control centers power and privilege on senior leadership, creating a clear line of demarcation between workers and executives. Although command-and-control management tactics have become somewhat diluted as decades progressed, the authoritarian approach eventually became widely associated with low employee morale and limited professional mobility for rank-and-file workers. Nevertheless, many corporate executives are conditioned to default to some version of the task-focused, command-and-control management style as everyday practice, which serves to continue upholding conventional structures of hierarchy and power.

Servant Leadership for a New Era

The rise of the civil rights movement in the 1960s and 1970s began to see popular sentiment shift toward promoting greater equity in the workplace. As a result, progressive federal acts, such as affirmative action on employment discrimination and the Pregnancy Discrimination Act of 1978, formally reshaped company values and policies that were implemented in response to the changing times. Part of this shift were emerging leadership theories that started trickling from academia into the mainstream introducing more supportive and flexible approaches to employee management.

Most notable of these was Robert Greenleaf's 1970s model of servant leadership. Greenleaf identified ten characteristics for leaders to develop for increasing company effectiveness, motivation, and performance: "listening, empathy, healing, awareness, persuasion, conceptualization, foresight, stewardship, commitment to growth of people, and building community" (Gandolfi & Stone, 2018, p. 265). These newly aspirational attributes directly challenged and stood in stark contrast to core command-and-control values of emotional detachment, rigid expectations, transactional engagement, opacity, and self-sacrifice in service of company goals.

The concept of servant leadership continued to evolve and gain momentum through the end of the 20th century, creating new models that built upon Greenleaf's original ideas. Two of these examples were transformational leadership and authentic leadership. Transformational leadership shifted the narrative from "leader as oracle" to "leader as collaborator," centering teams instead of managers through influence and inspiration, to build leadership pipelines and galvanize dynamic productivity. Authentic leadership was built upon transformational theory, adding values alignment that accentuates interdependence and personal accountability. This style requires selecting a leader who can demonstrate interpersonal expertise as well as functional in a way that comes across as genuine, not performative. These early models paved the way for human-centered leadership in the 21st century.

Human-Centered Leadership: Frameworks and Characteristics

Data in recent years signifies an accelerating momentum for a human-centric approach as a higher-order management style. A summary of the findings from Gartner's 2022 survey of over 200 HR leaders revealed that 90% said leaders must start focusing more on developing human-centered skills to ensure organizational success, while a separate survey of close to 3400 employees found that only 29% reported that their direct manager is a human-centered leader. While not presented as a formal framework, Gartner's research identified three elements that they concluded were predominant in human-centered leaders: authenticity (comfortable empowering self and others through genuine self-expression), empathy (capable of demonstrating respect and true care and concern for the well-being of employees), and adaptability (shows an ability to be flexible in their approach) (Gartner, 2022). Despite the fact that leaders across industries commonly exhibit a historical pattern of dismissing or distrusting data from HR teams, it would be prudent for executives to contemplate that Gartner's research also discovered that 37% more employees reported having increased engagement when reporting to a human-centered leader compared to employees who did not, which is meaningful when considering that highly engaged employees drive up to a 27% improvement in team productivity (Gartner, 2022).

Further MIT research cited by Harvard Business Publishing (2024) confirmed the importance of balancing psychological safety with accountability in a HCL style, finding that high psychological safety with low accountability suppresses intellectual honesty – a crucial process that's necessary for innovation to thrive – due to apprehension for appearing unsupportive. Yet in a survey of 3400 full-time employees, only 28% percent said their leader was skilled at establishing psychological safety, and even less – 22% – felt their leader was skilled at demonstrating intellectual honesty or facilitating constructive debate; similarly, 30% of leaders surveyed believed themselves to be skilled at creating psychological safety but just 24% felt the same about their capability for encouraging intellectually honest open debate (Harvard Business Publishing, 2024).

Comparison of HCL Models and Attributes

One concept worth examining involves the principles of human-centered leadership as presented by Josh Bersin, one of the world's leading workplace analysts and an expert in leadership and HR practices. In 2021, he released an executive report based on his year-long work with 400 senior HR leaders who identified human-centered leadership as a necessary business skill for managing an increasingly VUCA landscape. In it, Bersin (2021) proposes that the difference between traditional leadership and human-centered leadership is that the former focuses more on the optimization of business functions, systems, processes, and operating procedures, where HCL focuses on investing in people and their professional development via best practices like coaching and skills training to accelerate expertise, augment creative problem-solving, and stimulate innovation even during a crisis.

His proposal for a human-centered leadership model recognizes the need to integrate operational and relational mindsets with leadership skills. In collaboration with the 400 global HR execs, Bersin devised a high-level list of knowledge, behaviors, and skills that articulates the distinction between what an operationally/task-focused approach typically looks like compared to a human-centric one. The components are structured under three pillars that include mindsets and attitudes, skills and capabilities, behaviors and actions, with the overarching theme that mastering competence in "power skills"(the term Bersin uses for people skills) is equally as important as being a technical/functional skills expert (Bersin, 2021). Some examples offered as to how this shows up in everyday context are inclusion and psychological safety to align on new ideas, viewing culture-building and connection as being fundamental to sustaining financial growth and effective execution, and taking intentional measures to recruit diverse talent and perspectives for driving innovation (Bersin, 2021).

As proposed principles and models of HCL continue to emerge, the most comprehensive models of human-centered leadership to date have come from the healthcare sector. Available literature indicates that HCL in healthcare (HCL-HC) started to develop around 2015 in response to rising burnout and attrition metrics among physicians and hospital teams. Two models are presented here to compare their defining characteristics.

The first and most detailed example was developed by LeClerc, Kennedy, and Campis (2020). They contend that a foundational aspect of HCL is that it requires embracing a higher level of cognitive complexity to integrate relational thinking with the bottom-line mentality of linear thinking and conventional leadership in general. Acknowledging that linear thinking is useful when applied to managing operational policies and procedures, LeClerc et al. (2020) assert that human-centered leaders are comfortable flexing between linear and relational thinking and are significantly better positioned to harness the tension of this integrated thinking to facilitate greater organizational innovation. This aligns with the competing values framework embedded in the Brilliant Leadership model, which proposes that demonstrating dexterity of cognitive complexity enables leaders to seamlessly deploy situational behaviors and produce better outcomes overall.

Traditional leadership assumes that change originates at the top of the hierarchy, and the followers below execute the goals set by their leaders; in actuality, transformation begins from the center of a system and expands outward (LeClerc et al. 2020). Their framework for defining human-centered leadership begins with a focus on self – practicing self-awareness, self-care, and self-compassion – while focusing on others. This is achieved by mindfully demonstrating versatility in human-centric attributes situationally from three domains: Awakener (cultivates people), Connector (builds community), and Upholder (recognizes others' humanity), setting clear expectations that "the Human-Centered Leader…employs mindfulness to empower whichever combination or single attribute is required in the moment" (LeClerc et al. 2020, p. 121).

Another iteration of HCL in healthcare, the Human-Centered Leadership Mastery model, was proposed by Boehm and Phillips (2021) and is defined as "leading people with humanity" (p. 1). The model's structure resembles HCL-HC, with a three-part Mastery focus comprising Heartset (emotional intelligence attributes), Mindset (growth mindset attributes), and Skillset (business acumen attributes) developed along levels of Mastery breadth – leading self, others, and organizational excellence (Boehm & Phillips, 2021). Although neither the HCL Mastery model nor the HCL-HC specifically states creating psychological safety as a directive, each highlights different attributes necessary for establishing psychological safety. For example, the HCL Mastery model emphasizes skills like active listening, attunement to bias, humility and vulnerability that are more implied in HCL-HC, where HCL-HC overtly identifies behaviors of self-reflection and advocating for an environment of continuous learning and innovation that are implied in HCL Mastery.

Dr. Timothy Clark's (2020) four-stage framework for psychological safety also offers specific behavioral recommendations as to how managers can scale innovation by establishing unambiguous environments of psychological safety. Clark also advises leaders to focus on inclusion and belonging as the foundation for scaling psychological safety and innovation concurrently by encouraging ideas from as many diverse perspectives as possible. According to Clark, one of the errors leaders often make is unconsciously consigning the team to the status quo, which is the opposite of innovation. To avoid this, an action he recommends before sharing feedback is for leaders to first identify what their own status quo biases might look like – a trait common among senior executives (Clark, 2020).

Other studies have noted that fervent ambition for status and power tends to correlate with high levels of entitlement and ego and low tolerance for dissent, fostering a fixed mindset based in the leader's belief that their approach is the only "right" way. This blind-spot thinking results in leaders giving feedback that orients teams toward preserving the status quo instead of embracing innovation by open and thorough questioning of the status quo to uncover fresh insights (Clark, 2020).

Challenges to Executive Development of HCL Characteristics

There are real obstacles leaders face in developing acumen as human-centered leaders. In early 2024, Harvard Business Publishing shared a Leadership Fitness model designed to facilitate the creation of human-centered leaders. It does so by examining

Table 3.1   Five Factors Standing in the Way of Human-Centric Leadership Development

Insufficient skill development opportunities – subprime capability for behavioral versatility
Threat rigidity – driven by subconscious encoding schemas and personality systems
Belief on self – identity as a leader, binary discernments attached to bias for perceived validated leadership traits
Belief on others – organizational culture and core values, societal expectations for leadership behavior
Environment that tests endurance – stress from VUCA, burden of meeting increasingly intense expectations

five common challenges identified as executive barriers to embracing or developing human-centered leadership skills (Table 3.1).

In the context of the model, leadership fitness becomes evident through consistent execution of higher-order capabilities, such as recognizing and actively challenging their own biases, resisting the tendency toward binary thinking about right/wrong or good/bad leadership behavior that limits their ability to master behavioral versatility, and respecting their own endurance thresholds to effectively manage energy and avoid burnout (Harvard Business Publishing, 2024). However, it does clarify that while leadership fitness serves as the foundation for developing a human-centered leader, two important considerations must be acknowledged: an unambiguous comprehension of what HCL looks like in action and the results it should strive for – specifically, shifting the focus from *employee engagement* to *employee fulfillment* by helping teams better manage stress and prevent burnout while improving people's adaptability to ongoing change (Harvard Business Publishing, 2024).

Where all these frameworks align most closely with the concept of the Motivator in the Brilliant Leadership framework (see chapter 1) is their shared emphasis on the leader's responsibility to continually nurture greater self-awareness through exhibiting human-centric values of authenticity, personal reflection, inclusion and belonging, transparent communication, and accountability. By doing so, leaders can amplify innovation through psychological safety to an aspirational degree, where teams feel safe to challenge established assumptions without fear of ridicule or reprimand. Data from several studies conducted on the correlating relationship between innovation and psychological safety is explored further below.

The Relationship between Psychological Safety and Innovation

The data illustrating a strong relationship between psychological safety and innovation is compelling, with more studies being added with increasing regularity. One study examined this through the lens of a "bottom-line mentality" or BLM. Greenbaum et al. (2020) defined BLM as "one-dimensional thinking that revolves around securing bottom-line outcomes to the neglect of competing priorities" (p. 503). They posit that since BLM purposefully excludes focusing on anything identified as not having a direct impact on bottom-line results, it activates a collective "goal shielding" effect, demonstrated as a disregard for psychological safety (because it's regarded as peripheral to success), an increased tendency toward transactional communication, and minimized tolerance for risk – all of which directly inhibit creativity and innovation (Greenbaum et al., 2020).

Their study also illustrates that the higher BLM within a group, the more the impact on reducing psychological safety and innovative thinking, and suggests that this process can end up becoming the reflexive norm whenever there is pressure to achieve a specific required outcome if it is not recognized and intentionally disrupted (Greenbaum et al., 2020). Organizational studies measuring the effects of bottom-line mentality on teams are increasing; as the data on this topic expands, Greenbaum et al. (2020) suggest leaders proactively identify other success indicators beyond bottom-line achievement that signal support for mediating factors like psychological safety that have implications on the bottom line, especially if leaders observe teams who appear to be high in BLM agreement.

Daly and Sætre (2023) explored the relationship between psychological safety and innovation in the context of delivering unpleasant feedback, prefacing their findings by citing a recent survey of senior executives. In that survey, 85% of respondents cited fear as often or always being the primary impediment to innovation in their organizations, specifically, fear of criticism, uncertainty, and negative career impact (Daly & Sætre, 2023). For their study, data were aggregated from 120 MBS students (majority male and approximately 30 years old), from across a variety of industries who responded to select situational vignettes, each featuring statements of high or low commitment using a Likert scale methodology.

The results indicated a direct tie of psychological safety to innovation, with respect to not only an organization's ability to innovate but also the *willingness* of employees to innovate now or in the future. While this study chose a situational focus for exploring this dynamic – specifically, how leaders managed ending or interrupting innovation projects with teams – the consequences of low psychological safety are consistent across scenarios: employees who become less invested, less motivated, less confident, *and* more reluctant to share new ideas in the future (Daly & Sætre, 2023). As ideas are discretionary, the negative impacts of low psychological safety on an organization's capacity to innovate pose a significant threat to companies striving to achieve or maintain a competitive edge.

To help leaders course-correct this risk, Daly and Sætre (2023) offer recommendations for fostering greater psychological safety by investing in developing managers' interpersonal skills, concentrating on areas such as building and repairing trust, having difficult conversations, learning how to apologize, and practicing empathy. Additionally, providing education on emotional intelligence empowers managers with an enhanced perspective for recognizing potential biases and behavioral patterns that smother latent capacity for innovation by interfering with cultivating psychological safety.

Edmunson and Bransby (2023) aggregated a review of themes that have emerged from the research literature on psychological safety, several of which regard the impact of leadership attitudes on organizational mindset and its consequences for creativity and innovation. One of the themes from the studies they observed was how high degrees of change and uncertainty tended to curb the effects of psychological safety in small-to-mid-sized organizations, restraining a company's potential to innovate. This relates to an adjacent theme on learning behaviors that support creative thinking, such as knowledge sharing and voicing perspectives. They refer to a study that found environments where knowledge sharing was perceived as risky – i.e., sharing errors one had made or asking for help due to concerns it would reflect poorly on their competence and expertise – and reported a higher likelihood of *knowledge hiding* (reserving ideas and opinions), resulting in a failure to thrive due to reduced levels of psychological safety (Edmunson & Bransby 2023).

These organizational-level studies also indicated that creative organizations that intentionally center learning and psychological safety within their culture are better able to tolerate dynamic VUCA settings by facilitating risk-taking, which is highly favorable for teams involved in producing innovative work (Edmunson & Bransby, 2023). It requires the leader to willingly adopt a viewpoint of *not knowing* to model the attitude that recognizes speaking up as evidence of being highly invested in achieving a successful outcome. Similarly, a recurring theme across research literature is the impact of a leader's mindset and behavior on a team's psychological safety.

These authors' review of meta-analysis data confirms common observational insights, such as leaders with high competence in human-centered skills like active listening, transparent communication, encouraging dialogue and debate, and conflict resolution enhanced psychological safety; when the environment is considered unsafe to ideate freely or question assumptions, "preventable failures are likely and innovation suffers" (p. 70); and these consequences on team performance were greater in surroundings where rigorous knowledge complexity and creativity was the norm than for more predictable tasks. Speaking up to leaders is an act of professional courage involving interpersonal risk that leaders should reinforce through a demonstrated commitment to psychological safety (Edmondson, 2018). In other words, it's not enough to simply instate policies of open communication; displaying discipline for developing proficiency in "interpersonal skills…require[s] socially situated practice" (Anders, 2021, p. 6).

While data indicates that the ability of a leader to create an organizational culture that supports psychological safety to fuel creative thinking has the greatest effect on team innovation, there are tertiary relationships and situational scenarios that can either augment or undermine the leader's efforts that haven't been as closely examined.

Some suggestions for further research (Anders, 2021) include exploring more deeply how co-workers can disrupt psychological safety in a work setting, so much of the literature is concentrated on the role of the leader in creating psychological safety, but less so for the role that peers and teammates play in upholding it.

A similar case can be made for examining leaders' influence to create and sustain innovation in remote and hybrid work arrangements, which make up about two-thirds of US employment roles as of early 2024. Many leaders still feel ill-equipped in their ability to lead from a distance and default to old patterns of command-and-control or neglect remote team members despite good intentions, both of which undermine creativity, innovation, productivity, and turnover. This opens a door for many more research questions around how remote and hybrid environments channel or suppress psychological safety along with other crucial aspects of belonging: robust collaboration, time, and grace for learning at the moment, and feeling confident to share opinions and insights without fear of backlash.

Lastly, there is a burgeoning dialogue on which methods appear to work best for developing the human-centric skills and transformational mindset that brilliant leaders adopt to drive open innovation. Arguably, executive coaching is most effective for achieving transformational growth. Longenecker and McCartney's (2020) review of C-suite executives found that enhancing personal accountability was particularly effective in making positive progress toward developing a transformational mindset. Crevani et al. (2021) posit that coaching is effective at influencing behavioral change because the targeted outcome of executive coaching is designed to reflect a human-centered approach by focusing on the "human element of leadership as a non-coercive relationship seeking mutual beneficial outcomes, something that is more complex and distributed than how leadership practice has traditionally been understood" (p. 133).

Ultimately, the primary distinguishing factor for achieving long-term behavioral changes in leadership style is a leader's determination and dedication to intentionally exercising attributes of human-centered leadership daily. This assertion aligns with Taylor et al.'s (2019) conclusion that demonstrating sustained intrinsic motivation to improve and evolve – prioritizing coaching sessions, showing up ready to engage, implementing and experimenting with new behaviors in-between sessions, etc. – is a reliably indicative success factor for predicting a leaders' ability to sustain meaningful change.

There are practical actions one can take to begin developing this behavioral flexibility. Several of these recommendations are explored in the next and final part of this chapter.

Transition into Daily Business

As was shown above, a human-centered leadership style is the way to go in the 21st century. You have become familiar with central instruments and the characteristic features of human-centered leadership and their various dimensions and forms. Human-centered leadership reigns supreme over other leadership styles in the modern-day work environment because it gives employees the feeling of not only being a cog in a machine. Not only does it enable the workforce to thrive under constant pressure by providing them with trust and psychological security, but it is more suitable for the challenges of leaders in modern work environments and a shift from a leadership style that relies heavily on positional authority is indicated.

In the following section, ways of transferring your new knowledge about human-centered leadership will be shown. The behaviors and methods shown will help you to implement human-centered leadership in daily business life and thereby increase the productivity of employees by building trust and giving purpose. These methods are based on behavioral patterns that managers need to display and observe to communicate effectively and lead by example. As laid out by John C. Maxwell, "leadership ability is the lid that determines a person's level of effectiveness. The lower an individual's ability to lead, the lower the lid is on his potential" (Maxwell, 1998), it goes to show the importance of leadership ability. To succeed both in your individual goals and in the collective goals of your company, you need to constantly remind yourself of the importance of your own leadership ability. Challenging the status quo and constantly reevaluating your behavior is paramount to evolving as a leader.

Implementing the theory which will be explained later on and putting it into daily practice is not only a challenge in terms of communication. In addition to the leaders' sphere, the role of an organization that plays a vital part in the evolution of a leader will also be examined in terms of the ways an organization can support leaders in developing skills that are needed in daily business life. Often, there is a disconnectedness between a dogmatic approach and the transfer into the real world. Establishing and executing a human-centered and value-driven leadership style is no exemption. Virtual and agile work environments certainly don't make it easier for leaders to exercise said style. On the other hand, communication is the most powerful tool in those environments, which is why it is of utmost importance for leaders to adapt to these given circumstances.

Further, complications arise since some attributes that are necessary to lead in such a way cannot be trained. Emotional intelligence for example is a basis for all means of communication. Knowing how to maneuver all sorts of scenarios as well as knowing how to interact with different personalities is paramount. Getting involved with your employees, on the other hand, is just a matter of motivation and willingness to be a great leader. When those attributes align, communication becomes even more efficient since there is an overlap between a manager's personality and their nonverbal communication, which results in authenticity that builds trust between employees and the management.

Following through on a human-centered leadership approach not only is beneficial on a personal level but also has a direct influence on how employees perform. Creating an environment of open dialogue can go a long way in increasing productivity as well as fostering and nurturing the bond between the company and the employee. To create such an environment, one must follow a certain set of guidelines. Certain aspects of a manager's communication with his employees should be emphasized. On the one hand, it is important to communicate transparently. On the other hand, it is important to be cooperative. This enables a form of equality and breaks down hierarchical structures. It is the task of each manager to choose the best form of communication for each individual employee and to weigh up the pros and cons. In this context, it is equally important to respond to individual requests, such as facilitating one-to-one meetings as this shows the willingness to accommodate individual needs and therefore builds trust.

In daily business, care should be taken to formulate interim goals in projects wherever possible to increase motivation and the opportunity for feedback. It is important to find the right balance between constructive requests and excessive control that could compromise the autonomy of employees. In order to signal that employees have the necessary freedom to fulfill tasks, feedback should be given where appropriate and the manager should be available for any queries at any time. By refraining from constant control, employees can use the space they are given to find creative solutions in addition to getting empowered on a personal level. In addition to the abovementioned aspects, it is extremely important to have a sensitivity to social and cultural realities within the team/company to promote a culture that values all people equally.

For communication to be contemporary and engaging, it's paramount for managers and executives alike to try to listen actively and impartially, communicate clearly to ensure understanding, and keep a level head in all scenarios. They should also recognize and respect both their own needs and those of others and make sure these are considered when making decisions. Being mindful that their perceptions may differ from others', they must differentiate between observations, feelings, and interpretations. Moreover, they should actively seek feedback and appreciate diverse opinions as opportunities to expand their viewpoints. Another aspect that importance cannot be overstated is being accountable for one's actions. By showing accountability, a base layer of trust is created. Additionally, humility is a trademark of great leaders as they don't take anything for granted and is a value that is found to be part of so-called "Level 5 Leaders," which is regarded the pinnacle of leadership (Collins, 2005).

Managers should lead by example as this fosters an open way of communication and further breaks down hierarchical structures. All the required traits and skills must be transposed in a way employees can distinguish them because being the real version of yourself as well as being consistent in your leadership is critical to building strong relationships with your employees. By creating an inclusive environment where employees feel comfortable enough to express their ideas and opinions that might be off the beaten path even if they differ from the prevailing consensus leaders enable employees to be creative and possibly disrupt the status quo. Encouraging diverse perspectives unlocks creativity and drives innovation by exposing employees to the unknown and challenges the existing ways of thinking.

To foster a value-driven human-centered leadership style in the dynamic setting of daily business interactions, researchers and experts have developed various methods and strategies. One notable framework is Friedemann Schulz von Thun's communication square, which divides communication into four dimensions of content, which provide guidelines considering the interests of both communicators. This communication model delineates the following levels:

∎ Factual aspect: This aspect refers to the objective information being communicated such as data, facts (the "what").
∎ Self-expression: Self-expression involves the speaker revealing information about themselves by the way they are conveying the message such as emotions and attitudes. (the "me").
∎ Relationship aspect: The relationship sphere touches the nature of the relationship between the speaker and their listeners. It includes elements such as the level of trust and respect as well as the underlying hierarchy (the "we").
∎ Appeal: This aspect refers to what the speaker is trying to accomplish through the process of communication, which may include commands or suggestions (the "you").

Each of these dimensions plays a major role in facilitating effective leadership communication. However, it's important to recognize that they are interrelated components of a unified toolkit and must be considered in a holistic approach. Thus, when preparing for communication processes, managers should immediately identify their objectives for each dimension to minimize misunderstandings and maintain a clear line of communication. None of the mentioned aspects stand out and therefore all are of equal importance. In this context, it cannot go unmentioned that companies where prompt bilateral communication is being employed enjoy a competitive advantage since repetitive feedback loops and unnecessary correspondence are being taken out of the equation. To implement such a way of communication, a leader will set out clear pathways that ensure the most efficient and least time-consuming ways of communication.

Organizations play an important role in shaping and supporting leaders who need to exemplify value-driven leadership behaviors in their daily interactions. An organization needs to lay the groundwork by establishing a foundation of clear values and principles that serve as guiding lights across all operational aspects, including leadership conduct. It's paramount that these values are consistently communicated and deeply ingrained into the organizational culture since the coherence between the intrinsic motivation of leaders and the organizational culture leads to authenticity, which results in being trusted by employees and stakeholders alike.

Regarding assessment, organizations can employ various methods to evaluate leaders' alignment with said values. This includes regular performance evaluations that not only take into consideration which outcomes are produced but also delve into the ethical dimensions of decision-making and adherence to organizational values. Additionally, all-encompassing feedback mechanisms offer important insights into how leaders' actions are perceived by their colleagues, subordinates, and superiors.

To nurture that kind of engaging leadership style, organizations need to provide their executives with ongoing education and training opportunities to empower leaders in honing and reinforcing value-driven leadership behaviors. They can rely on a manifold of existing tools such as workshops, seminars, as well as tailored leadership development programs focusing on areas such as ethical leadership, emotional intelligence, communication, and conflict resolution. These initiatives equip leaders with practical strategies to integrate organizational values into their daily leadership practices.

Moreover, organizational leaders, especially executives and senior managers, must lead by example, representing the traits they expect from others. Their actions set the tone for the entire organization and serve as powerful models for aspiring leaders.

Emphasizing continuous improvement, organizations must create a culture of ongoing learning and development. This involves revisiting and reinforcing organizational values in a frequent manner, providing continuous support and resources for leadership growth, and actively seeking feedback from employees to identify areas for improvement.

By employing proactive assessment, education, and reinforcement of value-driven leadership behavior, organizations create a culture that is based on integrity, trust, and ethical excellence. This not only enhances organizational effectiveness and performance but also ensures long-term sustainability and earns stakeholder trust. It is also important to note that organizations should individually assess how they want to approach human-centered leadership and define what it should look like within the company to create a mission statement for leaders (Harvard Business Publishing, 2024).

Selection of Practical Guidelines and Examples

So much for the theory. In order to work out the best approaches for yourself, you need a certain amount of intuition and a degree of self-reflection to recognize where you still need to work on yourself. An essential aspect of effective leadership communication lies in its consistent application in everyday interactive business settings. To achieve this, leaders can rely on established best practices for guidance, though it's acknowledged that these may not cover every scenario comprehensively.

Applicable Best Practices

Let's now delve into a curated set of best practices concerning stylistic communication approaches to help you with enabling and establishing your personal style of leadership based on aforementioned values:

a. Active listening is a fundamental skill in effective communication, especially for leaders aiming to foster trust and understanding within their teams. Referring to Lyman K. Steil, active listening consists of four elements: perception, interpretation, assessment, and reaction. It requires managers to fully engage with the speaker, not just relying on passively hearing their words but also comprehending their message, both on a verbal and on a non-verbal level. Active listening is a skill that everybody can acquire to resolve conflicts more effectively. Active listeners establish a better basis of understanding, which leads to better decision-making that also includes all the necessary information.

b. Tell and Sell versus Ask and Listen is a question of concepts. Both concepts have their advantages but with regard to human-centered leadership the ask and listen approach is highly favorable since it aligns with the overarching theme of empowering employees. Both refer to behavioral patterns where in the case of the tell and sell concept, leaders provide their subordinates with a clear vision or message while explaining the value of that vision. On the contrary, the ask and listen approach is meant to solicit input by employees through the act of asking questions by a leader, which as a result will enable employees to come to solutions by self-reflection (Van Quaquebeke & Gerpott, 2023).

c. Understanding and encouragement play crucial roles in effective leadership communication. It's essential for leaders to truly grasp the perspectives of those they're communicating with to guide discussions effectively and establish rapport. By identifying the key issues at hand, leaders can address them constructively and foster solution-oriented dialogues. Moreover, providing encouragement to employees is vital for their morale and motivation. When leaders express support and belief in their team members, it empowers individuals to reach their full potential, ultimately boosting overall productivity and efficiency within the company. But it should also be mentioned that by providing encouragement and hence creating psychological security, intellectual honesty mustn't take a backseat. Accepting other opinions is important but leaders can't refrain from telling their employees if an idea is not leading to success (Dyer et al., 2023)

d. There is also a set of guidelines with regard to the content that is being communicated. Managers should follow the "CART" rule. ("Do I have everything in my cart?" is a control question one must answer before communicating a message).

Clarity, Consistency, and Completeness

Ensuring that the message is clear and easily understood by the audience: This involves using simple language, avoiding jargon, and providing specific information to convey the intended message effectively. By communicating clear messages, you also decrease the likeliness of conflict and frustration that can be a byproduct of being misunderstood.

In addition to the message being clear, the information being conveyed must also be consistent with communication of the past, present, and future to nullify the risk of contradicting oneself and thus losing credibility in the eyes of employees and possibly being misunderstood because ambiguous messages are being sent. It also shows mindfulness of your own words as well as a level of professionalism to be in line with past and future messages, which leads to an increased level of trust and respect.

To round out these attributes, a message must also be complete. To get a better grasp of the meaning, two different spheres must be considered: the expectation level of the addressee and the understanding horizon of the addressee. Differing horizons of understanding emerge because a leader views their message as sufficiently clear and comprehensible although employees perceive this differently as recipients. In such situations, leaders would benefit from explaining the reasons behind the information they are sharing because that way employees can get a better understanding as to why there might be an informational deficit, which at that specific point in time cannot be addressed.

Accuracy

Providing accurate and reliable information that serves as a basis for future tasks or projects. and avoiding misunderstandings and/or misinformation is of utmost importance. It's essential to verify facts, cite sources when necessary, and double-check information before communicating it to others. Additionally, delivering accurate messages facilitates understanding and collaboration between concerned parties since every recipient can rely on the same information. It also results in better decision-making because every decision being made is based on reliable information that has been verified by yourself beforehand leading up to the communication process.

Relevance

It is also paramount to share information that is relevant to the recipient only. In this respect, it is necessary to know what information the recipient needs for their tasks and to specifically tailor one's message accordingly to ensure its relevance and importance. Also, by sharing only relevant information you show your interlocutor that you value their time and attention by not oversharing as well as nullifying possible extractions or misunderstandings that could be caused by an informational overload.

Timeliness

Last but not least, communication has to come in a timely manner to ensure its usefulness to the audience. Sharing information prematurely can do a lot of harm since most of the time only questions arise as to why only partial information is being shared. If there is a need to share partial information, leaders must provide a reasoning behind that decision. Additionally, they need to provide updates once further information can be shared to ensure employees feel they are kept in the loop. Responding to inquiries or giving feedback in a timely manner is also key to fostering an environment of open communication and appreciation and signals attentiveness to employees.

Conclusion

It is not always easy to deal with the multitude of communicative processes that occur in working life daily. You must live up to your own standards as well as the expectations of your employees and the values of the company. The tools mentioned above are intended to serve this purpose. However, if you take these framework conditions to heart, you will be rewarded with an increased level of trust, conviction, productivity, and more creative solutions for which it is worth going the extra mile for yourself and your employees. To quote Bill Gates, "As we look ahead into the next century, leaders will be those who empower others".

Putting your employees first should be your main priority when it comes to fully embracing human-centered leadership. To add to that message, leaders not only need to empower others but also be light on their feet and embrace versatility (Kaiser et al., 2023). In a world that is rattled by crisis after crisis, the ability to adapt to a manifold of different circumstances has increased year after year. COVID-19 has shown how fragile the status quo is and highlighted the importance of versatility. That versatility must also be employed in the context of human-centered leadership by not falling back on past behavioral patterns but rather testing new formats and ideas continually since there is no perfect one-size-fits-all solution.

References

Anders, A. D. (2021). Human-centered leadership development: A communication-based approach for promoting authentic and transformational leadership. *International Journal of Business Communication, 2021*(11), 232948842110565. https://doi.org/10.1177/23294884211056558

Beddows, P., Bishop, D., Fracchia, E. C., Fuller, T., Moore, M., & Scordato, C. (2022). *Human-centered leadership*. Leading with Humanity: The Future of Leadership and Coaching – An Institute of Coaching Report. https:// instituteofcoaching.org /ioc-report-leading-with-humanity-the-future-of-leadership-coaching.

Bersin, J. (2021). *The big reset playbook: Human-centered leadership*. https://joshbersin.com/research/big-reset-2020/

Boehm, L., & Phillips, S. MD, MPH. (2021). *Human-centered leadership mastery model*. https://www.ceocoalition.com/wp-content/uploads/2023/09/human-centered-leadership-mastery-model.pdf

Clark, T. (2020). *The four stages of psychological safety*. Berret-Koehler Publishers, Inc.

Collins, J. (2005). Level 5 leadership: The Triumph of humility and fierce resolve. *Harvard Business Review*. https://hbr.org/2005/07/level-5-leadership-the-triumph-of-humility-and-fierce-resolve

Crevani, L., Uhl-Bien, M., Clegg, S., & By, R. (2021). Changing leadership in changing times II. *Journal of Change Management: Reframing Leadership and Organizational Practice, 21*(2), 133–143. https://doi.org/10.1080/14697017.2021.1917489

Daly, J. A., & Sætre, A. S. (2023). It is all about the bottom line: Group bottom-line mentality, psychological safety, and group creativity. *Frontiers in Psychology, 14,* 1060617–1060617. https://doi.org/10.3389/fpsyg.2023.1060617

Dweck, C. (2016). *Mindset: The new psychology of success.* Ballantine Books.

Dyer, J., Furr, N., Lefrandt, C., & Howell, T. (2023). Why innovation depends on intellectual honesty. *MIT Sloan Management Review.* https://sloanreview.mit. edu/article/why-inno vation-depends-on-intellectual-honesty/

Edmondson, A. C. (2018). *The fearless organization: Creating psychological safety in the work-place for learning, innovation, and growth.* John Wiley & Sons.

Edmunson, A., & Bransby, D. P. (2023). Psychological safety comes of age: Observed themes in an established literature. *Annual Review of Organizational Psychology and Organizational Behavior, 10,* 55–78. https://doi.org/10.1146/annurev-orgpsych-120920-055217

Gandolfi, F., & Stone, S. (2018, October–December). Leadership, leadership styles, and servant leadership. *Journal of Management Research, 18*(4), 261–269. https://www.lasnny.org /wp-content/uploads/2018/11/Leadership-Leadership-Styles-and-Servant-Leadership .pdf

Gartner. (2022, June 23). *Gartner HR research identifies human leadership as the next evolution of leadership* [Press release]. https://www.gartner.com/en/newsroom/press-releases/06-23 -22-gartner-hr-research-identifies-human-leadership-as-the-next-evolution-of-leadership

Greenbaum, R., Bonner, J. M., Mawritz, M. B., Butts, M. M., & Smith, M. B. (2020, July). It is all about the bottom line: Group bottom-line mentality, psychological safety, and group creativity. *Journal of Organizational Behavior, 41*(6), 503–517.

Harvard Business Publishing. (2024). *Leadership fitness: The path to developing human-centered leaders who drive employee fulfillment.* https://www.harvardbusiness.org/insight/ leadership-fitness-the-path-to-developing-human-centered-leaders-who-drive-employee -fulfillment/

Kaiser, R. B., Sherman, R. A., & Hogan, R. (2023). It takes versatility to lead in a volatile world. *Harvard Business Review.* https://hbr.org/2023/03/ it-takes-versatility-to-lead-i n-a-volatile-world

Leclerc, L., Kennedy, K., & Campis, S. (2020). Human-centered leadership in health care: An idea that's time has come. *Nursing Administration Quarterly, 44*(2), 117–126. https://doi .org/10.1097/NAQ.0000000000000409

Longenecker, C., & McCartney, M. (2020). The benefits of executive coaching: Voices from the C-suite. *Strategic HR Review, 19*(1), 22–27. https://doi.org/10.1108/SHR-06-2019 -0048

Maxwell, J. C. (1998). *The 21 irrefutable laws of leadership.* HarperCollins..

Richardson, N., Ph. D., & Antonello, M. (2023). *People at work 2023: A global workforce view.* ADP Research Institute. https://www.adpri.org/assets/people-at-work-2023-a-global -workforce-view/

Taylor, S. N., Passerelli, A. M., & Van Oosten, E. B. (2019, September). Leadership coach effectiveness as fostering self-determined, sustained change. *Leadership Quarterly, 30*(10). https://doi.org/10.1016/j.leaqua.2019.101313

Van Quaquebeke N., & Gerpott, F. H. (2023). Tell-and-sell or ask-and-listen: A self-concept perspective on why it needs leadership communication flexibility to engage subordinates at work. *Current Opinion in Psychology, 53*.

STRATEGY INNOVATION

2

Beyond Boundaries—How Leaders Create a Purpose-Driven Innovation

Chapter 4

Co-Creation, Strategic Visioning, and Iterative Loops

Alan T. Belasen and Lara Bertola

Anticipating emerging technologies requires vigilance, adaptability, and continuous drive innovation and growth. Brilliant leaders co-create a transformational vision that inspires and aligns stakeholders and envisions a future of success. They have the know-how to prioritize high-impact objectives with the greatest value to stakeholders, provide opportunities to assess skill gaps and priority areas for digital upskilling to execute the digital transformation, and promote ownership and shared accountability that empowers individuals and teams through delegation and autonomy. CEOs who excel in empowering lower levels generate 33% higher revenue streams for their organizations (Badal & Ott, 2015). These leaders focus on wins that can be spread throughout the organization and model the way with trustworthy leadership committed to the broader values of ethics, equity, and sustainability.

Brilliant leadership has been identified throughout this book as a critical leadership approach to guide organizations through unanticipated challenges. Brilliant leaders rely on their innovative thinking, high risk-tolerance, and behavioral flexibility to diagnose complex problems, mobilize collective intelligence, and promote adaptive solutions. They communicate with empathy during times of change and are able to build trust, reduce uncertainty, re-engage organizational members, drive learning through co-creation, enhance organizational resilience, and seize new opportunities.

This chapter centers on how shaping a human-centric culture through trustworthiness and empowerment allows forward-thinking leaders to balance constraints with creativity, promote divergent thinking, and build trust in their organizations. These mechanisms encourage shared leadership and collaborative behaviors, the means by which brilliant leaders navigate the challenges of the digital era and drive innovation throughout the organization.

DOI: 10.4324/9781003495307-6

Rethinking Leadership: Strategic Visioning

In today's ever-changing business environment, organizations have numerous chances to gain a competitive edge by incorporating digital technologies (Nyagadza, 2022) and new forms of leadership. Digital transformation affects how organizations operate and deliver value for their customers and requires forward-thinking leaders with the ability to reframe forms of organizing and rethink decision-making processes and strategies to foster innovation and agility. Notably, the age of technological innovation establishes a vision for organizations to reimagine how leaders operate, reshape their culture, and seize new opportunities.

The competitive tech-driven landscape is constantly evolving due to economic growth, changes in labor markets, demographics, and consumer preferences. Organizations now face unprecedented levels of volatility, uncertainty, , complexity, and ambiguity, also known as the "VUCA world" where unpredictable change becomes the norm (Doheny et al., 2012; Bennett & Lemoine, 2014; Millar et al., 2018).

Scholars generally agree that VUCA represents a strategic dilemma for organizations to stay ahead of the market by unlocking their competitive advantage through a dynamic interplay of strategy as a stretch and leverage (Domínguez et al., 2022) while preserving a sense of stability at the core of their organizational identity (Ravasi & Schultz, 2006). This dilemma influences the ability of organizations to effectively respond to the demands of a constantly fluctuating and uncertain environment while also rejuvenating their business strategies. It is also a key success factor in tackling the challenges posed by VUCA for large corporations to sustain their competitive advantage because exploitative and exploratory activities compete for scarce resources (Bodwell & Chermack, 2010; Martínez-Climent et al., 2019).

As organizations increasingly shift toward learning, exploration, and collaborative structures, the role of leadership in the digitalized environment becomes critically impactful. Brilliant leaders act purposefully and authentically, inspiring others to shape a business world that is not only technologically advanced but also socially conscious and human-centric.

Adaptive systems and successful disruptive innovation require a regeneration sequence of outcomes with iterative feedback loops and a guiding star: the visionary brilliant leader who combines a human-centric approach, trustworthiness, and execution excellence. A brilliant leader with the vision and capacity to simultaneously optimize the current business model through exploitation and inspire new ventures and outcomes through exploration.

The ability to be ambidextrous is essential. Ambidextrous leadership focuses on a dual logic: (a) a humanistic or collaborative approach to develop ideas and initiate innovation; and (b) a managerial or rationalistic approach, which is concerned with the efficient use of resources to implement innovation (Belasen, 2000). In healthcare, this dual focus matches the conditions for a successful adaptive organization, with clinical and administrative champions that facilitate the transformation to value-based care and population health (Belasen, 2019).

Iterative Loops

Brilliant leaders are resilient. They initiate ambidexterity by creating a compelling vision of success that draws on current resources and capabilities and promotes learning and forward-thinking by inspiring intrapreneurship and exploration. They use a style that encourages the coexistence of conflicting goals and that requires members to adopt integrative solutions. They model the way by encouraging organizational members to adopt exploratory and exploitative behaviors, recognize competing tensions, articulate explicit goals and metrics for new initiatives, boost the collective intelligence of the organization, and build a culture of collaborative innovation (Belasen, 2022).

Isaacs and Ancona (2019) suggest three strategies for initiating and sustaining the value of collaborative innovation: communicating strategically, cultivating new ideas collectively, and removing barriers to innovation implementation. Iterative loops of feedback are integral to these three strategies, allowing brilliant leaders to harness the insights and energy of employees at all levels of the organization. In so doing, brilliant leaders leverage the collective intelligence of their employees and position their organizations for the future.

Communicating strategically. Brilliant leaders crowdsource ideas for the new vision and mobilize support for that vision. The Defense Advanced Research Projects Agency (DARPA), the innovative government agency focused on transformational breakthroughs in national security, uses a set of simple questions based on the Heilmeier Catechism principles to think through and evaluate proposals. The answers to these questions map well into innovative thinking that focuses on industry conditions, competition, risks, costs and benefits, why you, why now, and milestones.

- What are you trying to do? Articulate your objectives using absolutely no jargon.
- How is it done today, and what are the limits of current practice?
- What is new in your approach and why do you think it will be successful?
- Who cares? If you are successful, what difference will it make?
- What are the risks?
- How much will it cost?
- How long will it take?
- What are the mid-term and final "exams" [that will allow you to measure] success?

Cultivating new ideas collectively. Adaptive organizations gain access to open innovation through collaborative networks or ecosystems that exist along the lines of the supply chain with diverse stakeholders (Belasen & Rufer, 2013). With open access to multiple channels of communication, consumers and employees have become major players in the mass consumption, co-creation, and distribution of information (Belasen & Luber, 2017). At W. L. Gore, if new ideas gain support, change advocates schedule regular peer review sessions with people from manufacturing, R&D, sales and marketing, and other relevant areas of expertise to evaluate the usefulness of the new ideas. Senior leaders review the ideas and use their knowledge of resources and capabilities, and market/technology trends to promote a new strategy.

In another example, Corning, NY, rejuvenated its innovation pipeline using a set of simple rules derived from successful past innovations:

■ address new markets with more than $500 million in potential revenue
■ leverage the company's expertise in materials science
■ represent a critical component in a complex system, and
■ be protected from competition by patents and proprietary process expertise.

Removing barriers to innovation implementation. Brilliant leaders remove major barriers to innovation by clearing the way for promising new projects and getting innovation teams the resources they need. NASA's leaders solicit their employees for new ideas by giving people more time, money, recognition, and dedicated physical space for innovation. Others may focus on reducing process requirements for innovations, for instance, fast-tracking low-cost missions and giving special treatment to high-potential technologies. Proposals may include an element of innovation to encourage informed, appropriate R&D risk, to counter the agency's risk-averse culture.

Given the complexity of this system, considerable focus is placed on fostering transparent communication, active collaboration, and innovative thinking, which are essential for achieving the organization's goals (Mattessich & Johnson, 2018). It seems reasonable to ask, what does this transformation mean for leaders? Leaders should encourage transparent communication and actively seek feedback from their teams. This demands significant courage as it may disrupt the status quo, requiring the refinement of existing skills and the cultivation of new ones in order to adapt to changing workplace requirements.

Shared Leadership

In contrast to the past, where leadership scholars focused on traits, the past few years have witnessed a flurry of energy and attention aimed at understanding networked leadership which fosters an environment of engagement, high-commitment, and ownership. This form of collaborative leadership is viewed "as a dynamic, interactive influence process among individuals in groups for which the objective is to lead one another to the achievement of group or organizational goals or both" (Pearce & Conger, 2002, p. 1).

Thus, the emphasis is not only on enhancing current skills but also on developing new skills suitable for meeting the changing needs of modern work settings. Traditional leadership is morphing from a solo approach to co-leadership, a form of shared leadership between two or more individuals with complementary strengths and abilities. Each co-leader takes on distinct, though often overlapping leadership roles.

Mobilizing an organization to adapt its behaviors and strategies to not just survive but flourish in new and challenging business environments is crucial (Holbeche, 2023). Without such proactive change, any company today would struggle to maintain relevance and competitiveness. Indeed, the ability to inspire people at all levels of the organization to embrace adaptive work is a defining characteristic of brilliant leadership in a fiercely competitive digital world. In a rapidly evolving business landscape marked by technological advancements, global dynamics, and shifting consumer demands, the capacity to mobilize resources and drive organizational change has become indispensable for achieving sustained long-term success.

Progress toward more participative models of leadership is gaining momentum due to the increasing recognition that these approaches not only promote inclusivity and ethics but also prove to be more effective in navigating the intricate challenges and swift changes within today's business environment. Sustained advocacy, comprehensive education, and impactful demonstration of the advantages of shared leadership will play a crucial role in propelling this cultural shift forward. Some evidence comes from the healthcare industry.

An important pathway for shifting the traditional leadership landscape is to rethink the entrenched solo leadership model, typically headed by an executive with business skills, with a shared leadership model that casts the net wide to include expert leaders. At its core, shared leadership is emerging as a vital strategy for transforming organizations faced with increasing complexity.

Shared leadership promotes robust communication structures by providing broader competence, continuous learning, iterative feedback loops, and joint responsibility for operations and services. Co-leaders develop synergistic relationships fostered by trust, acceptance, and the mutual understanding of when to take initiative and when to step back and allow peer leaders to step in.

Shared leadership leverages the combined strengths of peer leaders for better outcomes. Research shows that more diverse and inclusive management teams make better decisions up to 87% of the time, are faster 50% of the time, and deliver 60% better results (Larson, 2017). In healthcare, two variants of co-leadership platforms are *dyads* and *triads*, and both have the potential to transform hospitals and healthcare organizations (Belasen, 2019). In a *dyad,* the two co-equal partners bring their unique perspectives to create win-win outcomes. In health settings, the two co-leaders are an administrator and a physician. Administrators bring business skills essential for managing productivity and cost-effective delivery of care to populations. Physicians bring clinical expertise for determining health initiatives, providing high-value patient care, assuring quality and patient safety, and assessing clinical outcomes. In a *triad*, nurse managers join the leadership team. The value of nurse management to patient care and improving hospital quality and efficiency is promoted via shared accountability in a physician-nurse-administrator leadership structure. Through a relational approach to leading, dyads and triads create action pathways into a new era of quality-based, team-driven care.

Instituting dyad or triad leadership structures creates opportunities for dealing with complexity through effective collaboration and shared experiences. Dyad leaders who appreciate the value of cooperation also encourage teams to meet broader, emerging goals through inter-professional collaboration and teamwork. A survey of 868 Insights Council members by the *New England Journal of Medicine* (Swensen & Mohta, 2017) found that 72% use a dyad leadership model in their organizations and 85% believe that the dyad works effectively. A more recent survey of healthcare leaders by the Medical Group Management Association (MGMA, 2019) with 1303 applicable responses found that 77% of the respondents indicated that their organizations utilize a physician and administrator (dyad) leadership team model.

A related approach to shared leadership is distributed leadership, a concept that empowers individuals across organizational lines to assume leadership roles. In a distributed leadership model, policymaking and influence are dispersed throughout the organization, allowing for greater adaptability, transfer of best practices, innovation implementation, joint accountability, and empowerment of individuals and teams. One of the best examples of distributed leadership comes from academic institutions where faculty and staff share leadership responsibilities through governance and membership in committees with rotated roles. This approach recognizes that effective leadership can come from various academic programs and disciplines within the university rather than being centralized by the administration.

Some scholars view digital transformation as incentivized by distributed leadership (as opposed to being run by a digital officer) due to the need for mutual responsiveness and transparency (Lorentzen, 2022). It is reasonable to believe, however, that a more holistic approach that combines transactional and transformational styles of leadership (see Chapter 1) is essential for developing and implementing innovation. Where transactional leadership has been more paternalistic, with leaders creating a vision, outlining specific performance targets, and focusing on results, transformational leaders inspire performance through commitment (not command) structures, use empathy and emotional intelligence, and empower and energize employees through transparent and open communications.

Trustworthy Leadership

The true test of effective leadership does not occur when everything is running smoothly. It occurs during unanticipated events when employees defer to leaders for guidance and emotional support, and when it is critical to make smart choices that are also ethical. Periods of major or continuous disruptions may trigger distrust that challenges leaders to demonstrate characteristics of trustworthiness more reliably or focus on response strategies to regain stability.

Trustworthy leaders demonstrate strong emotional intelligence (EI) skills that can be a game changer when it comes to tackling disruptions. Strong emotional intelligence facilitates interactions and collaborative behaviors, essential for dealing with stressful situations. They are effective in promoting psychological safety and in enabling positive and enduring outcomes in teams and organizations.

Trustworthy leaders have the humility to reveal their weaknesses and defer judgment to experts or delegate important tasks to competent team members. Integrating vulnerabilities into the range of the leader's behavior increases authenticity and reflects dependability that not only enhances leadership attributes of self-awareness and empowerment but also encourages followers' preference to trust these leaders (Jiang et al., 2022). This is important since building and sustaining trust in organizations is also an effective form of mobilizing individuals and teams during disruptions. During disruptions, the trust employees have in their leaders replaces the perceived threat with perceptions of safety, benevolence, and integrity (Kelloway et al., 2012).

Indeed, a trustful relationship between leaders and employees is critical as it increases employee commitment and motivation to pursue organizational goals. Brilliant leaders are sensitive, attuned, and responsive to moments of differences, and feel responsible for working with those differences. They focus on the common purpose, are inspirational, and project trustworthiness and empathy to ensure that organizational members remain calm and engaged.

Brilliant leaders acknowledge uncertainty, communicate with compassion, show understanding, and are empathetic. They rely on informal means of communication to promote collaborative structures and use messaging that appeals to collective values and history to reinforce public trust and stakeholders' acceptance (Belasen & Belasen, 2019). When the communication is clear, empathetic, transparent, and frequent, internal dialogues are more positive, and members show more confidence in their own ability to perform, and, at the same time, trust the ability of leaders to lead during disruptive times.

Disruptions expose leaders to vulnerabilities in how they access, interpret, and embrace sensemaking credibly and accountably. Leaders can devise a well-synchronized communication plan that includes responses to early warning signals of a threatening crisis and action pathways to deal with the unexpected (Belasen & Eisenberg, 2023). These action pathways must be credible, transparent, and carried out by leaders who convey honesty and inspire joint accountability essential for human-centric organizations (United Nations, 2020).

Cultivating traits of transparency, credibility, accountability, and honesty enables brilliant leaders to have the skills needed to embody trust and be prepared for disruptions. Transparency enables trustworthy leaders to learn from others and update their thinking. Accountability reflects the importance of complying with regulations and communicating important information or directions to stakeholders. Credibility reinforces important goals and interests and the need to be open to feedback. Honesty enables the trustworthy leader to promote openness and commitment to implementing decisions, while holding members to high standards of truthfulness. These traits help brilliant leaders prioritize empowerment and commitment, strengthen relationships, encourage informed decisions through open communication, and inspire people to improve collaboration and sustain the human-centric workplace.

Balancing Constraints and Creativity

The rapid advancements in technology, the shifting global landscape, and the changing expectations of employees have created a new playing field for leaders. As technological advancements reshape industries and transform the way we work, leaders need to adapt and redefine their roles to navigate the new work environment.

Successful leaders foresee change, seize opportunities, and inspire their teams to achieve high performance. They value new ways of empowerment and collaboration. By balancing constraints with creativity, leaders can push boundaries and encourage innovative thinking (Moussa et al., 2018). This shift is prompted by the digital age, which demands a brilliant leader who prioritizes creativity, collaboration, and inclusivity.

The effect of these constraints on creativity and innovation has attracted substantial interest across various fields. Very often, when businesses talk about digital transformation, the focus is more on "digital" rather than on "transformation" (Boyatzis, 2008). Technology appears to be prioritized. While leveraging digital technologies for innovation is fine, the people ultimately drive change through the organization (Chatterjee et al., 2023). For an organization to succeed, its workforce needs to develop the right digital mindset and possess digital competencies. Even if leadership is about engaging in communication and collaboration, and being open to receiving input from those they lead, this can be a daunting experience that demands courage from leaders.

Business executives, especially, are not accustomed to sharing their private feelings and thoughts with colleagues, and the pursuit of change starts with the initiative of the individual – in this case, the leader. Basic and intermediate levels of aquired digital literacy skills could include a fundamental understanding of mobile devices, coding, social media messaging , use of internet platforms, intergroup dialogue, critical and independent thinking, openness, and insightfulness (Maxwell et al., 2023), while change leadership involves effectively balancing the driving and restraining forces of change and supporting employees in adapting new work methods. For instance, the fear of losing one's job is a significant issue for many employees. If individuals perceive the change as a threat to their interests, resistance will emerge. Addressing employees' short-term concerns about how the change will benefit them long-term is also crucial. Over time, a higher level of trust will be established, reducing the potential for resistance.

Therefore, before implementing any digital transformation projects, the top management team must understand the underlying reasons and importance of such initiatives for the organization's success. They need to fully support these projects and show proactive dedication by actively participating in related activities, ensuring early alignment of leadership, and securing their unwavering commitment at the beginning of any digital transformation project. This means holding meetings with executive leadership to prepare the organization for upcoming changes. The main goal is to align management expectations and address key issues related to the digital transformation process (Hoe, 2022). Therefore, the top management team must possess a comprehensive understanding of the underlying reasons and profound significance of digital transformation for the organization's long-term success. This entails conducting thorough deliberations with executive leadership to prepare the organization for impending changes and harmonize managerial expectations while tackling pivotal issues pertaining to the digital transformation process.

Leadership in the digital age goes beyond just implementing technology; it requires a deep understanding of the potential benefits and limitations of digital tools, as well as an effective strategy to drive organizational success. By engaging in these proactive measures and fostering strong leadership commitment, organizations can pave the way for a smoother and more successful digital transformation process, ultimately driving positive organizational outcomes and achieving strategic success.

Co-Creating a Culture of Innovation

Leaders need to model the way in promoting a culture that embraces change within the organization, creating an environment that encourages experimentation and views failures as necessary steps toward success. Leaders must actively support the planned digital transformation while also ensuring open communication, conducive to innovative thinking and actions (Bilal et al., 2021).

Leaders must not only adapt to technological advancements but also actively engage in sourcing and guiding their implementation in order to fortify their organization's competitive edge and ensure its sustained advantage. Brilliant leaders successfully navigate digital transformation and act as catalysts for cultivating cultures of innovation that permeate every facet of their organizations. At the core of this effort is blending co-creation and strategic planning techniques into the foundation of a company's culture. One common drawback in digital transformation projects is overlooking the human aspect of change, leading to a focus on technical solutions rather than people-centered considerations (Ross et al., 2006).

However, at its core, digital transformation involves a cultural change, requiring a shift from traditional to modern operational approaches that embrace diversity and inclusivity essential for driving innovation. By creating environments that empower individuals to be themselves and promoting shared leadership models, organizations can tap into the potential of their diverse workforce, facilitating the emergence of new ideas.

Notably, scholars stress the significance of sparking intellectual curiosity and fostering divergent thinking by incorporating principles that prioritize humanity, sustainability, and ethics in organizational operations (Allen et al., 2019), which have been recognized as crucial elements for driving significant change (Millar & Price, 2018; Nauman et al., 2022).

Building on this foundation, Megheirkouni & Mejheirkouni (2020) suggested that the leadership development process is the period that extends from when an organization identifies its weaknesses to when it adopts and implements a specific leadership development program that helps leaders or managers overcome these weaknesses. However, the evolving digital landscape demands that leadership adopt new capabilities focused on securing long-term sustainability for organizations. To succeed in the technological era, traditional leadership styles may not be sufficient. Leading in disruptive times requires blending conventional leadership types and embracing new approaches to foster innovation within organizations.

Effectively guiding organizations through the complexities of today's digital landscape demands a nuanced blend of traditional leadership principles and evolving methodologies, meticulously crafted to ignite innovation within the organization. In recent research conducted by Strasser et al. (2022), it was suggested that leaders are expected to take on various roles beyond traditional expectations, including serving as community mentors, content curators, network analysts, and social entrepreneurs.

The framework emphasizes the evaluation of dominant institutions and institutional changes introduced by social innovators based on their level of institutionalization across three dimensions: width (broad and coherent influence), depth (structural and cultural embeddedness), and length (persistent and evolving reproduction). These authors also identified network leadership roles and practices that support the development of transformative capacity that can expand, disseminate, or enhance institutional changes. Therefore, the focus is not on individual leaders holding formal leadership positions in this context but rather on network leadership and even distributed leadership discussed above.

Previous discussions in social innovation policy and research have often revolved around "heroic individuals," but social innovation networks or ecosystems involve a range of actors and organizations working together to shape social innovation. However, this approach consists of a multitude of interconnected actors and organizations that collectively shape and co-create social innovation (Pel et al., 2017). This multifaceted leadership approach emphasizes the vital need for brilliant leaders to actively embrace digital progress to bolster their organization's competitive advantage amidst swift technological advancements. Leaders who are unwilling or unable to engage at this level and undertake this approach will fail to identify the core opportunities and risks associated with digital transformation (Türk, 2023).

Encouraging Divergent Thinking

Leading through disruptive times necessitates leaders to account for and address diverse perspectives, help followers recognize and understand the impetus for change, and give followers ownership of change implementation to ensure lasting impact. Furthermore, leaders must prioritize the development of an environment that fosters flexibility and autonomy and plays an important role in managing resources to ensure the long-term viability of businesses (Wasono & Furinto, 2018).

Encouraging divergent thinking through a culture of innovation derives its impetus from holistic organizational frameworks. These frameworks ought to be deeply attuned to the evolving dynamics of the information/knowledge economy, characterized by relentless transformation, global interconnectedness, and the necessity for swift adaptation. Leading in today's digital era calls for an emphasis on new approaches to empowerment and cooperation, along with a deliberate equilibrium between limitations and innovation. Anghel (2019) explored deeper into the concept of compliance in digital transformation, emphasizing not just change processes and integrating systems with new technologies but also the need to act with foresight and pioneer innovation.

Smart leaders adapt proactively to the rapid fluctuations within their industries and changing consumer preferences, envisioning shifts before they fully manifest, seizing emerging opportunities, and rallying their teams toward achieving optimal performance. Leadership in this new era should be rooted in principles of empowerment and adaptability aimed at unleashing the full potential of managers and employees. By establishing a transparent information system and nurturing a culture that prioritizes empowerment, leaders can foster an environment conducive to creativity and innovation with an ethos of inclusivity and diversity. Moreover, organizations can effectively harness the potential power of co-creation and purpose-driven innovation to successfully navigate through various complexities presented by this digital age while instigating meaningful change.

Prior research has shown that simply adopting digital technology is not enough for organizations to thrive in the digital era, which demands a leader who prioritizes creativity, collaboration, and inclusivity. Digital leaders are vital for transforming business strategies, so organizations must acknowledge this shift and adjust their leadership approaches accordingly (Cortellazzo et al., 2019). Fostering environments that encourage active participation and communal decision-making allow organizations to tap into the boundless potential of diverse teams. By moving beyond traditional hierarchical structures and promoting a culture of diversity and inclusivity, these organizations leverage the collective intelligence of their members to address complex challenges and drive innovation.

While constraints may seem like shackles that bind, they possess the latent power to serve as catalysts for ingenious thinking. It is through the act of breaking free from the confines of conventional wisdom and embracing audacious, unconventional approaches that organizations unleash the full spectrum of creativity inherent within their teams, birthing a cornucopia of novel solutions that defy expectations. Exploring further into the concept of co-creation involves fostering a mindset that values intellectual curiosity and encourages different ways of thinking. Organizations can cultivate a culture that prizes curiosity, fueling innovative exploration and encouraging individuals and teams to seek unconventional solutions (Baer, 2012; Gino et al., 2017). This requires a deep-rooted dedication to turning vision into reality and navigating challenges with determination and perseverance.

Visioning That Brings Together Stakeholders

Integrating stakeholders into the formulation of a shared vision and goals not only empowers them with a sense of ownership and commitment but also fosters collaboration and alignment toward common objectives. This underscores the significance of stakeholder involvement in strategic decision-making processes, acknowledging their invaluable contributions to organizational direction and purpose. Similarly, transparent communication channels between leaders and stakeholders not only build trust and mutual understanding but also serve as conduits for disseminating pertinent information about decisions and organizational strategies, thereby promoting accountability and engendering greater support and cooperation.

Leaders who embody ethical principles inspire confidence and loyalty among stakeholders while also enhancing organizational credibility and reputation, creating an environment conducive to long-term success and viability. Furthermore, engaging stakeholders in the strategic planning process facilitates the synthesis of diverse perspectives and insights, enriching the strategic discourse and enhancing the adaptability of organizational strategies. By incorporating stakeholder feedback into decision-making processes, leaders can proactively identify emerging challenges, seize latent opportunities, and tailor strategies to align with evolving market dynamics and stakeholder expectations.

However, effective stakeholder engagement transcends episodic interactions. It necessitates sustained and concerted efforts in continuous relationship building in which leaders invest time and resources in cultivating robust relationships with stakeholders. Through regular dialogue, feedback mechanisms, and responsiveness to stakeholder needs, leaders can cultivate an ecosystem of trust and goodwill, thereby laying the groundwork for sustainable growth and prosperity (Attanasio et al., 2022).

By assessing stakeholder satisfaction and loyalty, leaders can glean valuable insights into the efficacy of their engagement strategies and make informed, data-driven decisions to optimize organizational performance and enhance stakeholder relationships. The benefits from both of these perspectives are vital for sustainability. However, stakeholder engagement should also be viewed as an opportunity for social learning. It is a social process where diverse stakeholders come together in a common forum to learn about each other's values, reflect upon their own values, and ultimately strive to create a shared vision and objectives.

Conclusion

This chapter focused on the challenge brilliant leaders face to co-create a transformational vision that inspires and aligns stakeholders and promotes a future of success. They have the know-how to execute digital transformation and the relational skills to influence collaboration and joint accountability that empower individuals and teams through delegation and autonomy. These leaders traverse innovation while embodying qualities such as empathy, resilience, and agility needed to create purpose-driven innovation. They empower their teams during disruptive times, build trust, minimize ambiguity, and exploit new opportunities.

The chapter advanced the power of rethinking leadership by moving beyond traditional forms of leadership toward shared leadership and distributive leadership and employing strategic visioning that brings together stakeholders by highlighting the new purposes, values, and goals for scaling and sustaining change and innovation. Trustworthy leadership that promotes empowerment and collaboration is instrumental in balancing institutional constraints with new ideas by breaking existing boundaries and promoting innovative thinking. This chapter also described the dynamics of co-creation that encourage diversity of people and perspectives, bringing together stakeholders to support the goals of digital transformation and further explore new solutions that embrace humanity, sustainability, and ethics.

References

Allen, S., Cunliffe, A. L., & Easterby-Smith, M. (2019). Understanding sustainability through the lens of ecocentric radical reflexivity: Implications for management education. *Journal of Business Ethics, 154*, 781–795.

Anghel, D. (2019). The ground rules for managers and leaders in the change management process of digitization. *CAL, 20*, 37–42.

Attanasio, G., Preghenella, N., De Toni, A. F., & Battistella, C. (2022). Stakeholder engagement in business models for sustainability: The stakeholder value flow model for sustainable development. *Business Strategy and the Environment, 31*(3), 860–874.

Badal, S. B., & Ott B. (2015). Gallup - Delegating: A huge management challenge for entrepreneurs. *Business Journal.* https://news.gallup.com/businessjournal/182414/delegating -huge-management-challenge-entrepreneurs.aspx

Baer, M. (2012). Putting creativity to work: The implementation of creative ideas in organizations. *Academy of Management Journal, 55*(5), 1102–1119.

Belasen, A. T. (2000). *Leading the learning organization: Communication and competencies for managing change.* SUNY Press.

Belasen, A. T. (2019). *Dyad leadership and clinical integration: Driving change, aligning strategies.* Health Administration Press.

Belasen, A. T. (2022). *Resilience in healthcare leadership: Practical strategies and self-assessment tools.* Routledge.

Belasen, A. T., & Belasen, A. R. (2019). The strategic value of integrated corporate communication: Functions, social media, stakeholders. *International Journal of Strategic Communication, 13*(4). https://doi.org/10.1080/1553118X.2019.1661842

Belasen, A. T., & Eisenberg, B. (2023). Building trust for better crisis communication: Lessons for leadership development, Chapter 7. In N. Pfeffermann & M. Schaller (Eds.), *New leadership communication - inspire your Horizon* (pp. 93–110). Springer. https://doi.org/10 .1007/978-3-031-34314-8_7

Belasen, A. T., & Luber, E. (2017). Innovation implementation: Leading from the middle out. In N. Pfeffermann & J. Gould (Eds.), *Strategy and communication for innovation: Integrative perspectives on innovation in the digital economy* (pp. 229–243). Springer.

Belasen, A. T., & Rufer, R. (2013). Innovation communication for effective inter-professional collaboration: A stakeholder perspective. In N. Pfeffermann, T. Minshall, & L. Mortara (Eds.), *Strategy and communication for innovation* (2nd ed., pp. 227–240). Springer.

Bennett, N., & Lemoine, G. J. (2014). What a difference a word makes: Understanding threats to performance in a VUCA world. *Business Horizons, 57*(3), 311–317.

Bilal A., Siddiquei A., Asadullah M. A., Awan H. M., & Asmi F. (2021). Servant leadership: A new perspective to explore project leadership and team effectiveness. *International Journal of Organizational Analysis, 29*(3), 699–715

Bodwell, W., & Chermack, T. J. (2010). Organizational ambidexterity: Integrating deliberate and emergent strategy with scenario planning. *Technological Forecasting and Social Change, 77*(2), 193–202.

Boyatzis, R. E. (2008). Leadership development from a complexity perspective. *Consulting Psychology Journal: Practice and Research, 60*(4), 298–313.

Chatterjee, S., Chaudhuri, R., Vrontis, D., & Galati, A. (2023). Influence of managerial practices, productivity, and change management process on organizational innovation capability of small and medium businesses. *European Business Review, 35*(5), 839–859.

Cortellazzo, L., Bruni, E., & Zampieri, R. (2019). The role of leadership in a digitalized world: A review. *Frontiers in Psychology, 10*, 456340.

Doheny, M., Nagali, V., & Weig, F. (2012). Agile operations for volatile times. *McKinsey Quarterly, 3*(1), 126–131.

Domínguez, B., Orcos, R., & Palomas, S. (2022). To be different or to be the same when you are a small firm? Competitive interdependence as a boundary condition of the strategic balance perspective. *Long Range Planning, 56*(2), 102289. https://www.sciencedirect .com/science/article/pii/S002463012200108X

Gino, F., et al. (2017). Why curiosity matters. *Harvard Business Review, 95*(5), 94–101.

Holbeche, L. (2023). *The agile organization: How to build an engaged, innovative and resilient business.* Kogan Page Publishers.

Hoe, S. L. (2022). *Digital transformation: Strategy, execution and Technology.* Auerbach Publications.

Isaacs, K., & Ancona, D. (2019). 3 Ways to build a culture of collaborative innovation. *HBR.* https://hbr.org/2019/08/3-ways-to-build-a-culture-of-collaborative-innovation

Jiang, L., John, L. K., Boghrati, R., & Kouchaki, M. (2022). Fostering perceptions of authenticity via sensitive self-disclosure. *Journal of Experimental Psychology: Applied, 28*(4), 898–915. https://doi.org/10.1037/xap0000453

Kelloway, K. E., Turner, N., Barling, J., & Loughlin, C. (2012). Transformational leadership and employee psychological well-being: The mediating role of employee trust in leadership. *Work Stress, 26,* 39–55. https://doi.org/10.1080/02678373.2012.660774

Larson, E. (2017). New research: Diversity + inclusion = better decision making at work. *Forbes.* https://www.forbes.com/sites/eriklarson/2017/09/21/new-research-diversity-inclusion-better-decision-making-at-work/?sh=1045bea84cbf

Lorentzen, A. C. R. (2022). Digital transformation as distributed leadership: Firing the change agent. *Procedia Computer Science, 196,* 245–254. https://doi.org/10.1016/j.procs.2021.12.011

Maxwell, K. E., Nagda, B. R., & Thompson, M. C. (2023*). Facilitating intergroup dialogues: Bridging differences, catalyzing change.* Taylor & Francis.

Martínez-Climent, C., Rodríguez-García, M., & Ribeiro-Soriano, D. (2019). Digital transformations and value creation in international markets. *International Journal of Entrepreneurial Behavior & Research, 25*(8), 1603–1604.

Mattessich, P. W., & Johnson, K. M. (2018). *Collaboration: What makes it work.* Fieldstone Alliance.

Megheirkouni, M., & Mejheirkouni, A. (2020). Leadership development trends and challenges in the twenty-first century: rethinking the priorities. *Journal of Management Development, 39*(1), 97–124.

MGMA. (2019, October 31). *Better together: Most healthcare leaders report using a dyad leadership model.* https://www.mgma.com/data/data-stories/better-together-most-healthcare-leaders-report-us

Millar, C. C., Groth, O., & Mahon, J. F. (2018). Management innovation in a VUCA world: Challenges and recommendations. *California Management Review, 61*(1), 5–14.

Millar, J., & Price, M. (2018). Imagining management education: A critique of the contribution of the United Nations PRME to critical reflexivity and rethinking management education. *Management Learning, 49*(3), 346–362.

Moussa, M., McMurray, A., & Muenjohn, N. (2018). Innovation and leadership in public sector organizations. *Journal of Management Research, 10*(3), 14–30.

Nauman, S., Bhatti, S. H., Imam, H., & Khan, M. S. (2022). How servant leadership drives project team performance through collaborative culture and knowledge sharing. *Project Management Journal, 53*(1), 17–32

Nyagadza, B. (2022). Sustainable digital transformation for ambidextrous digital firms: Systematic literature review, meta-analysis and agenda for future research directions. *Sustainable Technology and Entrepreneurship, 1*(3), 100020.

Pearce, C. L., & Conger, J. A. (2002). *Shared leadership: Reframing the hows and whys of leadership.* Sage Publications.

Pel, B., Dorland, J., Wittmayer, J., & Jørgensen, M. (2017). Detecting social innovation agency; methodological reflections on units of analysis in dispersed transformation processes. *European Public and Social Innovation Review, 2,* 110–111.

Ravasi, D., & Schultz, M. (2006). Responding to organizational identity threats: Exploring the role of organizational culture. *The Academy of Management Journal, 49*(3), 433–458. http://www.jstor.org/stable/20159775

Ross, J. W., Beath, C. M., & Goodhue, D. L. (2006). Develop long-term competitiveness. through IT assets. *MIT Sloan Management Review, 47*(3), 31–38.

Strasser, T., De Kraker, J., & Kemp, R. (2022). Network leadership for transformative capacity development: Roles, practices and challenges. *Global Sustainability, 5*, e11.

Swensen, S., & Mohta, N. S. (2017, August). Leadership survey ability to lead does not come from a degree. *New England Journal of Medicine, Catalyst*, August,. https://www .primarycareprogress.org/wp-content/uploads/2017/11/Insights-Council-August-2017 -Leadership-Survey-Report-Ability-to-Lead-Does-Not-Come-from-a-Degree.pdf

Türk, A. (2023). Business competencies for a strategic model suitable for digital transformation. In P. Vardarlıer (Ed.), *Multidimensional and strategic outlook in digital business transformation: Human resource and management recommendations for performance improvement* (pp. 205–216). Cham: Springer International Publishing.

United Nations. (2020). *Accountability, integrity, and transparency in times of crisis.* https:// unglobalcompact.org/academy/accountability-integrity-and-transparency-in-times-of -crisis

Wasono, L. W., & Furinto, A. (2018). The effect of digital leadership and innovation management for incumbent telecommunication company in the digital disruptive era. *International Journal of Engineering and Technology, 7*, 125–130.

Chapter 5

Transforming Business: Coping with Paradoxes in Purpose-Driven Innovation

---

Jaap Boonstra

The future of our world is up for debate. We are confronted with climate change, geo-political tensions, polarization in society, demographic issues, disruptive technologies, poverty, and health issues. Many social issues affect people directly, and they want to do something about it. They envision a future, bring allies together, and get to work. Small initiatives lead to innovative and values-driven alliances with a positive impact on our society. The mission of a values-driven alliance is to make positive changes in our society. Because of the societal mission and the scope of values-driven alliances, collaboration is complex and full of paradoxes. This chapter presents eight paradoxes that provide insights into how to deal with irreconcilably opposed views and resulting actions in the life cycle of values-driven alliances.

The chapter provides insights into the dynamics of innovative values-driven alliances and how leaders and professionals deal with paradoxes in the alliances' life cycle and in their communication and decision-making processes. The values, motives, and competencies of brilliant leaders are explored and discussed. The Global Alliance for Banking on Values is used as a case study to inspire scholars and practitioners to deal with the paradoxes that arise in creating purpose-driven alliances and managing innovative alliances with the aim of supporting societal transformation. In addition to understanding the dynamics of alliances and the essential qualities of values-driven leaders, this chapter provides inspiration for people who want to contribute to a better

DOI: 10.4324/9781003495307-7

world, by working together with others. Leaders, professionals, and change masters are invited to reflect on their own capabilities in creating and managing values-based alliances and on the values, motives, and competencies of their own leadership in the collaborative transformation to create a better and more sustainable world.

Playing with Paradoxes in the Life Cycle of Alliances

There are many models for the life course of alliances (De Man, 2013). Based on my own experiences, I distinguish four phases in the alliance life cycle: forming, building, developing, and evolving alliances. The phases are not successive stages but form a dynamic and continuous pattern full of paradoxes.

Forming alliances lays the foundation for the alliance. In this phase, the initiators find each other in a common ambition. It is the phase of getting to know each other and exploring possibilities to strengthen each other. Building trust is essential in this phase (De Man et al., 2010). In the building phase, the search for a common identity is central (Kourti, 2021). New members join, and the common ambition is further elaborated (De Rond & Bouchikhi, 2004). In the building phase, the focus is on bringing together the ambitions of the members and achieving a common goal (Das & Kumar, 2007). The original initiators are committed to the open and active involvement of all members so that unnecessary tensions and possible conflicts are prevented (Das & Teng, 1998). In the developing phase, the alliance faces the task of continuing to innovate and adapt as the context changes (Koza & Lewin, 1998). Innovation may require reforming the network and admitting new partners. This can put existing relationships and identities under pressure (Das & Teng, 2000). When evolving alliances, recognizing and handling stagnation is a challenge, and perhaps the alliance has to transform its mission, strategies, and goals, and reconsider criteria for partnership.

Dealing with Paradoxes

A paradox consists of two seemingly irreconcilable opposing views and related actions, which exist simultaneously and are each meaningful and defensible (Smith & Lewis, 2011). Contradictions take the form of a paradox when both poles of the contradiction manifest themselves at the same time, are mutually tense, but meanwhile do not exist separately (Van Twist & Vermaak, 2022). Paradoxes are so embedded in the daily actions and interactions of organizational life that they become difficult to spot or are too intertwined in systems of contradictions (Fairhurst, 2019).

This raises the question of how we should deal with tensions and paradoxes in the life cycle of organizations and alliances. A failure to address emerging paradoxes could reinforce paralyzing inertia in the development of organizations (Mastio et al., 2021).

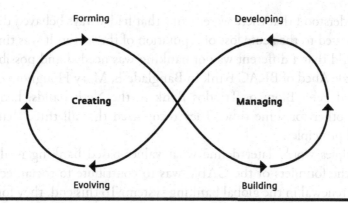

Figure 5.1 Life Cycle of Values-Driven Alliances. Adapted from: Boonstra, J.J. & Eguiguren, M. (2023), p.18.

Paradoxes reflect the strategic choices we face as we begin to work together in alliances. Paradoxes can create discomfort because both sides of a paradox are necessary for healthy interplay. The tension of paradoxes keeps organizations and teams alive, prevents a one-sided focus, encourages action, and invites you to step out of your comfort zone. It stimulates the joint search for alternatives and new unconventional possibilities (Miron-Spektor et al., 2011). The challenge for leaders and members in the alliance is to position themselves in the field of tension that the paradox evokes without choosing one of the extremes (Hoebeke, 2004).

Van Twist and Vermaak (2022) describe four action perspectives to deal with paradoxes. The first is to endure the tension created by the paradox and endure relational discomfort by putting the essence that binds the players first and acknowledging the tension between the poles as something that comes with it if you want to make a difference together. A second possibility is to unravel the paradox by investigating, reversing, deepening, and stating that the poles do not fight each other but actually need each other. A third action perspective is the art of balancing. Now it is a matter of making the dynamics of the paradox manageable by seeking balance and making combinations of views and related actions. A fourth perspective is to transcend the paradox in which players explore new possibilities together and learn to experiment. In alliances, recognizing and dealing with paradoxes can help members find new opportunities in the face of problems, tensions, and strategic choices.

Forming Alliances

In 2008, a financial crisis broke out in the United States with a major impact on our world. As a result, the banking system was scrutinized, and the global financial system was called into question. In this context, leaders of three values-based banks initiated conversations that resulted in the creation of the Global Alliance for Banking on Values (GABV) a year later. After the financial crisis, the banking sector was quite weak, but the bankers understood that there were banks that had always behaved differently and had not contributed to the acute loss of reputation of the sector. It was time to make it clear to the world that a different way of banking was needed and possible. The three bankers, Sir Fazle Abed of BRAC Bank in Bangladesh, Mary Houghton of ShoreBank in Chicago, and Peter Blom of Triodos Bank in the Netherlands, had known and respected each other for some time. They recognized that all three shared the same aspirations and principles.

These principles would later define what values-based banking is all about. The initial goal of the founders of the GABV was to contribute to social, economic, and environmental renewal in the global banking system. To this end, they formulated five action points to which they wanted to commit themselves:

- *Take leadership*: Bringing together value-based banks to work for a better and just world.
- *Joining forces*: Promoting the value-based banking model as an alternative to the traditional banking models that led to the financial crisis.
- *Showing solidarity*: Bringing together leaders who develop ideas and exchange experiences about sustainable financial models, working methods, and organizational forms.
- *Intensify cooperation*: Focusing on far-reaching economic and social cooperation by values-driven banks.
- *Provide practical solutions*: Bringing together bank executives, management, and young talent to improve value-based banking practices.

With these ideas in mind, ten like-minded banks were invited to a first meeting to discuss the establishment of the GABV in March 2009 in the Netherlands. In the first founding meeting, there was no automatic consensus on the alliance's mission and goals. Some banks had a strong focus on sustainability, others were more focused on changing social values and culture, and still others focused on poverty reduction and social inclusion. Some banks had been working on their banking model for decades, while others were just getting started. All were committed to economic and social development and recognized the importance and potential of money as a tool and driver of social renewal. During the meeting, the invited members transcended their mutual differences and formulated a common mission: to develop, define more clearly, and grow values-driven banking to create an alternative to traditional financial systems.

Dealing with Paradoxes in Forming Alliances

In this section, we describe two paradoxes in the formation phase of the GABV, both of which are essentially about trust.

Trust in People and Trust in Systems

There is a difference between trust in people and trust in systems (Boonstra & Smith, 2010). Reliance on systems concerns the design and functioning of alliances, the management model, the measurement of performance, and the control systems used. Trust between people is about trusting the other person as a person. A definition of trust is when we say that we trust someone or that someone can be trusted, we implicitly mean that there is a good chance that an action of the other person will be beneficial to us or at least not harmful (Kaats & Opheij, 2023). Based on mutual trust, we consider whether to participate in an alliance. In values-driven alliances, the initial phase mainly revolves around mutual trust (Camps et al., 2004). At the same time, clear agreements are needed on investments, cost allocation, and revenues to prevent conflicts of interest from arising and alliances falling apart due to insufficient reciprocity. Systems help to create a framework in which trust is anchored.

At the GABV, friendship and mutual respect between the three founders played an important role. They shared a vision of how the conscious use of money could contribute to improving society. It was relatively easy for them to gather like-minded colleagues to work together to change the financial sector. Mutual trust was essential for the thirteen bankers who founded the GABV. Due to the limited number of members and mutual trust, the statutes and governance model were simple, and the financial arrangements transparent, with the costs of the new alliance being borne by the members, taking into account their size and financial capabilities. The three initiating banks were also prepared to make up for any shortfalls in the first few years.

Rely on Feeling and on Reliable Analyses

A paradox in the formation of values-driven alliances is how much time is invested in trusting each other in the early stages and the time spent in careful analysis of the reputation and reliability of the partners (Das & Teng, 1998). An accurate analysis helps to reduce risks and value everyone's contribution. It contributes to the prevention of opportunistic behavior by one of the partners. Continuing to analyze for too long raises the question of whether the person performing the analysis trusts the other and can be trusted. The emotional appeal is supplanted by rational analysis. Particularly at the beginning of alliance formation, it is essential to spend time on personal trust and to give space to feelings, motives, and individual involvement (Hoffmann & Schlosser, 2001). Building solely on trust can later lead to disillusionment if it turns out that the partners have little to offer each other. That is why it is also relevant to make everyone's contributions visible.

In the formation of the GABV, working from feeling was more important than an accurate analysis of the position of the members. In the early years, new members were invited by the initiators and admitted based on personal relationships and reputation. Regardless of the importance of trust, the GABV was aware of the need to be analytical as well. You can't claim to be a values-driven alliance if you can't demonstrate your positive impact on society and explain why you're different from other players in the banking industry. This is why the GABV started working early in its life cycle on the GABV Scorecard: an analytical tool that translated the principles of values-based banking into hard indicators. In subsequent years, the scorecard was used to monitor the performance of existing members and show the differences between the banks and the rest of the industry. At the GABV, trust and attention to detailed analysis have gone hand in hand almost from the start.

Building Alliances

Drawing on the strength of their collaboration, in 2013 the directors of member banks discussed what it takes to make the global financial system more people-centric and stable, and what stakeholders, including banks, regulators, governments, and customers, can do to make this happen. The GABV thus clarified its intentions to change the financial world. In 2014, the GABV mission statement was rewritten as

> The GABV will represent and advance the values-based banking movement by raising public awareness of values-based banking and building a strong GABV profile based on a growing number of members with a broader global reach, an increase in the number of customers, and a greater social impact.

However, the GABV was not yet ready to accomplish this mission. At the end of 2014, the GABV had only 24 members, and most of the banks came from Europe and North America. The global network had not grown for four years, and its members almost exclusively represented the Western world. Expansion and global broadening were necessary. The governance of the GABV also required improvement. The board was still in the hands of the three initiators. The coordination of activities was carried out by a few part-time professionals who were seconded to the GABV from a few member banks and reported to the chairman of the GABV. The ambition of the alliance was clearly higher than what could be achieved with the existing members and their capabilities, resources, and structures.

In the course of 2014, the members of the GABV decided to strengthen the alliance by appointing an executive director who reports to the board. The biggest challenge for the new director was to professionalize the organization and realize the global expansion. By 2019, the GABV had grown substantially to 62 members and 16 supporting partners, and the alliance was much more balanced with 45% of members from outside the Western world. The board of the GABV was restructured, with changes to the statutes and the addition of regional departments. Member services grew rapidly, mainly through further development of the Values-Based Banking Scorecard and the creation of communities of practice for staffing, marketing, and communications.

Dealing with Paradoxes in Building Alliances

In the building stage, two paradoxes are explored that concern the balancing between content and process and the recognition and handling of conflicts.

Balancing between Content and Process

The paradox between content and process is especially visible during the building phase because the number of members increases while the initial intentions of the initiators remain relevant to the vitality of the network. New members and stakeholders admitted to the alliance must understand and believe in the ambitious dreams of the initiators. The growth of the alliance puts pressure on the content side to develop more precise goals, align activities, ensure quality, and measure results. At the process level, it is about creating and adjusting the shared mission and bringing beliefs together (Kaats & Opheij, 2023).

It is also about maintaining collaborative relationships, dealing with tensions and conflicts, and choosing and embedding new partners (Baron & Besanko, 1999). Building alliances is a balancing act between focusing on the process of collaboration and focusing on content with tangible results (Kale & Singh, 2007). Content and process refer to and need each other, but the orientation of the two is fundamentally different. The challenge is to bridge these differences.

At the GABV, communities of practice helped create informal interactions between experts from member banks working on a substantive theme. However, it was almost impossible to create new communities of practice without the explicit support of the board chairmen. In 2015, a risk management community of practice was initiated by a small enthusiastic group of experts. Despite their enthusiasm and the expertise of the participants, that community of practice had to stop its content activities two years later due to a lack of support from the board members to look at risk management from different perspectives. This cooled the involvement of the group members and forced them to give up. Process and content must go hand in hand to be able to take initiatives that fall outside existing frameworks. Other communities of practice have been successful in staffing, marketing, and communications. Huge steps have been taken in developing the scorecard to determine the social impact and financial robustness of values-driven banking and to compare it with traditional banks.

Valuing Conflict and Avoiding Conflict

Organizations involved in building a broader alliance often have to deal with a diversity of parties that pursue their own interests in addition to the common interest. A shared mission can unite these interests, but it is sometimes difficult to formulate concrete goals. A constructive dialogue can contribute to a solid mission and vision that binds the members of the alliance (De Bruijn & Ten Heuvelhof, 2007). When developing and rethinking a mission, disagreements and relational conflicts can arise. The challenge is to take these conflicts seriously and make use of them (Kaats & Opheij, 2023). Power conflicts in which one party can dominate the other parties are destructive to a sustainable partnership and must be avoided. Conflicts about investments, property rights, and the distribution of proceeds can also better be prevented by making clear agreements in advance.

At the GABV, two conflicts were on the table during the building phase. One of these was the request for a board change by several members. From the beginning, the board was in the hands of the three founders. There were no clear agreements for the replacement of board members, and the decision-making process was unclear to many members. The board of the GABV itself argued for a reform of the management model while retaining the principles of simplicity, transparency, and acceptance. By questioning itself, the tensions quickly disappeared, and space was created for a new governance model in which more members had input. A more existential tension appeared around the need for growth. There weren't enough members to make a global impact, and most of the members were based in the Western world. This jeopardized the alliance's credibility as a global player and rendered its mission to change the financial sector infeasible.

Despite the awareness of the need for growth, some members were less than happy with the alliance's growth rate. They raised questions about the values of some of the new members and the eligibility criteria used to bring them on board. This subcutaneous tension persisted for a few years but gradually dissipated as existing members and newcomers came into contact and got to know each other better. Personal contacts and interactions instilled trust. Better use of the scorecard to analyze candidate banks also helped to address criticism of the admission of new members. In a way, a new common framework on eligibility criteria was formed between the existing and the new members, and the tension could be overcome.

Developing Alliances

With stable governance, a better global presence, more diversity in member banks, several well-designed services, and visible social impact, it was time to evaluate the ambition of the GABV and review the strategic vision. The new mission and vision for the GABV was a continuation of the previous mission but now with more coherence and more focus on changing the global financial system:

> Our shared mission is to change the banking system so that it is more transparent, economic, social, and environmental sustainability, and consists of a broad range of banking institutions serving the real economy. Our vision is to expand and strengthen the practice of values-based banking. The GABV wants to lead a financial system that

promotes social justice, responds to the climate crisis, and delivers real and lasting prosperity and well-being for all.

The new mission and vision set the tone for action in the new phase. In 2019, the GABV announced its "Climate Change Commitment" initiative, whereby members voluntarily commit to measuring and reporting the carbon footprint of their lending and investment portfolios in line with the Paris and Cairo Climate Statements. This initiative is part of the GABV's wider commitment to lead positive change in the financial sector. The participating institutions intend to influence the banking industry by demonstrating that banks can assess and report on their greenhouse gas emissions. Most GABV banks are also signatories to the Partnership for Carbon Accounting Financials (PCAF). This is an emerging platform to create methodologies to assess and disclose carbon emissions in the financial sector. Partly due to the efforts of the GABV, more than 270 financial institutions have signed the declaration, including some of the largest financial institutions in the world. They have committed to review, disclose, and account for the carbon emissions of their loans, investments, and insurance financing.

Dealing with Paradoxes in Developing Alliances

The evolution phase is about consolidating the alliance and, at the same time, developing the alliance further. This involves two paradoxes about stability and agility, and open and closed networks.

Stability and Agility

All alliances face changes in the global environment and uncertainties about the future. To deal with these changes, resilience and agility are essential (Van der Steen, 2017). With resilience, the alliance retains its core and finds strength from a shared ambition and a stable identity. In agility, the alliance has high adaptability that is based on mutual trust, intensive communication, and a challenging mission (Cullen et al., 2000). The more smoothly and quickly an alliance can adapt to change, the more value it will create in the long run for its partners and wider society. At the same time, stability is necessary to achieve financial and social results (Boonstra & Eguiguren, 2023). Developing alliances is a balancing act between the pursuit of stability and agility. The shared ambition and underlying values and principles contribute to a stable identity, which makes the alliance resilient. At the same time, a challenging mission invites flexibility in broadening activities and taking new initiatives (Bamford et al., 2003).

At the tipping point between the building and evolution phase, the GABV developed a new vision with more focus on changing the financial system in the world. The strategy focuses on expanding the alliance and its activities, strengthening its visibility and impact, and taking the lead in initiatives that contribute to a better and more sustainable world. Due to the larger size of more than seventy members, the decision-making processes must be followed more strictly and transparency in decision-making must be increased. However, the nature of the alliance has not changed, and its activities are still based on a shared mission with freedom of action by each member to contribute to this mission within the guiding principles of values-driven banking.

Open Network and Closed Network

An open network stimulates access to new knowledge and information that can be important for innovation. An open network also offers opportunities to allow new perspectives when cooperation has stalled and to break through tensions in established relationships. A closed network with strong relationships stimulates trust, and this trust is necessary to share information and invest in the relationship. This paradox is about the constant balancing between the security of a closed network and the creativity of an open network (Ferreira et al., 2020).

Strong relationships between members promote trust and reciprocity and enable the transfer of complex and tacit knowledge (Strašek et al., 2020). Perhaps, open alliances are more suitable for generating ideas, and closed alliances are more suitable for realizing those ideas. This raises the question of how open alliances for idea generation can be combined with more closed alliances for idea realization.

The GABV is an open network by nature as its open character is embedded in the ambitious mission to change the global banking system. After a fast-growing expansion, the growth rate during the development phase is much lower. Slow growth makes it easier for existing members to strengthen their interactions with other members and become more embedded in the organization's values. This allows them to derive more tangible and intangible value from their alliance membership. In the evolution phase, there is room for a limited number of new members per year. The admission criteria and the robustness of the recruitment and entry of new members have already been strengthened during the building phase, preventing tensions and misunderstandings. The GABV combines the strength of the existing GABV network with the initiation of open platforms to measure and disclose carbon emissions, thereby increasing its impact.

Evolving Alliances

Essentially, the GABV has always been a group of banks and banking cooperatives that are at the forefront and share a mission to change the financial system. Members want to actively use finance to achieve sustainable development for people, communities, and the environment. Despite the GABV's changes in its life stages and its more radical approach to achieving its mission, the essence of the alliance has remained unchanged. However, there are developments that invite transformation.

Changes in the financial sector, including the emergence of cryptocurrencies, new forms of banking, and the unparalleled growth of regulation, are causing most banks to rethink how they offer their banking services and to shift a growing share of business activities to less-regulatory areas. is. In response, the GABV can develop and offer a global platform on which value-based banks and other financial service providers offer their services, together with other providers of, for example, renewable energy, home insulation, sustainable agricultural products, and local social enterprises that bank with GABV banks and meet the criteria of the GABV. Several government initiatives target the financial sector to accelerate the transition to sustainable finance. As a result of these changes, the marketing efforts of many mainstream financial institutions are focused on promoting sustainability and the United Nations Sustainable Development Goals. This is often done in a way that resembles the "greenwashing" of existing activities, without the institutions interpreting their policies and operations differently. In this context, the GABV can more than ever live up to its leading role in values-driven banking.

Another strategic theme is how the GABV can collaborate with policymakers and regulators in promoting sustainable finance. Another factor is that the current regulatory burden is largely aimed at systemic banks to keep the global financial system in check. For the GABV, the question is how the alliance can take a leading role in a radical shift from current regulations to a broader system for promoting sustainable finance in which care for the environment and human dignity are central.

Dealing with Paradoxes in Evolving Alliances

Evolving alliances is about finding a balance between consolidation and co-creation and between social impact and economic significance.

Consolidation and Co-Creation

In values-driven alliances, the members work together on their mission in co-creation. They want to create a better future and contribute to a prosperous, just, and sustainable society. In creating an attractive future, the energy focuses on generating appealing ideas of what a desirable future could be and taking initiatives to realize these ideas (Duysters & De Man, 2003). The paradox means that the alliance continuously renews itself in a process of co-creation between the members. On the other hand, an alliance needs consolidation to provide quality to its members and achieve results to invest in the future (Gulatti, 1995). If the alliance's mission and vision doesn't match its current capabilities, disbelief ensues. If the ambition isn't challenging enough or just more of the same, disillusionment ensues. The essence is to find a balance between a challenging and at the same time realistic vision of the future that people want to work on with energy to bring that future a step closer (De Rond & Bouchikhi, 2004).

Given the developments in the banking sector, but also given the history and development of the GABV, it is likely that the paradox of consolidation and co-creation will be approached in a balanced way. One of the distinguishing features of the GABV since its foundation has been the way the alliance adheres to its essence and guiding principles and offers its members room to pioneer a human way of banking. Co-creation has always been a natural way of working together among the members, so in the transformation phase, there is a good chance that imagining a viable new future will take shape in co-creation involving all members.

Social and Economic Significance

In values-driven alliances, social significance is central to the mission that binds the members. Without social significance, there is a good chance that the alliance will fall apart. Ultimately, no partnership can survive without economic significance. Societal and economic significance go hand in hand (Sakara et al., 2012). Economic significance is relevant to be able to continue to invest in the alliance with a view to the social significance and future results. For the involvement of the partners in values-driven alliances, the economic significance is relevant and social significance is central. If the alliance performs adequately and achieves results, there is also economic significance for each member of the alliance.

The GABV is a good example of how social and economic significance go hand in hand. Since 2012, the GABV has published an annual survey comparing the performance of value-based banks and banking cooperatives with the largest banks in the world. In the annual surveys of economic growth, profit, financial stability, resilience, and contribution to the real economy, it is striking that the conclusions are the same over the years.

Despite serious disruptions to the financial markets and the real economy due to, for example, the financial crisis and the COVID-19 pandemic, value-based banks continue to outperform mainstream banks (Kocornik-Mina et al., 2021). This positive result is rooted in values-driven banking principles. The GABV has convincingly demonstrated that serving the real economy leads to better and more stable financial returns.

Brilliant Leadership in Innovative Alliances

The world of leaders is complex and confusing (Clegg et al., 2021; Crevani et al., 2021). To make sense of this complexity, we need to embrace multiple perspectives and capabilities to create and manage alliances for a sustainable world. Leadership in innovative and values-driven alliances is about strengthening the power of the community to shape its own future and independently realize sustainable changes based on a common ambition and shared values. Interesting about this definition is that anyone can be a leader by taking the initiative and asking others to join in. No formal position is required for this. This makes brilliant leadership a shared activity rather than a role or characteristic of an individual.

Sense Makers and Change Poets

Brilliant leaders in alliances are sense makers and change poets (Weick, 2011). Sensemaking is based on the interaction of people in their relationships between the alliance, the members of the alliance, and the people and dynamics in the environment of the alliance. People create meanings based on an external stream of events and dreams, and the values and beliefs they share (Sparr, 2018). These values and beliefs arise from events in the past and shape our view of events in the present day.

Values and beliefs are nurtured by history, stories, and earlier events and maintained by the expectations of people about how they should behave. Brilliant leaders are values-driven and search for ways to break through entrenched patterns. This requires knowledge of the basic assumptions that unite the people. Only if they know the values and beliefs, can they create space for new practices, and from these new practices, new pictures of reality and distributed leadership can emerge (Edwards, 2015).

Organizational stories add to the daily language and make way for new understandings to arise. In the daily routine, patterns of cooperation will change, and people begin to act collectively and make sense of what is going on. Through their actions, they add to the flow of events.

Global View

Brilliant leaders are global leaders in the sense that they have a global view, being open to what is going on in the world, and being aware of a host of events of all types (Gehrke, et al., 2024). This is not merely a matter of knowing what is going on globally and locally but of keeping an eye open for unique local events and actions, spotting differences, and capitalizing on them. This global view thus goes hand in hand with an awareness of the local situation (Beer et al., 2023). Being aware of your local situation requires an open mind and the willingness to enter difficult areas and engage in dialogue with others (Weick, 2011). The traits of the biomimetic leader correspond well with the needs of leaders in values-based alliances (Olaizola et al., 2021).

Collaborative Mindset

Brilliant leaders are social leaders and are constantly aware of relationships and collaboration. In current organizational practices, collaboration is increasingly important (Boonstra, 2023). It is not just about the collaboration between leaders and followers, or between various professionals within departments, but also about the collaboration between organizations, for example, in the context of alliances and networks. This requires leaders to be capable of strategic foresight and collaboration.

The new forms of collaboration are concerned with team spirit, being able to deal with differences, and trust; they are also more concerned with listening than with talking. Collaboration in purpose-driven alliances requires social awareness, that is, being able to enter social relationships and create shared leadership in building social networks (Conger & Pearce, 2003). Social awareness contributes to trust and the development of people, teams, and organizations.

Analytical View

Brilliant leaders have an analytical view on complex issues. This is necessary to unravel complexity, understand the dynamics behind it, and examine how these dynamics can be tackled; good analysis is usually half the battle. By sharing the results of your analysis, you create a sort of base from which a common understanding can be generated to serve as a starting point for tackling problems in a continuous learning process (Holmqvist, 2003).

This concerns hard data and soft events that are difficult to clarify. To reach a fully-fledged analysis, it is necessary to be familiar with customer processes, and therefore to have conversations at all levels within the company and with people from outside, such as customers, suppliers, funders, and supervising authorities. The essence is to be aware of any of your own assumptions that could lead to bias. An analytical view contributes to being able to handle ambiguity and uncertainty; a careful analysis is the foundation of the fourth perspective, that is, a view on change processes and inter-organizational learning.

Ethical Awareness

Brilliant leaders are ethical-aware. They recognize that the experience of change itself and the dissonance it creates, fuels new thinking, and instigate new discoveries and innovations that can revitalize the health of organizations, communities, and the world. Finding the balance among and between simultaneous and sometimes contradictory demands for economically, socially, and environmentally sustainable solutions is a compelling leadership opportunity ultimately grounded in a personal ethic that reaches beyond self-interest (Ferdig, 2007).

Transformational Power

Brilliant leaders are transformational leaders. A considered view on change processes does not entail the untargeted mobilization of the aspirations and motivations of all the people in the alliance; it is more concerned with the well-considered initiation of change (Miles et al., 2005). Conscious change means establishing the cause and the intention of the change, assessing its nature and impact, determining the desired direction as well as the most fitting change strategy and required actions, and finally, selecting the people required to make the change a success. The key concept is transformational awareness. Transformational awareness contributes to sensitivity to what moves people and to the commitment and self-assurance of the people involved.

Reflective Look

Brilliant leaders have a reflective look at what is happening, including clarification of your own role as a leader and professional (Ladkin, 2020). This requires taking a break and distancing yourself so that you can look back at your experiences and your own behavior. Thoughtful reflection means looking at ongoing experiences and patterns that appear. One appropriate question here may be how it is possible that, time and again, you end up in a certain type of uncomfortable situation. Or what were the driving forces behind the successes you achieved? This is a matter of self-awareness, and self-awareness is the art of understanding your own moods, emotions, and energy, understanding your own behavior and behavioral patterns, and taking account of the effects of your behavior on others. A reflective view enhances self-awareness and contributes to self-confidence and learning capacity.

Conclusion

In this final section, the focus is on the significance of values-driven alliances and the essence of brilliant leadership in innovative values-based alliances.

Creating and Managing Values-Driven Alliances

Creating and managing values-driven alliances is an ongoing collaborative process between members. In adapting and changing during the life cycle of these alliances, there are always more members involved in the change process rather than a centralized power that can initiate and steer the needed changes. Members create and manage the alliance through dialogue between people from different backgrounds who work together and challenge each other in an ongoing process of change and development. They envision a sustainable future together, try to find their way in an unpredictable world, and make a collaborative effort to shape their future. In alliances, leadership is a responsibility of the many, not of the few (By, 2021).

This perspective on transformational change reveals that innovation is not the task of the individual but rather an adaptive quality of the many to collectively shape their environment. This means that members deal with unexpected events and moments of uncertainty while creating opportunities to develop and enjoy doing so. The ambition of the alliance is part of an ongoing dialogue about the meaning of the alliance and the member organizations within society. People in alliances make choices about how they interact with each other. This creates social groups that create and maintain cultural norms and values together. In their collaboration, they discover and experience the world around us and give meaning to what we see and find relevant.

Dealing with Paradoxes

Managing innovation is invariably managing paradoxes and a balancing act between continuity and transformation (Nasim & Sushil, 2011). Within the GABV, paradoxes were discussed and interpreted by members, and the tensions investigated. Often this started with recognizing unequal positions between members and including all perspectives. Then it was about articulating the shared mission and guiding principles of the alliance. In doing so, it was essential to reassess tensions and provide room for contradiction to feel the discomfort. Only then was there room to combine perspectives and steer on guiding principles and shared values. Transcending perspectives arose in an open dialogue with all members and through learning experimentation. Leaders' sensemaking about paradoxes to other members is based on their own sensemaking processes and stimulates others to engage in paradoxical sensemaking and their subsequent reactions to paradoxical tensions (Sparr, 2018).

Communicating

Communicating about innovation and collaboration in values-driven alliances is a continuous process in which people engage in dialogues with each other to explore and clarify problems and ambitions further. They are invited to make themselves heard and asked if they want to produce ideas and contribute to change. It is precisely in these interactions that meaning is generated, and a story is created about the dream and ambition that generates involvement. A profound development of the alliance only succeeds when the communication reaches the deeper layers of the identity of the alliance and the people involved can exchange meanings and share values.

Promoting informal communication between members, investing in the community so that members get to know each other in depth, evaluating the strength of purpose of members and making sure there is alignment with the purpose of the group, as well as a clear and transparent governance system, and the celebration of successes and milestones in collective results are some of the activities that build trust during all phases of the alliance life cycle. Offering and appreciating small wins in trust building is helpful. Actions to begin identifying who to build trust with or starting with modest joint actions are ways to get started without having to deal with all aspects of trust building at the same time.

Brilliant Leadership

Leadership is about activities that people undertake together. It is about ambitions they share, goals they want to realize, and dreams they want to make come true. Leadership is, therefore, also about giving meaning to events, creating meaning, and celebrating success. It is about an interplay between leaders and followers. No leader acts autonomously. Good leaders know how to follow, and they are committed to turning followers into leaders. Collaborative activities and teamwork are aimed at achieving results. These can be concrete goals, or they can involve realizing an attractive vision of the future.

Brilliant leadership means realizing transformational changes. The change is not enforced but focuses on creating a desirable future without disqualifying the past. It is about maintaining identity and what is valuable while shaping innovation. In conclusion, brilliant leadership in alliances is a social process in which an individual member of a group gives meaning to events and, together with others, creates a vision of the future, maintains relationships, and organizes cooperation to jointly shape a desirable future.

Future of Values-Driven Alliances

Over the past twenty to thirty years, we have seen an astonishing acceleration of change in our society. These changes are not always for the better and sometimes even threaten people and life on our planet. In this context, values-driven alliances will increase in number and value. Together we have opportunities to start and develop values-driven alliances in which we can work together on current social and human challenges. Creating and developing sustainable alliances can be summed up with the question: what are we going to do together to shape a valuable future? Answering that question is about seeking connection, identity, and meaning to contribute to the future of a community and wider society. From this perspective, leadership is the collective pursuit of delivering on purpose (By, 2021).

The meaning of values-driven alliances is not only in improved innovative mindset, but also in a stronger image, or the development of new services and products that make a difference in the world around us. The main value of these alliances is their collective capacity to contribute to the challenges of our society by placing prosperity and human dignity above economic development.

References

Bamford, J. B., Comes-Casseres, B., & Robinson, M. S. (2003). *Mastering alliance strategy*. Jossey Bass.

Baron, D. P., & Besanko, D. (1999). Informal alliances. *The Review of Economic Studies, 66*(4), 743–768. https://doi.org/10.1111/1467-937x.00107

Beer, A., Sotarauta, M., & Bailey, D. (2023) Leading change in communities experiencing economic transition: Place leadership, expectations, and industry closure. *Journal of Change Management, 23*(1), 32–52. https://doi.org/10.1080/14697017.2023.2164936

Boonstra, J. J. (2023). Reflections: From planned change to playful transformations. *Journal of Change Management, 23*(1), 12–31. https://doi.org/10.1080/14697017.2022.2151149

Boonstra, J. J. & Eguiguren, M. (2023). *Alliances for sustainable futures. Creating and managing purpose-driven alliances.* Edward Elgar.

Boonstra. J. J., & Smith, G. A. C. (2010) Vertrouwen: Een gelaagd fenomeen [Trust: A layered phenomenon]. *M&O, Tijdschrift voor Management en Organisatie, 64*(6), 3–16.

By, R. T. (2021). Leadership: In pursuit of purpose. *Journal of Change Management, 21*(1), 30–44. https://doi.org/10.1080/14697017.2021.1861698

Camps, T., Diederen, P., Hofstede, G. J., & Vos, B. (2004). *The emerging world of chains and networks: Bridging theory and practice.* Reed Business.

Clegg, S., Crevani, L., Uhl-Bien, M., & By, R. T. (2021). Changing leadership in changing times. *Journal of Change Management, 21*(1), 1–13. https://doi.org/10.1080/14697017.2021.1880092

Conger, J. A., & Pearce, C. L. (2003). A landscape of opportunities: Future research on shared leadership. In C. L. Pearce & J. A. Conger (Eds.), *Shared leadership: Reframing the hows and whys of leadership* (pp. 285–303). Sage. https://doi.org/10.4135/9781452229539.n14

Crevani, L., Uhl-Bien, M., Clegg, S., & By, R.T. (2021). Changing leadership in changing times II. *Journal of Change Management, 21*(2), 133–143. https://doi.org/10.1080/14697017.2021.1917489

Cullen, J. B., Johnson, J. L., & Sakano, T. (2000). Success through commitment and trust: The soft side of strategic alliance management. *Journal of World Business, 35*(3), 223–240. https://doi.org/10.1016/s1090-9516(00)00036-5

Das, T. K., & Kumar, R. (2007). Learning dynamics in the alliance development process. *Management Decision, 45*(4), 684–707. https://doi.org/10.1108/00251740710745980

Das, T. K., & Teng, B. S. (1998). Between trust and control: Developing confidence in partner cooperation in alliances. *Academy of Management Review, 23*(3), 491–513. https://doi.org/10.5465/amr.1998.926623

Das, T. K., & Teng, B. S. (2000). Instabilities of strategic alliances: An internal tensions perspective. *Organization Science, 11*(1), 77–114. https://doi.org/10.1287/orsc.11.1.77.12570

De Bruijn, H., & Ten Heuvelhof, E. (2007). *Management in networks. On multi-actor decision making.* Taylor & Francis.

De Man, A. P. (2013). *Alliances: An executive guide to designing successful strategic partnerships.* Wiley.

De Man, A. P., Roijakkers, N., & De Graauw, H. (2010). Managing dynamics through robust alliance governance structures. *European Management Journal, 28*(3), 171–181. https://doi.org/10.1016/j.emj.2009.11.001

De Rond, M., & Bouchikhi, H. (2004). On the dialectics of strategic alliances. *Organization Science, 15*(1), 56–69. https://doi.org/10.1287/orsc.1030.0037

Duysters, G. M., & De Man, A. P. (2003). Transitory alliances: An instrument for surviving turbulent industries? *R&D Management, 33*(1), 49–58. https://doi.org/10.1111/1467-9310.00281

Edwards, G. (2015). *Community as leadership.* Edward Elgar.

Fairhurst, G. T. (2019). Reflections: Return paradox to the wild? Paradox interventions and their implications. *Journal of Change Management, 19*(1), 6–22. https://doi.org/10.1080/14697017.2018.1552505

Ferdig, M. A. (2007). Sustainability leadership: Co-creating a sustainable future. *Journal of Change Management, 7*(1), 25–35. https://doi.org/10.1080/14697010701233809

Ferreira, J., Coelho. A., & Moutinho, L. (2020). Strategic alliances, exploration and exploitation and their impact on innovation and new product development: The effect of knowledge sharing. *Management Decision, 59*(3), 524–567. https://doi.org/10.1108/md 09 2019 1239

Gehrke, B., & Claes, M. T. (Eds.). (2014). *Global leadership practices: A cross-cultural management perspective*. Palgrave MacMillan.

Gehrke, B., Pauknerova, D., Claes, M. T., & Aust, I. (2024). Introduction to global leadership practices. In *Global leadership practices: Competencies for navigating in a complex world* (2nd ed., pp. 2--24). Edward Elgar Publishing. https://doi.org/10.4337/9781035308088 .00011

Gulati, R. (1995). Social structure and alliance formation patterns. A longitudinal analysis. *Administrative Science Quarterly, 40*(4), 619–652. https://doi.org/10.2307/2393756

Hoebeke, L. (2004). Dilemmas and paradoxes in organizational change processes: A critical reflection. In J. J. Boonstra (Ed.), *Dynamics of organizational change and learning* (pp. 149–175). John Wiley & Sons. https://doi.org/10.1002/9780470753408.ch9

Hoffmann, W. H., & Schlosser, R. (2001). Success factors of strategic alliances. *Long Range Planning, 34*(3), 357–381. https://doi.org/10.1016/s0024 6301(01)00041 3

Holmqvist, M. (2003). A dynamic model of intra- and interorganizational learning. *Organization Studies, 24*(1), 95–123. https://doi.org/10.1177/0170840603024001684

Kaats, E., & Opheij, W. (2023). *Learning to collaborate. Creating conditions for promising cooperation*. Boom.

Kale, P., & Singh, H. (2007). Building firm capabilities through learning: The role of the alliance learning process in alliance capability and firm-level success. *Strategic Management Journal, 28*(10), 981–1000. https://doi.org/10.1002/smj.616

Kocornik-Mina, A., Bastida-Viancanet, R., & Eguiguren Huerta, M. (2021). Social impact of purpose driven banking: Successful practices and a continuity framework. *Sustainability, 13*(14), 7681–7711. https://doi.org/10.3390/su13147681

Kourti, I. (2021). Managing the identity paradox in interorganizational collaborations. *European Management Review, 18*(4), 445–459. https://doi.org/10.1111/emre.12485

Koza, M. P., & Lewin, A. Y. (1998). The co-evolution of strategic alliances. *Organization Science, 9*(3), 255–264. https://doi.org/10.1287/orsc.9.3.255

Ladkin, D. (2020). *Rethinking Leadership: A new look at old questions*. Edward Elgar.

Mastio, E. A., Clegg, S. R., Pina e Cunha, M., & Dovey, K. (2021). Leadership ignoring paradox to maintain inertial order. *Journal of Change Management*, Published online, 1–19. https://doi.org/10.1080/14697017.2021.2005294

Miles, R.F., Miles, G., & Snow, C.C. (2005). *Collaborative entrepreneurship: How communities and networked firms use continuous innovation to create economic wealth*. Stanford University Press.

Miron-Spektor, E., Gino, F., & Argote, L. (2011). Paradoxical frames and creative sparks: Enhancing individual creativity through conflict and integration. *Organizational Behavior and Human Decision Processes, 116*, 229–240. https://doi.org/10.1016/j.obhdp .2011.03.006

Nasim, S., & Sushil. (2011). Revisiting organizational change: Exploring the paradox of managing continuity and change. *Journal of Change Management, 11*(2), 185–206. https://doi .org/10.1080/14697017.2010.538854

Olaizola, E., Morales-Sánchez, R., Eguiguren Huerta, M. (2021). Biomimetic leadership for 21st century companies. *Biomimetics, 6*(1), 47–56. https://doi.org/10.3390/ biomimetics6030047

Sakara, S., Bodur, M., Yildirim-Öktem, Ö., & Selekler-Göksen, N. (2012). Social alliances: Business and social enterprise collaboration for social transformation. *Journal of Business Research, 65*(12), 1710–1720. https://doi.org/10.1016/j.jbusres.2012.02.012

Smith, W. K., & Lewis, M. W. (2011). Towards a theory of paradox: A dynamic equilibrium model of organizing. *Academy of Management Review, 36*(2), 381–403. https://doi.org/10 .5465/amr.2011.59330958

Sparr, J. L. (2018). Paradoxes in organizational change: The crucial role of leaders' sense giving. *Journal of Change Management, 18*(2), 162–180. https://doi.org/10.1080/14697017 .2018.1446696

Strašek, A., Pušavec, F., & Likar, B. (2020) Open innovation and business performance improvement in strategic business alliances. *Journal of Contemporary Management Issues, 25*(1), 133–144. https://doi.org/10.30924/mjcmi.25.1.8

Van der Steen, M. (2017). Anticipation tools in policy formulation: Forecasting, foresight, and implications. In M. Howlett & I. Mukherjee (Eds.). *The international handbook of policy formulation* (pp. 182–197). Edward Elgar. https://doi.org/10.4337/9781784719326.00018

Van Twist, M., & Vermaak, H. (2022). Paradoxen: werk maken van ongemak [Paradoxes: Making work of discomfort]. *M&O, Tijdschrift voor Management en Organisatie, 76*(5/6), 152–175.

Weick, K. E. (2011). Reflections: Change agents as change poets – On reconnecting flux and hunches. *Journal of Change Management, 11*(1), 7–20. https://doi.org/10.1080/14697017.2011.548937

CULTURAL INNOVATION

3

How Leaders Shape a Culture of Innovation through Collaborative Technologies, Risk Tolerance, and Empowerment

Chapter 6

Co-creating Purposeful Change: From the Individual to the Organization

Aurelie Cnop and Andrew Mountfield

The COVID-19 pandemic has irrevocably altered the global workplace landscape, catalyzing profound reflections on work-life balance, professional fulfillment, and organizational loyalty (Klotz, 2021). This section provides a theoretical overview and introduces the overarching theme of the post-pandemic redefinition of work purpose, dissecting the emergence of new professional priorities, the quest for meaningful work, and the implications for employees and organizations alike (Tan & Marissa, 2023; Nourkova & Gofman, 2023; Liske et al., 2023). In doing so, we set the stage for a deeper investigation into the evolving dynamics of the workforce.

Post-COVID-19 Workforce Dynamics

Emergence of the "Great Resignation"

The "Great Resignation" phenomenon, characterized by a significant number of employees voluntarily leaving their jobs, has been attributed to various interconnected factors (Fry, 2022; Weinstein & Hirsh, 2023). Firstly, the COVID-19 pandemic catalyzed a reevaluation of work-life balance priorities among employees globally. The sudden shift to remote work arrangements forced many to reassess their relationship with work, prompting some to seek more flexibility, autonomy, and purpose in their professional lives (Boston-Fleischhauer, 2022). According to a survey conducted by Microsoft in 2021, 41% of global workers were considering leaving their current employers due to a

DOI: 10.4324/9781003495307-9

desire for flexible remote work options. Additionally, the pandemic-induced economic uncertainty spurred individuals to reflect on their career paths, leading to a heightened sense of discontentment with their current roles (Sull, 2022).

Secondly, there has been a growing dissatisfaction with traditional workplace structures and cultures. Employees, particularly from younger generations such as Millennials and Gen Z, are increasingly prioritizing values alignment, inclusivity, and a sense of belonging in their workplaces. According to a Gallup (2021) report on "the state of the global workplace", only 36% of U.S. employees feel engaged in their jobs, highlighting a widespread issue of disengagement in the workforce. This dissatisfaction has been exacerbated by reports of workplace burnout, inadequate support from employers, and a lack of opportunities for career advancement. As a result, many employees have opted to resign from their positions in search of organizations that offer a more supportive and fulfilling work environment.

Despite efforts by employers to address some of these concerns, such as implementing hybrid work models and prioritizing employee well-being initiatives, the "Great Resignation" continues to impact the labor market. According to data from the U.S. Bureau of Labor Statistics (2021), a record 4.4 million workers voluntarily quit their jobs in September 2021. Furthermore, the trend has persisted with a survey by the Society for Human Resource Management (2022) reporting that 35% of U.S. employees were considering quitting their jobs within the next 12 months. These statistics underscore the ongoing challenges faced by employers in retaining talent and adapting to the evolving expectations of the modern workforce. As organizations navigate the post-pandemic landscape, addressing issues related to work-life balance, career development, and workplace culture will be essential for mitigating the impacts of the "Great Resignation" and fostering a more engaged and productive workforce.

Dissatisfaction with Extrinsic Rewards

In recent years, there has been a noticeable shift in the priorities of employees, with intrinsic factors gaining precedence over extrinsic rewards in influencing their job satisfaction and overall engagement (Weinstein & Hirsh, 2023; Ferrazi & Clementi, 2022). Traditionally, organizations have relied on extrinsic rewards such as salary, bonuses, and benefits to attract and retain talent. However, research indicates that intrinsic factors, such as job satisfaction, work-life balance, and a sense of purpose, have become increasingly important in shaping employees' perceptions of their workplaces and driving their decision-making processes (Fuller & Kerr, 2022; Gulati, 2023).

Job satisfaction, often considered a cornerstone of employee engagement, encompasses various aspects of the work environment, including the nature of the job itself, relationships with colleagues and supervisors, and opportunities for growth and development. Studies have consistently shown that employees who are satisfied with their jobs are more likely to be productive, motivated, and committed to their organizations.

According to a Gallup (2023) report on "the state of the Global Workplace", highly engaged teams see a 21% increase in profitability. Conversely, dissatisfaction with work can lead to decreased morale, higher turnover rates, and reduced organizational performance. As a result, organizations are recognizing the importance of fostering a positive work culture and providing employees with opportunities to find meaning and fulfillment in their roles.

Work-life balance has also emerged as a critical factor influencing employees' decisions to stay or leave their jobs. In today's fast-paced and interconnected world, many employees struggle to maintain a healthy balance between their professional and personal lives. Long working hours, constant connectivity, and job-related stress can take a toll on employees' well-being and productivity. A study by the American Psychological Association found that 44% of workers reported experiencing high levels of stress due to workload. Consequently, organizations are under pressure to implement policies and practices that support work-life balance, such as flexible work arrangements, paid time off, and wellness programs. By prioritizing work-life balance, organizations can improve employee satisfaction, reduce burnout, and enhance overall organizational performance.

Furthermore, a sense of purpose has become increasingly important for employees seeking fulfillment in their work. Beyond financial compensation, employees are looking for opportunities to make a meaningful impact and contribute to something greater than themselves. According to a survey by Deloitte (2022), 73% of employees who say they work at a "purpose-driven" organization are engaged, compared to just 23% of those who don't. Organizations that align their mission and values with employees' personal beliefs and aspirations are more likely to attract and retain top talent. By fostering a sense of purpose among employees, organizations can cultivate a strong sense of commitment, loyalty, and engagement, driving positive outcomes for both employees and the organization as a whole.

Pursuit of Meaningful Work – Seeking Purpose through Employment

An increasing number of workers are now prioritizing meaningful engagement and purpose in their professional endeavors (Ferrazi & Clementi, 2022). This paradigm shift is reshaping not only individual job choices but also broader career aspirations and lifestyle decisions. To understand this trend, it's essential to examine the psychological and social underpinnings that drive individuals to seek purpose and fulfillment in their work.

One of the key theories that sheds light on this phenomenon is the Self-Determination Theory (SDT), proposed by psychologists Ryan and Deci (2000), SDT suggests that humans have innate psychological needs for autonomy, competence, and relatedness, and when these needs are satisfied, individuals experience greater motivation, engagement, and well-being. In the context of work, employees are more likely to feel fulfilled and satisfied when they have opportunities to exercise autonomy in their roles, develop their skills and competencies, and build meaningful relationships with colleagues and supervisors.

Moreover, Maslow's Hierarchy of Needs offers insights into the hierarchical nature of human needs and motivations. According to Maslow (1954), once basic physiological and safety needs are met, individuals seek higher-order needs such as belongingness, esteem, and self-actualization. In the workplace, employees are increasingly prioritizing self-actualization needs, which encompass personal growth, fulfillment, and the realization of one's potential. This aligns with the desire for meaningful engagement and purpose in professional endeavors, as individuals seek work that allows them to make a meaningful contribution and derive a sense of fulfillment from their efforts.

Social identity theory also plays a significant role in shaping individuals' career aspirations and decisions (Hogg, 2016). According to this theory, people derive a sense of identity and self-esteem from the groups to which they belong, including their profession or career field. As societal values shift toward prioritizing purpose and impact, individuals are motivated to align their career choices with their personal values and identity. This may involve seeking out organizations and roles that align with their beliefs and offer opportunities for meaningful contributions to society.

Furthermore, the rise of social media and digital connectivity has facilitated the sharing of narratives and experiences related to meaningful work, inspiring others to seek similar opportunities for fulfillment (Greenhow & Robelia, 2009; Williams et al., 2012). Through online communities and platforms, individuals can connect with like-minded professionals, share insights and resources, and gain validation for their pursuit of purpose-driven careers (Khan et al., 2021). This sense of belonging and validation reinforces the importance of purpose and meaning in professional endeavors, further fueling the trend toward prioritizing meaningful engagement in the workforce (Kasperiuniene & Zydziunaite, 2019).

The Overlooked Potential of Stayers

While much attention has been given to those leaving their positions, there exists a significant cohort of employees who choose to stay with their organizations through turbulent times. These individuals, often referred to as "stayers," demonstrate a high level of loyalty, commitment, and resilience even in the face of challenges (Breitling et al., 2021; Gulati, 2022). While their decision to remain may stem from various factors such as job security, career stability, or a sense of duty, "stayers" represent a valuable resource for organizations seeking to navigate change and drive innovation (Holtom et al., 2021).

One of the key strengths of "stayers" lies in their deep institutional knowledge and experience within the organization. Having weathered previous storms and transitions, these employees possess a wealth of insights, best practices, and lessons learned that can be invaluable during times of change. Their familiarity with the organization's culture, processes, and stakeholders enables them to navigate complex challenges more effectively and identify opportunities for improvement and growth (Newton, 2023).

Moreover, "stayers" often serve as role models and mentors for their colleagues, embodying the values and resilience needed to thrive in dynamic environments (Horoszowski, 2020; Goldner & Mayseless, 2009). Their steadfast commitment to the organization can inspire others to remain engaged and focused, fostering a sense of stability and continuity amid uncertainty. By actively engaging with "stayers" and leveraging their influence, organizations can cultivate a culture of resilience, adaptability, and continuous learning, which are essential for driving transformative growth and innovation (Blake-Beard, 2009).

Furthermore, "stayers" possess a unique perspective on the organization's strengths, weaknesses, and areas for improvement. Their insider knowledge and long-term perspective enable them to identify inefficiencies, bottlenecks, and outdated practices that may hinder progress. By empowering "stayers" to voice their insights and ideas for change, organizations can tap into a rich source of internal expertise and drive meaningful improvements that enhance efficiency, productivity, and competitiveness.

Additionally, "stayers" can play a crucial role in fostering collaboration and cohesion within teams and across departments. Their commitment to the organization's mission and values creates a sense of shared purpose and belonging, which can transcend individual differences and foster a spirit of collaboration and innovation. By harnessing the collective energy and creativity of "stayers," organizations can overcome silos, break down barriers to communication, and cultivate a culture of collaboration and teamwork that drives transformative change (Thokozani & Maseko, 2017; Nongo & Ikyanyon, 2012).

Understanding the Diversity of Stayers

Interestingly, within the group of "stayers," three distinct "buckets" have emerged, each with different perspectives in terms of agency. The first bucket, known as "the Corporate Conformists," typically consists of individuals who adhere closely to organizational norms and practices, finding comfort in the predictability and structure of the corporate environment (Nia et al., 2021). The second group, "the Value-Driven Millennials," prioritize meaningful work that aligns with their personal values and societal contributions, often seeking roles and projects that reflect their commitment to making a positive impact (Bannon et al., 2011). The third bucket, dubbed "Gen Z – Wellbeing-Prioritizers" focuses on maintaining firm boundaries between work and nonwork life, emphasizing the importance of mental health and work-life balance (Hayes, 2021; Ganguli et al., 2022).

Despite their loyalty and decision to stay, these groups exhibit a common trend: a sense of pessimism within the confines of the organization contrasted with optimism about opportunities and changes outside of it. This dichotomy highlights the complex interplay between individual aspirations, organizational culture, and the broader socioeconomic landscape, underscoring the need for organizations to understand and address the diverse needs and expectations of their steadfast employees to harness their full potential in driving forward-looking change.

Organizational Change, Agency, and the Complexity of Engagement

This section examines the tension between collective change within a system and individual agency and proposes a practical approach related to change through clarity of corporate purpose. It further addresses several key problems associated with balancing system change and supporting agency. Lastly, it proposes a framework of six factors to support purposeful change.

Change: Top-Down and Bottom-Up

To understand what we mean by purposeful change, we should first examine what influences change itself. Notably, we are part of a broader context which both provides opportunities but also restraints, that we will characterize as a system. Central to the definition is to ensure that parts of the system should not be isolated from other parts, which we take as our starting point. Examples of system components may be beliefs or values concerning what society expects good citizens to do and how they should have, the laws and regulations of the country which we live in, and from an organizational perspective, corporate objectives, individual targets, the management and leadership system in general, and the business ecosystem of which these are part. What these systems or system components have in common is their dual function of providing a structure for behavior or actions while at the same time restricting these through, for example, legal restriction or social mores.

The system as a conceptual framework is often rooted in a common scientific understanding of systems, derived from what we understand to drive engineering, physical sciences, mathematics, or computer systems. But in a social or corporate context, these systems are often so complex that we are unable to fathom our own contributions, how they work in terms of cause-and-effects, and yet we talk about system change, change leadership and so forth, as though they were mechanisms. Furthermore, we may feel part or even a victim of the system, be this at a societal or an organizational level, often because these systems are characterized by their scale, their complexity, and their unpredictable dynamics.

In doing so, we risk thinking of organizations as objects that can and need to be reduced to their component parts to, as a minimum, attempt to grasp their workings at this microscopic level, in the hope of making them do what we want. But this reductionist view of organizations leads to the assumption of a fully deterministic model, in which we are simply required to understand its individual components to grasp the whole. This ignores first the practical challenges of modelling a complex and dynamic set of relationships which implicitly have no borders and fails to appreciate that these systems may have properties that go beyond the sum of their parts, each explicitly interacting with the other. We will return to what higher purpose properties of systems might be later in this section in our discussion of purpose.

A second set of arguments are often set in juxtaposition to the scale, complexity, and dynamics of a system, in which we may see ourselves as simply a cog in the machine, and abandon hope of having influence (Mayer, 2024). These oppose the idea of the system to beliefs concerning free will and agency. This perspective argues that individuals possess free will and are both capable and responsible for their decisions, actions, and for what they fail to do.

To what extent is "free will", broadly speaking the ability to act at one's own discretion, compromised by the "system" discussed above? Two school of thought have been proposed, which can be described as the "optimist" and "pessimist" view of human agency (see for example Bortolotti, 2018). Optimists are those who argue that while determinism may influence decision-making of individuals, this is not sufficient to eliminate its importance. Pessimists can be described as those who believe that determinism limits our moral agency in such significant ways that we cannot act of our own free will.

One aspect that can be derived from this second pessimist perspective is that in the face of a deterministic view, individuals can "learn" to have incapacity, in other words, to form the view that they have no influence over the system through their own agency. It does not require a huge leap of imagination to link these learned perceptions to managerial or leadership practices at a micro-level understanding of organizational culture, or more broadly, to societal norms and practices. Why is this discussion important?

Depending on which set of arguments we choose to apply, change will be viewed as a separate and different concept. From a system perspective, change implies addressing the major levers of the system, acknowledging its relationship not simply to its components but the forces that create and maintain the system itself. From an agency perspective, we view the individual and their relations to others as being the source of the motivation for creating change. To the extent that they can overcome their "incapability" to act through their conviction that change is possible, then free will represents the factor determining whether change occurs.

However, it is difficult to escape the conclusion because of our own lived experience in organizations that both perspectives are at work, and that adopting a perspective that acknowledges the existence and significance of systems, while understanding and leveraging the importance of agency is the appropriate response. This chapter chooses to frame its arguments from an "optimist" view of determinism. We would argue that "wicked problems" illustrate the importance of taking this dual perspective. It is recognized that environmental and social challenges can be understood from a system viewpoint, in the sense that planetary boundaries constrain our ability to act indefinitely as we have since the Industrial Revolution in terms of production, consumption, and, perhaps, political systems.

Yet, without the agency of individuals and their coalitions of interest acting as a focal point for alternatives, it is difficult to imagine change occurring other than because of a financial, social, and environmental collision with the system boundaries. Embracing both collective and individual choice appears not simply appropriate but inevitable. Our question is how do these dual perspectives interact at a corporate level and what roles do corporate system leadership and agency at an individual or group level play.

Purpose: A Working Definition for System Leadership and Individual Agency

Discussing purpose both from the system and from the individual perspective leads inevitably to a conflict that is embedded in the economic history of the last two centuries, namely, that of self-interest vs. the interests of the collective. Any resolution of this apparent collision of goals needs to move beyond the simple motivation of collective rather than individual interest via compliance or incentives, to a recognition that collectively we are better at solving problems than as individuals, but that problem-solving initiative can often result from the agency of individuals. What is required is a framework where we recognize both the good and the harm of our actions, and a shared definition of purpose that articulates this.

What does this mean for corporations? We argue that they exist primarily to solve problems and that organizations are created precisely since they require a diverse set of individual skills and motivations to achieve this. The result in this case is indeed greater than the sum of its parts. But what solutions emerge from this combination, and how do we manage and measure both the harm and the good they do? Equally, if we recognize individual agency, then surely, we must acknowledge that individuals will attempt to realize their own values and act in their own self-interest. What implications does this apparent conflict between collective, or system purpose have with that articulated by individuals?

For this chapter, we adopt the British Academy's definition of purpose (British Academy, 2017), namely producing profitable solutions from the problems of people and the planet, and not profiting from creating problems. While the focus of this research has been on the corporation rather than the individual, we argue that it can be a bridge between the two perspectives. The definition implies a system perspective recognizing the existence of costs and benefits associated with exploiting sources of environmental and social value, not currently always reflected in profit. Further, it articulates principles that can serve to focus the problem-solving abilities related to individual agency.

While the British Academy research selected a range of factors that were required in order to create a framework around purpose and its operationalization, we aim to address briefly questions that illustrate the challenge of bridging the gap between leadership system and individual agency levels. These can be summarized as follows: The strategy problem – the primacy of investor interests; the leadership problem – the reconciliation of top-down articulation of objectives and increasingly senior generations of staff; the agency problem – the challenge of enabling the optimist perspective; the problem of top-down vs emergent objectives – can change be planned or does it simply emerge?; the scope problem – is the incremental the enemy of the transformational? We conclude this section with a framework of factors that require the balancing of the corporate leadership system with the agency of the individual, if the organization is to act as a problem-solver for people and the planet without succumbing to the temptation of profiting from causing further problems.

The Strategy Problem

A classic challenge to individual agency that addresses change while remaining within the stated purpose framework is the apparent primacy of shareholders above all other stakeholder groups, even if short-term shareholder financial goals cause problems for the sake of additional profit. While some authors (Bruner, 2013) argue that this is a matter of regulatory compliance and the protection of corporate reputation, a purpose-driven strategy will require the articulation of guidance and governance which goes beyond those win-win examples (e.g., less waste results in lower cost) to clarity concerning the inevitable trade-offs between different objectives and their related actions. The purpose definition suggests that financial but also social and environmental benefits and costs must form the basis for strategic decision-making.

The Leadership Problem

As described in the first section of this chapter, personal values and individual purpose have evolved and represent a challenge to a leadership system often characterized by command-and-control thinking. We outlined the new employee expectations and the emergence of the three groups: "Corporate Conformists" (Group 1), who identify with and adhere to the organizational norms and practices, often rooted in command-and-control leadership systems; "Value-Driven Millennials" (Group 2), who prioritize meaningful work, and, "Gen Z – Wellbeing-Prioritizers" (Group 3), who stress the importance of boundaries between work and nonwork life.

The Agency Problem

As noted, the tension between the optimist and the pessimist view of determinism is related to the belief of the individual that they through their agency can create purposeful change. The pessimist view when transferred to the corporation can be illustrated by those who for example by their experience or through what they have absorbed through the culture of the organization that this change is either impossible or unhelpful to them as individuals within the leadership system. This learned incapacity is of course influenced by the strategy and leadership arguments illustrated above, but one might equally suggest that organizations may also differ in this respect despite coming from the same industry.

For example, exploratory research (Mountfield et al., 2021) within the fast-moving consumer goods and retail industry confirmed that individual agency for sustainability goals, despite their articulation by senior management, was low in organizations with shareholder-driven strategies and command-and-control style leadership systems. The only exceptions to this behavior occurred when long-term stakeholder strategy and distributed leadership systems existed.

The Planned vs. Emergent Strategy Problem

Strategists distinguish between planned and emergent strategies (see, for example, Mintzberg et al., 2009). From the perspective of systems and individual agency, planned strategies traditionally reflect an understanding of the organization that requires a process-driven, cascade and agreement of objectives throughout the corporation, distributing resources and aligning targets. Nevertheless, it is recognized that emergent strategies exist in all organizations.

These are generally the result of the agency of individual managers at more junior levels than those responsible for strategy, who redefine objectives and reallocate resources to reflect their own understanding of the organizational and competitive environment and their own interests. If these initiatives lead to success and are communicated to senior management, these emergent elements can become institutionalized into the formal planned strategy of the organization. This "problem" reflects the co-existence of both a leadership system and individuals exercising agency to adjusting the objectives set by the system and is generally agreed (see for example Mintzberg et al., 2009) to be an almost universal characteristic of organizations.

The Scope Problem

From an organizational viewpoint, are there limits to individual agency, even when acting from an optimist perspective of determinism? At what stage is it necessary for individual, emergent, exploratory, or experimental acts of agency to be institutionalized and to become, so to speak, part of the system itself? To formulate the problem in this way may be interpreted as sliding into a pessimist perspective, based on the argument that the system can only be changed by insinuating oneself into the institution itself. Mountfield et al. (op cit) argue that for certain types of organizations, namely those with a cultural bias toward command-and-control, top-down target-setting, and rewarding target fulfillment, this may be the case. But it is noteworthy, that a minority of organizations in this research project had long histories of delegating authority to lower levels in the organization, even to the extent of formally reallocating resources to allow for transformational change to business models.

While the issue analyzed in the research addressed change related to sustainability, the outlier organizations did not simply adopt incremental measures to meet this challenge. Instead, they can be argued to have previously institutionalized the ability to continuously adapt. In other words, they may be said to have incorporated the optimist perspective of agency into both their leadership system and their culture of delegating high degrees of strategic freedom and building on traditions of agency at lower levels of the organization.

The scope problem leads, as outlined in Section 1, to questions concerning the homogenous nature of those members of the organization who are not mandated to set top-down strategic objectives and are active at both the middle and the lower organizational levels. As we outlined, we identify Group 3 who may be said to have a common pessimistic view of opportunities within the organization, while remaining more optimistic about life outside it. This complexity derives from the interactions between the individual, the organizational, and the broader socioeconomic factors that make up the ecosystem of those who work in organizations. These factors are expressed in the degree of agency that individuals within these groups demonstrate both within and outside the organization concerning corporate and individual purpose and how this manifests itself in terms of social and environmental values and behaviors.

Balancing the Leadership System and Individual Agency

In this section, we propose a framework for purposeful change that balances the requirements for a leadership system with those of agency. In doing this, we extend an existing set of factors originally formulated for the operationalization of purpose (Barby et al., 2021). It is worth repeating the definition of purpose, namely "producing profitable solutions from the problems of people and planet, and not profiting from creating problems". In addition to the original factors comprising "motive" (what problem are we solving?), "measurement" (how do we express financial but also social and environmental costs and benefits?), and "monetarization" (what are financial values equivalent to social and environmental outputs?), we propose three additional factors chosen to support the operationalization of purpose.

We aim to build bridges between the leadership system and individual agency: "Management" (how can purpose-driven problem-solving be embedded in management processes and decision-making?), "method" (what is the appropriate balance between planned and emergent change activities?), and lastly, "mobilization" (how do we avoid the trap of the pessimist perspective?). In outlining these factors within the proposed framework, we distinguish between those aspects related to the leadership system and those rooted in agency.

In Table 6.1, we propose that the different framework elements need to be adapted both in terms of content and communication to the expectations of each of the three groups described above. The priorities can be seen as broad-brush descriptions of the agency drivers and as recognition of the different priorities set by the groups described above. What consequences does this have in organizations in terms of leadership and communication practice?

In the next section, we examine the case study of a "composite" company, based on different real events, as it introduces organizational change through the approaches that it uses as it operationalizes its purpose. This provides an illustration of the framework used above and explores the possibilities and limits of building bridges between a system and an agency perspective in a given organization. As always, this case is not designed to demonstrate good or poor management but to encourage discussion of leadership and communication options around engaging for agency.

Case Study

The composite case study example is a multinational, publicly quoted, research-driven life sciences company, with operations in many locations and many 1000s of employees who span all three of the groups described above. Like many organizations in its industry, the company is facing both regulated and emergent demands on its social and environmental objectives and actions, which are perceived in different ways by members of the three groups. This situation is made more complex by a changing business environment, in which new elements from outside the organization influence and infiltrate management practices at a company and functional level. As noted, these influences are perceived in different ways by members of the three groups, who filter them by the degree to which short- and longer-term benefits to these different internal actors are recognized.

Whereas Group 1 will wait for these influences to be identified and internalized by senior management, Group 2 embraces the increasing importance of social and environmental factors, is motivated by the opportunities these provide, and support emergent strategies that build on these. Group 3, however, while supporting the impact that these factors will generate, is less likely to engage voluntarily with opportunities within the firm to exercise agency, and is more likely to be skeptical of the possibilities of change within the organization, preferring to be agentic outside the company.

These differing perceptions and levels of engagement affect the second stage of emergent strategy development. Changing external environments may lead to challenges at the middle management level, and in the absence of clarity of what the strategic reaction will be from senior management, this influence often leads to emergent experiments (see for example Mintzberg et al., op. cit.) around conceptualizing and applying social and environmental factors in day-to-day decision-making. Group 2

Table 6.1 Bridges between the Leadership System and Individual Agency

	Leadership system	Agency
Motive	Set broad strategic change aims; initiate and allocate resources to relevant change programs; provide clarity concerning operational trade-offs	Encourage exploration and experimentation around change aims; recognize and reward strategic risk-taking; demonstrate linkages between organization and broader society. *Group 2 priority; Group 3 (broader society)*
Measurement	Create standardized financial, social, and environmental measurement frameworks and apply these consistently across strategic initiatives to support system change	Reduce measurement burden through standardization and minimization of individual performance management through encouragement of team goals. *Group 1 priority*
Method	Balance corporate initiatives with experimentation and exploration; ensure rapid decision-making concerning experiments and ensure institutionalization of successful projects	Encourage the spirit of innovation through exploration and experimentation; accept (and celebrate) fast failure; support individuals' efforts and encourage collaboration. *Groups 2 and 3 priorities*
Management	Align minimalist planning and steering processes with target culture; ensure the integration of measurement and methods into management processes	Maximize distributed leadership structures to encourage agency and usage of degrees of freedom through to team and individual levels. *Group 2 priority*
Monetization	Install internal social and environmental currency as part of day-to-day decision-making and remain consistent at senior levels	Devolve operationalization of strategic change aims through the cascade of social and environmental currency to the level of the team. Consider related incentives for more senior staff. *Groups 1, 2, and 3 priorities*
Mobilization	Demonstrate commitment through consistency; reward and recognize change-consistent behaviors at all levels; reduce second-guessing operations to the minimum	Enable continual learning of individuals and teams through incremental and transformational change activities both within and outside the organization. *Groups 2 and 3 priority*

takes the lead in these experiments, with Group 1 waiting to see whether these initial experiments will be successful before joining where they see benefits. However, Group 3 remains detached unless they see the possibility of engaging with these experiments beyond the boundaries of the organization, an argument for viewing these complex problems as an ecosystem with multiple actors. Where experiments are viewed as successful by senior management, these insights pass from emergent to deliberate strategy and are legitimized within the organization and become part of management practice.

As might be expected, Group 1 is most enthusiastic about this institutionalization of strategy, which allows for formal setting and measurement of goals, broken down to targets for individual performance. This deliberate strategy and its results are communicated internally within the organization, capturing again the attention and agency of Group 2, and externally through voluntary reporting and preparation for formal disclosure, which in turn influences the ecosystem, which may lead to a greater engagement from Group 3.

The framework in Table 6.2 describes the different leadership and communication needs of the three groups, reflecting the need to adapt strategies to meet changing external requirements, while maintaining engagement and agency.

Conclusion

The "Great Resignation" has led to significant introspection among employees about their personal values and work relationships, compelling organizations to address broader questions of corporate purpose and accountability to both shareholders and stakeholders. This evolution drives the need to reexamine the role of agency in shaping both deliberate and emergent strategies, particularly its impact on leadership and communication practices.

Among those staff who choose to "stay" with organizations, we identify three groups of employees: "Corporate Conformists" (Group 1), who identify with and adhere to the organizational norms and practices, often rooted in command-and-control leadership systems, "Value-Driven Millennials" (Group 2), who prioritize meaningful work, and lastly, "Gen Z – Wellbeing-Prioritizers" (Group 3), who stress the importance of boundaries between work and nonwork life.

We proposed a framework that addresses the multiple requirements of the management of change and the encouragement of agency, covering the following factors: Motives, measurement, method, management, monetization, and mobilization, and stress the need to adapt agency-related actions to the differing expectations of the three groups described. As demonstrated in our case study, such adaptations are crucial and must reflect the unique circumstances of each organization – their competitive environment, strategy, structural makeup, and culture – to maximize individual agency and organizational engagement.

Table 6.2 Communication

	Leadership system	Agency
Motive	Identify emergent changes to the strategic environment and signal these within the strategy process, recognizing that factors will be complex and ambiguous.	Provide clarity to Group 1, where strategically appropriate; engage Group 2 with targeted opportunities to influence discussion; and avoid purely internal focus for Group 3.
Measurement	Create standardized financial, social, and environmental measurement frameworks, but ensure that measurement is linked to resource allocation	Initial focus on project goals and measurement as a priority for Group 1 (who often may be the more senior staff); measure and communicate the resource allocation across the portfolio of initiatives
Method	Balance corporate initiatives with experimentation and exploration; fail fast; institutionalize changes to strategy	Support individuals' efforts and encourage collaboration across functions for Group 2; encourage cross-ecosystem perspectives and engagement for Group 3.
Management	Ensure the management process acknowledges and supports experimentation with formal frameworks	Provide Group 1 with clear objectives, priorities, and experimentation expectations, while allowing Group 2 (and 3 where possible) to encourage agency and usage of their own degrees of freedom through to team and individual levels
Monetization	Install internal social and environmental currency as part of day-to-day decision-making and remain consistent at senior levels	Devolve operationalization across all groups of strategic change. Consider, where already in place and robust, the linkage of social and environmental goals to incentives / variable compensation.
Mobilization	Acknowledge the "rules of engagement" of different groups and communicate in a targeted fashion	Enable continual learning of individuals and teams through incremental and transformational change activities both within (Group 2) and outside the organization (Group 3), while maintaining engagement of Group 1 through the incorporation of initiatives into a formal management goal system.

The Leadership for Agency Framework presented above is aligned with and integrates the Brilliant Leadership Framework, which encompasses strategy innovation, open innovation, cultural innovation, and business innovation.

- Strategy innovation can be deployed to create visionary and creative leadership strategies that resonate with Corporate Conformists while inspiring Value-Driven Millennials and Gen Z employees with disruptive and dialogic approaches that emphasize work-life balance and meaningful engagement.
- Open innovation practices, which highlight moral ethics, empathy, and authenticity, can foster a workplace culture that better aligns with the evolving values of these groups, enhancing dialogue and mutual respect across the organization.
- Cultural innovation, focusing on continuous improvement and inter-functional collaboration, can help align the organization's internal practices with its broadened accountability to stakeholders, reinforcing a culture of integrity and consistent ethical behavior.
- Finally, business innovation can drive the organization's transformation by optimizing processes and aligning the brand's promise with its operational practices, ensuring that all stakeholders, including employees, feel a part of the organization's journey toward innovation and excellence.

By employing these elements of the Leadership for Agency Framework, organizations can navigate the complex dynamics of the modern workplace and lead through periods of significant disruption with agility and strategic foresight.

References

American Psychological Association. (2021). *Stress in America 2021: One year later, a new wave of pandemic health concerns.* https://www.apa.org/news/press/releases/stress/2021/one-year-pandemic-stress-essential

Bannon, S., Ford, K., & Meltzer, L. (2011). Understanding millennials in the workplace. *The CPA Journal, 81*(11), 61.

Barby, C., Barker, R., Cohen, R., et al (2021, January 23). *Measuring purpose: An integrated framework* (January 23, 2021). https://ssrn.com/abstract=3771892

Blake-Beard, S. (2009). Mentoring as a bridge to understanding cultural difference. *Adult Learning, 20*(1–2), 14–18.

Bortolotti, L. (2018). Optimism, agency, and success. *Ethical Theory and Moral Practice, 21,* 521–535. https://doi.org/10.1007/s10677-018-9894-6

Boston-Fleischhauer, C. (2022). Reversing the great resignation in nursing: More things to consider. *The Journal of Nursing Administration, 52*(6), 324–326.

Breitling et al. (2021). 6 strategies to boost retention through the great resignation. *Harvard Business Review.* https://hbr.org/2021/11/6-strategies-to-boost-retention-through-the-great-resignation

British Academy. (2017). *Future of the corporation.* https://www.thebritishacademy.ac.uk/programmes/future-of-the-corporation/

Bruner, C. M. (2013). Conceptions of corporate purpose in post-crisis financial firms. *Seattle University Law Review, 36,* 527.https://digitalcommons.law.uga.edu/fac_artchop/1135

Deloitte. (2022). *2022 Global human capital trends.* https://www2.deloitte.com/us/en/insights/focus/human-capital-trends.html

Ferrazi, K., & Clementi, M. (2022). The great resignation stems from a great exploration. *Harvard Business Review.* https://hbr.org/2022/06/the-great-resignation-stems-from-a -great-exploration

Fry, E. T. A. (2022). Resigned to the 'great resignation.' *Journal of the American College of Cardiology, 79*(24), 2463–2466.

Fuller, J., & Kerr, W. (2022). The great resignation or the great rethink. *Harvard Business Review.* https://hbr.org/2022/03/the-great-resignation-or-the-great-rethink

Gallup, Inc. (2023). *State of the global workplace: 2023 report.* https://www.gallup.com

Gallup, Inc. (2021). *State of the global workplace: 2021 report.* https://www.gallup.com/work-place/350123/united-states-canada-workplace-trends.aspx

Ganguli, R., Padhy, S. C., & Saxena, T. (2022). The characteristics and preferences of Gen Z: A review of multi-geography findings. *IUP Journal of Organizational Behavior, 21*(2), 79–98.

Goldner, L., & Mayseless, O. (2009). The quality of mentoring relationships and mentoring success. *Journal of Youth and Adolescence, 38*, 1339–1350.

Greenhow, C., & Robelia, B. (2009). Old communication, new literacies: Social network sites as social learning resources. *Journal of Computer-Mediated Communication, 14*(4), 1130–1161.

Gulati, R. (2022). The great resignation or the great rethink. *Harvard Business Review.* https://hbr.org/2022/03/the-great-resignation-or-the-great-rethink

Gulati, R. (2023). The great resignation stems from a great exploration. *Harvard Business Review.* https://hbr.org/2022/06/the-great-resignation-stems-from-a-great-exploration

Hayes, A. M. (2021). *The emotional, mental, and spiritual well-being of gen Z: Perceived social media messages.* Masters Theses. 825. https://digitalcommons.liberty.edu/masters/825

Hogg, M. A. (2016). *Social identity theory.* Springer International Publishing.

Holtom, G. et al. (2021). Are you trying to retain the right employees? *Harvard Business Review.* https://hbr.org/2021/10/are-you-trying-to-retain-the-right-employees

Horoszowski, M. (2020). How to build a great relationship with a mentor. *Harvard Business Review.* https://hbr.org/2020/01/how-to-build-a-great-relationship-with-a-mentor

Kasperiuniene, J., & Zydziunaite, V. (2019). A systematic literature review on professional identity construction in social media. *SAGE Open, 9*(1), Article 2158244019828847. https://doi.org/10.1177/2158244019828847

Khan, T., Nahar, R., Hassan, F., Halder, S., & Khan, Z. H. (2021). Employees' perception on involvement in social media and performance in workplace: A study on banking profes-sionals in Dhaka City. *AIUB Journal of Business and Economics, 18*(1), 99–112.

Klotz, A. (2021). The great resignation has quitting become too cool. *BBC Worklife.* https://www.bbc.com/worklife/article/20230411-the-great-resignation-has-quitting-become -too-cool

Liske, C., Tutticci, N., & Diño, M. J. S. (2023). Joy at work and vocational identity during COVID-19: A structural equation model. *Journal of Nursing Scholarship, 55*(5), 1058–1067. https://doi.org/10.1111/jnu.12795

Maslow, A. H. (1954). *Motivation and personality.* Harpers.

Mayer, C. (2024). *Capitalism and crises: How to fix them.* Oxford University Press.

Microsoft. (2021). The next great disruption is hybrid work—Are we ready? *Work Trend Index.* https://www.microsoft.com/en-us/worklab/work-trend-index

Mintzberg, H., Ahlstrand, B., & Lampel, J. (2009). *Strategy safari: A guided tour through the wilds of strategic management.* FT Press.

Mountfield, A., Hrajnoha, K., Koh, L., & Lascenko, L. (2021). Barriers to implementing sustainability experienced by middle managers in the fast-moving consumer goods and retail sector. In S. Teerikangas, H. Onkila, N. M. P. Bocken, & S. C. A. Thomé (Eds.), *Research handbook of sustainability agency.* Edward Elgar Publishing, 75–92.

Newton, D. (2023). Retaining the best of your culture amid organizational change. *Harvard Business Review.* https://hbr.org/2023/11/retaining-the-best-of-your-culture-amid-organizational-change

Nia, S. J., Vakili, Y., Hassanpour, A., & Alabbas, S. A. K. (2021). A model of antecedents and consequences of employee social conformity in organization. *Multicultural Education, 7*(10), 16–25.

Nongo, E. S., & Ikyanyon, D. N. (2012). The influence of corporate culture on employee commitment to the organization. *International Journal of Business and Management, 7*(22), 21–28.

Nourkova, V., & Gofman, A. (2023). Everyday heroes: Graphical life stories and self-defining memories in COVID-19 medical volunteers. *Journal of Personality, 91*(1), 85–104. https://doi.org/10.1111/jopy.12683

Ryan, R. M., & Deci, E. L. (2000). Intrinsic and extrinsic motivations: Classic definitions and new directions. *Contemporary Educational Psychology, 25*(1), 54–67.

Society for Human Resource Management. (2022). *State of the workplace study 2021-2022.* https://www.shrm.org/content/dam/en/shrm/research/SHRM-State-of-the-Workplace-report-2021-2022.pdf

Sull, D. (2022). Toxic culture is driving the Great Resignation. *MIT Sloan Management Review, 63*(2), 1–9.

Tan, S., & Marissa, K. L. E. (Eds.). (2023). *Discourses, modes, media and meaning in an era of pandemic: A multimodal discourse analysis approach.* Routledge and Taylor & Francis.

Thokozani, S. B. M., & Maseko, B. (2017). Strong vs. weak organizational culture: Assessing the impact on employee motivation. *Arabian Journal of Business and Management Review, 7*(1), 2–5.

U.S. Bureau of Labor Statistics. (2021, October). *Economic news release: Job openings and labor turnover summary.* https://www.bls.gov/news.release/archives/jolts_10122021.htm

Weinstein, M. L., & Hirsch, P. M. (2023). For love and money: Rethinking motivations for the 'great resignation'. *Journal of Management Inquiry, 32*(2), 174–176. https://doi.org/10.1177/10564926221113060

Williams, D. L., Crittenden, V. L., Keo, T., & McCarty, P. (2012). The use of social media: An exploratory study of usage among digital natives. *Journal of Public Affairs, 12*(2), 127–136.

Chapter 7

Techno-Survive vs. Techno-Thrive: The AI-Responsive Leadership Framework

Leigh Thompson

The advent of generative AI marks a paradigm shift in leadership and for many, a "shock" to the leadership mindset. This chapter delves into how leaders' emotional, cognitive, and behavioral responsiveness with regard to generative AI affects team morale, decision-making, and performance. We explore the potential for leaders to either excel (thrive) or struggle (wither) amidst the novel leadership challenges that AI poses. Our inquiry centers on the perception and impact of generative AI, steering clear of its technical complexities. Thus, our focus is not on the technical or computational intricacies of AI, but rather on how the adoption and inclusion of generative AI affect the emotions, cognitions, and behaviors of leaders and their teams, particularly with respect to decision-making. By examining and understanding the human experience of relationships with AI, leaders can better navigate its integration, thereby enhancing team performance, communication efficacy, and organizational effectiveness.

Introducing the *AI-Responsiveness Leadership Framework* (ARLF), we underscore the importance of leaders' openness to AI adoption and understanding the leadership implications. Specifically, the ARLF framework focuses on the influence of generative AI on leaders' emotional-attitudinal responses, cognitive thinking and judgment processes, and behavioral action choices. This model examines how leaders' emotional, cognitive, and behavioral responses to AI can profoundly shape their effectiveness and, by extension, team performance. We scrutinize both the positive and negative outcomes of leaders' AI interactions on their teams and the broader organization. Specifically, the focus is on how leaders and teams may either diminish, adapt, or flourish under the influence of generative AI.

DOI: 10.4324/9781003495307-10

AI and Digital Leadership

The key premise of AI is that it can generate superior solutions, with increased speed compared to human experts (Bughin et al., 2018; Agrawal et al., 2018). For the purposes of this chapter, AI refers to

> systems designed by humans that, given a complex goal, act in the physical or digital world by perceiving their environment, interpreting the collected structured or unstructured data, reasoning on the knowledge derived from this data and deciding on the best action(s) to take (according to pre-defined parameters) to achieve the given goal. AI systems can also be designed to learn to adapt their behavior by analyzing how the environment is affected by their previous actions.
>
> **(The European Commission, 2018, p. 1)**

AI has extensive capabilities and is able to analyze its own environment and make its own decisions independently to control and improve itself (Peifer et al., 2022). The spectrum of AI is vast and consists of assisted, augmented, and autonomous intelligence (Vocke et al., 2019).

"*Digital Leadership*" is the term that refers to how human leaders can successfully lead teams and their direct reports in virtual contexts, which include AI platforms (Banks et al., 2022). In the digital era, there is a renewed focus on followers because of the lack of formal roles and the realization that followers are evaluating signals sent by leaders (Bastardoz & Van Vugt, 2019). In this sense, leadership in the digital era is a social influence process.

Thus, AI clearly has a seat at the professional business table. Bluntly speaking, AI means that strategic interactions and relationships between humans and artificial agents are increasingly the norm. Moreover, Moore's Law states that technological power doubles about every 18–24 months while the cost of technology decreases (Brock & Moore, 2006). Increased interactions and relationships raise critical questions about the role and relationship between human business leaders and AI. The behavior of humans changes when they interact with intelligent systems.

In this chapter, we focus on how leaders perceive, treat, and respond to AI at an emotional, cognitive, and behavioral level. Specifically, we focus on how the presence of AI affects leaders' emotions, motivations, cognitive and decision-making processes, and ultimately their behaviors and enacted strategies. To be effective in the digital era, leaders need to carefully consider their "relationship with" and "response to" generative AI. Self-examination of one's relationship with AI is critical in predicting whether leaders will "thrive" or merely "survive" now that AI has a seat at the management table.

The AI-Responsive Leadership Framework

For most leaders, the seemingly sudden launch of ChatGPT in 2022 (Roose, 2023), represented a shock to the system, forcing leaders and companies to ask questions and seek answers that many had never contemplated. Accordingly, there are emerging anxieties among business leaders pertaining to AI that center on unknown AI capabilities and outcomes (Keating & Nourbakhsh, 2018). Left unchecked and unexamined, these anxieties have personal, social, and organizational costs.

Historically, people have generally been skeptical or negative about the opinions generated by algorithmic machines, but when it comes to AI, people are anxious, yet more receptive. The plethora of AI "successes" showcased in the media, including the ability to win in the *Go* abstract strategy board game (Siau & Wang, 2018), and a variety of other games (Odeh 2023) has led many people to respect AI. AI's impressive decision-making and strategy is not limited to abstract games; AI has higher accuracy in predicting neuropathology on the basis of MRI data, compared to skilled radiologists (Vollmuth et al., 2023) and also in the domain of genetics (Vilhekar & Rawekar, 2024). With respect to business and professional qualifications, AI earns the highest scores on CPA, CMA, and CIA certification exams (Eulerich et al., 2023).

Given the undeniable superiority of AI across many domains, what is the CEO's (leader's) view of AI? One study of 384 respondents concerning the perceived role of AI in leadership revealed that leaders regard AI skills as essential for business continuity (Alblooshi et al., 2023). A PwC global survey revealed that "CEOs believe AI will be a catalyst for reinvention that will power efficiency." And, "70% of CEOs expect AI to significantly change the way their business creates, delivers and captures value in the next three years" (PwC, 2024, p. 1). Nearly 50% of CEOs believe their current business will not be viable in a decade if they don't address megatrends, including technological challenges, reflecting their position to address these challenges. Workforce skills, cybersecurity, misinformation, legal liabilities, and reputation are listed among the AI-notable technological challenges (PwC, 2024).

We introduce the AI-Responsive Leadership Framework (ARLF) to identify and organize how leaders' responsiveness to and relationship with AI affect their own leadership style and effectiveness as well as that of others (see Table 7.1). The ARLF framework considers three critical dimensions: leaders' emotions and feelings regarding AI, particularly with respect to morality and ethics, as well as anxiety versus curiosity; their cognitions and decision-making regarding AI; and their behaviors and actions.

Self-Awareness

A guiding assumption of the AI-Responsive Leadership Framework is that to be effective in the digital era, leaders need to be aware of their own reactions to AI as well as those of others. Such awareness is critical for adjusting one's own leadership style and

Table 7.1 AI-Responsive Leadership Framework

Dimension	Description	Key practices
Emotion Felt & Expressed emotion; perceptions of morality; attitude shaping	Self-awareness of one's own social-emotional-motivational state with respect to AI Understanding and empathizing with how others, direct reports, clients, customers, stakeholders, and other functional groups are feeling with respect to AI	• Reduce AI anxiety by improving socio-technical literacy • Awareness of "moral outrage" and identifying moral violations • Consider "roboethics" • Awareness of personality traits, including innovativeness, extraversion, and neuroticism
Cognition Decision-making; transparency; (rationally) evaluating options	Ability to engage in conscious, planful decision-making; evaluating data and information, identifying and optimizing choices; and reflective thought processes with respect to AI Accurately perceiving how others make decisions, think through problems and choices with respect to AI	• Explainability & Transparency: share and understand algorithms • Awareness of the "AI social proof" hypothesis • Purposeful trust considerations (benevolence and competence) • Co-creative systems; COFI (co-creative framework for interaction)
Behavior & Action Putting ideas into action; enacting strategy, communicating	Actions and behaviors in short-and-long-term with respect to AI Active management of others' behavior, actions, and strategy with respect to AI	• Thoughtful consideration of human–AI interaction (e.g., video-conference vs. immersive) • Identify key team roles (e.g., coordinator, creator, perfectionist, doer) • Identify key performance metrics for feedback purposes • Human–AI tuning

influencing others. For each of these dimensions, we focus on how leaders can thrive, survive, or wither. Leaders who feel anxious, threatened, and immobilized by AI will likely wither and retreat; leaders who merely accept AI and passively approach it will survive; leaders who actively examine, embrace, test, and question their relationship to AI will thrive.

Social Awareness

It is one thing to identify and understand one's own response to the introduction and presence of AI; it is quite another thing to empathize with the perspective of others. Leaders need to understand how their own socio-emotional reactions to generative AI strongly impact those of their team.

Leaders' Emotional Responsiveness to AI

The mere mention of AI stirs emotion in people. Leaders' emotional reactions to AI, such as outrage, anxiety, fear, excitement, skepticism, or appreciation, impact their subsequent decision-making, as well as team morale. Let's consider how the mere presence of AI affects leaders' emotional responses.

AI Anxiety

AI anxiety refers to the risk that superintelligence could result in the demise of humans (Bostrom, 2014). *AI anxiety* is different from *computer anxiety* (apprehensiveness related to a lack of computer skills), primarily because AI has the ability to make autonomous decisions and operate without human control (Li & Huang, 2020). A key predictor of AI anxiety is socio-technical illiteracy (Lemay et al., 2020). Li & Huang (2020) identified 8 factors that lead to AI anxiety, including privacy violation anxiety, bias behavior anxiety, job replacement anxiety, learning anxiety, existential risk anxiety, ethics violation anxiety, artificial consciousness anxiety, and lack of transparency anxiety. To be effective in the digital era, leaders need to be aware of the likely causes of AI anxiety and take steps to proactively remove or diminish the factors that can trigger AI anxiety.

Moral Outrage and Anger

Probably the topic that has garnered the greatest media attention is the morality of AI, with media portraying AI software as committing moral violations such as racism, sexism, spreading hate, or polluting people's minds (Shank & DeSanti, 2018). *Moral outrage* refers to an intense emotion that motivates people to shame and punish those who are believed to be violating norms. Moral outrage is intensified in the digital era with people "raging" online (Crockett, 2017). Viral online shaming, motivated by moral outrage, can lead to the immediate downfall of leaders and their companies.

Moral foundations theory argues that there are 6 domains of human morality, including: care/harm; fairness/cheating; loyalty/betrayal; authority/subversion; sanctity/degradation; and freedom/oppression (Graham et al., 2009; Haidt, 2012). A key leadership question concerns the perception of moral violations when businesses use AI. In one investigation, people's emotional response to the morality of seven real-world events was examined. When a moral violation actually occurred, only 43.5% of participants reported that they were "sure" that a moral violation occurred. Moreover, when participants perceived a moral violation to have actually occurred, they blamed AI, but not the organization, programmer, or the users of the AI program.

The *algorithmic outrage deficit hypothesis* explains why people seem to hold humans to a higher moral code than AI entities (presumably programmed by humans). According to the algorithmic outrage deficit hypothesis, people are *less* outraged by algorithmic discrimination than by human discrimination. For example, when blatant gender discrimination was made in hiring practices, people were *less* morally outraged by an AI entity (algorithm) but *more* outraged by a human who discriminated (Bigman et al., 2023). The implications for effective leadership are particularly critical. Leaders need to be aware that stakeholders will judge and scrutinize human decision-makers more harshly than AI entities and hold human leaders accountable for AI-driven decisions. For this reason, leaders are advised not to passively delegate decisions to AI but to act as stewards and oversee AI-based decisions.

Roboethics

Another question concerns how people, and leaders, in particular, treat AI entities. On the one hand, AI machines are not humans, and so people might not be held accountable to the same social politeness norms that guide human-to-human interaction. Bluntly stated, people may be hesitant to chastise a human member of their work team when a mistake is made but may feel justified in chastising an AI entity that makes the same mistake. The emerging field of "*roboethics*" focuses on how people are expected to treat and interact with non-human AI entities (Tzafestas, 2018). Curiously, groups, as compared to individuals, differ in terms of robot acceptance and treatment. One field study examined human-robot interaction as people received directional information from a humanoid robot. As compared to individuals, groups interacted more often, for longer, and more positively with the robot; and people within the groups followed the social norms set by the groups (Fraune et al., 2019). These results are particularly interesting because they seem to overturn the classic "bystander effect," in which people often are less likely to take prosocial action when in the presence of others (Darley & Latané, 1968.)

Guilt

People feel different intensities of emotion and engage in different behaviors when interacting with AI technologies (e.g., chatbots) versus humans. Specifically, studies of consumers in the retail industry revealed that moral intention (e.g., intention to report an error) was *more* likely when people interacted with humans than AI entities; moreover, moral intention decreased as people considered the AI machine less humanlike.

This is considered a decline in morality because people are not holding others (such as team members) to the same social-ethical standards. This decline in morality is caused by the fact that interacting with non-humans (AI machines) decreases feelings of guilt (Giroux et al., 2022). However, when humans believe that AI machines have been deliberately programmed to be unethical, their moral outrage increases. For example, people are more outraged by AI-programmed vehicles that kill discriminately than indiscriminately, and even more outraged when the AI machine is programmed to kill a less-preferred group (e.g., an elderly person over a child) than an AI-powered machine that indiscriminately kills (De Freitas & Cikara, 2021). Effective leaders need to encourage their teams and direct reports to hold AI entities to the same moral standards as humans.

Personality Traits

Some research indicates that certain personality traits are more receptive to AI. One investigation measured people's personal innovativeness in information technology as well as the "big five" personality traits (extraversion, agreeableness, conscientiousness, neuroticism, and openness) and then correlated the results with AI in terms of sociality and functionality (Park & Woo, 2022). Overall, the more innovative people were, the more positive their attitudes toward AI across all dimensions. Curiously, the more extroverted a person was reported to be, the more negative their attitudes were toward AI. Agreeableness was associated with both positive and negative emotions (toward AI) and positively related to sociality and functionality. The more conscientious a person was, the less negative emotions they felt toward AI and the more functionality. Neuroticism was related to negative emotions, but high in sociality. In sum, the relationship between personality dimensions and attitudes toward AI is complex.

Implications for Leadership: Building Emotional Awareness

In sum, investigations suggest that the mere presence of AI changes human behavior, in particular, by increasing anxiety and outrage. To facilitate a thriving emotional response in the face of human–AI interaction, leaders need to be forewarned about the possible negative emotional reactions to AI. Rather than being passive, leaders must self-manage their own emotional responses. Such self-management should not simply be limited to human–AI interaction. Indeed, an essential aspect of successful leadership in the digital era is to understand and empathize with how others, including direct reports, clients, customers, stakeholders, and other functional groups are feeling with respect to AI. In the digital era, effective leaders set the stage for techno-thriving by embodying positive emotions. Followers are particularly attentive to the emotional state of their leaders, and the more power that a person has, the more their own emotional state, such as mood, is felt by others (Anderson & Thompson, 2004).

One study examined the effectiveness of leaders' charismatic signaling through the use of charismatic leadership tactics (CLTs) such as using metaphors, posing rhetorical questions, expressive hand gestures, animated voices, and certain facial expressions), when formally-defined leadership roles did not exist (Tur et al., 2022). The key finding was that CLTs drive evaluations of leaders in virtual contexts.

Leaders' Cognitive Adaptability and Decision-Making

Arguably, the core of a leader's job is to make decisions, which depends upon thoughtful cognition and rationality. Cognition, rationality, impartiality, and transparency are critical for effective leadership in the digital era. In this sense, leaders need to make purposeful, planned decisions with regard to their reliance upon AI.

Economic Rationality and AI

Formal models of decision theory underlie rational models of decision-making in companies and firms (Harre, 2021). The principle of expected utility theory is guided by the assumption that agents make choices as if they were maximizing a utility function. In this regard, AI has clearly demonstrated its superiority over even the most skilled humans in a variety of games and decision-making situations that have an empirically demonstrable superior solution (e.g., Go and chess). The question is not whether AI can outperform humans in demonstrable decision-making (it clearly does!), but rather, how much *autonomy* should leaders grant to AI for the purposes of optimizing decisions. Thoughtful leaders in the digital era will not passively delegate strategic decision-making to AI but instead, thoughtfully act as stewards.

Explainability and Transparency

Explainable artificial intelligence refers to the idea that AI and human decision-makers are expected to justify and explain their decisions (Miller, 2019). For human decision-makers, explainability refers to transparency; for AI, this would mean that programmers would share their algorithms and answer questions about programming assumptions and criteria. Many AI applications are not adopted or used or trusted because of a lack of trust on behalf of their users (Linegang et al., 2006; Stubbs et al., 2007). Thus, by building more transparent and explainable AI systems, leaders and their teams will be more receptive to and trusting of intelligent agents. Indeed, studies reveal that human–AI team (HAT) performance improves on decision-making tasks when AI explains its recommendations, because it increases the chance that humans will accept AI's recommendation, regardless of its correctness (Bansal et al., 2021).

This finding is reminiscent of social psychology's famous *mindlessness effect*, wherein people fail to thoroughly process information (Langer, 1992). Thus, explainability represents a challenge for teams because humans need to vigilantly examine explanations generated by AI systems. The implications for leadership are challenging because merely providing an explanation (even if clearly wrong or absurd) can lead people to blindly accept it. Therefore, leaders must instill a heightened level of vigilance.

Decision-Making and Power

Through most of organizational history, power has occurred in the context of human interaction. One implication of power in human interactions is that it generally increases goal orientation (e.g., powerful people are more goal-focused) and it activates social role expectations (Fast & Schroeder, 2020). The digital era allows interactions between humans and AI entities. According to some researchers, the experience of using power with AI entities may lead to some unintended consequences, including greater action orientation, decisiveness, confidence, independence from others, and freedom from constraints (Fast & Schroeder, 2020).

To the degree that people perceive an AI entity as human (e.g., Alexa or Siri digital assistants), they may also experience power over it. Moreover, people tend to be simultaneously afraid as well as attracted to AI entities, almost viewing them as "divine, god-like" robots (Spatola & Urbanska, 2020).

Cognitive Biases and Decision-Making

In one humorous episode of NBC Universal's *The Office* (Schur, 2007), Michael Scott uses an intelligent agent to get driving directions and drives his car into a lake. Even though the body of water is completely visible, Michael ignores his own instincts of the dire situation and follows (the obviously wrong commands) the intelligent agent. A key axiom of social psychology and behavior is that people look to the behavior of others when deciding how to behave (Pratkanis, 2007; Cialdini, 2009).

Psychologically, people have two desires that influence their behavior: they want to avoid social censure and be "liked" and they also want to appear competent and knowledgeable (be "right"). Cialdini referred to this as *"social proof"* – the idea that people look to the behavior of others as proof that they are doing the right thing, with the most straightforward idea being that if others are behaving in a particular way or choosing something, then it must be a good idea. So far, this sounds sensible and even advisable. But this raises questions about how much people are willing to be influenced by AI when it comes to making decisions.

One series of studies examined the *AI social proof hypothesis*. The idea was that because AI entities are thought to be superior and all-knowing, they would be particularly influential in facilitating social proof. But, would this mean that people would blindly make obviously wrong and illogical decisions? In the study, participants had to make an urgent decision in a critical situation when they were unable to determine which action was correct. Here was the twist: some participants had to make a decision without any input or hints; other participants were given the option of consulting AI before making their decision. The experiment was constructed such that the AI consultant would make a completely absurd (wrong) decision. When participants were forced to make a decision without any AI input, they actively tried to find some premise for their own behavior and act in a thoughtful manner. This is exactly what would be desired in a management setting. However, when participants had the option of consulting an AI entity that made an absurd decision, over one-third of the participants copied the (absurd) AI opinion without any thought or recourse. And 85% copied a senseless action when observing an AI robot (Klichowksi, 2020).

Implications for Leadership

The research clearly suggests that because AI entities have demonstrated superior performance in several domains, leaders and decision-makers may be more accepting of their suggestions and decisions. However, to be effective in the digital era, leaders need to hold AI systems to a heightened level of accountability. This begins with explainability and transparency.

Leaders' Behavioral Strategies with AI

In this section, we take on the question of how the mere presence of AI can change actual behavior and business strategy. We have reviewed research that suggests that there are two possible pitfalls: On the one hand, leaders and their teams may be resistant to AI, due to anxiety; on the other hand, people may be too accepting of AI and not question its presumed superiority, even when they should.

Human Stupidity and Brain Drain

Human stupidity is a (published) pejorative term that refers to the fact that, well, AI and technology serve to make people less smart or effective. An early experiment revealed that the mere presence of a smartphone, even when turned off, reduces human cognitive capacity, particularly for people who are dependent upon their smartphones (Ward et al., 2017).

Individual Job Performance

A hallmark finding of social psychology is the *"social facilitation effect,"* which refers to the simple, yet, powerful observation that the presence of others, whether collaborators or merely audience members, facilitates performance on a number of behavioral and cognitive tasks (Zajonc, 1965; Cottrell et al., 1968; Bond & Titus, 1983). People run faster and solve problems more efficiently in the presence of other humans. The question is raised then, about how the mere presence of AI affects human performance. One study tested how a human-driven versus AI-driven companion affected people's behavioral performance (Sutskova et al., 2023). The presence of a human-driven companion had a stronger impact on human performance than the AI-driven companion, by actually worsening performance in both accuracy and reaction times.

Further research has attempted to disentangle the *mere presence effect* (MPE) versus the feeling of being observed by an audience (the *audience effect* (AE), Sutskova, 2023). The answer to how a human-minded versus AI-driven companion affects performance depends on whether the interaction takes place via videoconference or an immersive humanoid companion. When the interaction took place via videoconference, both MPE and AE *facilitated* human performance; however, when the interaction took place in an immersive in-lab experience, MPE and AE *hindered* the performance.

Team Performance

One study examined the performance of human-only, human–AI, and AI-only teams in a simulated emergency response management scenario (McNeese et al., 2021). Human-only teams performed worse than human–AI teams and AI-only teams had the highest performance.

Team Roles

When humans and AI collaborate in teams, roles within the team need to be clearly identified and articulated for the HAT (human–AI team) to be effective. One qualitative study identified four consistently important roles for AI-based teammates: coordinator, creator, perfectionist, and doer (Siemon, 2022).

How AI Affects Humans

What are the implications of interacting with AI on subsequent behavior, with humans? One study examined how people who received "smart replies" via algorithms behaved in subsequent interactions with others (Hohenstein et al., 2023). People who received "smart replies" from an AI entity were more likely to increase their speed of communication, use positive emotional language, and positively evaluate conversation partners. However, when people suspected that the other party was using algorithmic responses, people responded more negatively. This raises complex questions for leaders because whereas it would be tempting to lead customers and clients to believe they are interacting with a human, when this is not the case is deceptive and unethical.

Another study examined how people performed in mock job interviews with either the belief that they were being interviewed by a human recruiter, AI system, or AI system with a humanlike interface (Liu et al., 2023). Job candidates were *less* socially present and had greater feelings of uncertainty when they thought they were interacting with an AI system, versus a human; but they had a faster rate of speech and fewer silent pauses.

How Humans Perceive AI Entities

The characteristics of AI entities, such as teammates, impact how they are perceived by humans. One study examined how eight small teams perceived an AI agent that manifested either a gentle and cooperative conversational style or a blunt and uncooperative communication style (Milella et al., 2023). People were more satisfied when interacting with the cooperative AI entity than the blunt communicator; and people were more receptive when they believed the AI entity was a female, versus a male, confirming the gender stereotype that associates females with gentle and cooperative personality traits.

For human–AI teams (HATs; Harris-Watson et al., 2023) to be successful, human members will need to be receptive to their AI teammates. Perceived warmth and competence (benevolence and ability) are keys to building successful teams. One study examined human receptivity to a new AI teammate and found that perceived warmth and competence are important, with perceived ability (competence) as particularly important for knowledge utilization and acceptance, and warmth as important for team viability.

Competitive Versus Collaborative Choice

The above research suggests that people imbue too much blind trust in AI, even to the extent of ignoring their own judgment. Unconsciously, people behave differently when they believe they are interacting with a human versus an intelligent (non-human) agent, holding constant the information and messages they receive from the other party. A review of 162 experimental studies using computer players revealed that humans usually adapt to computer players even without any detailed prior information about them, but they often act more selfishly as well as rationally in their presence (March, 2021).

Team Trust and Performance

A key question is how people will perceive and treat AI team members. One study examined how people treated a human versus an AI team member based on actual performance (i.e., either superior or inferior; Dennis et al., 2023). Most people expected AI team members to be higher in ability and integrity, but lower in benevolence; and most people reported lower process satisfaction when working with an AI team members. When the AI team member performed well (superior), people perceived less conflict than with a superior human team member. This suggests that AI team members are likely to be accepted into teams, but that benevolence-based trust may be lacking.

Another investigation examined trust and performance in three types of teams, composed of three persons (either: all humans; two humans and one AI; or one human and two AI) (Schelble, et al., 2022). Human–AI teams (HATs) were similar to all-human teams in terms of the iterative development of human cognition, related to communication, but HATs were different in terms of their action-related communication and explicitly stated goals. Human–AI teams trusted teammates less when they were AI; and perceived less shared cognition with AI teammates versus human teammates.

Implications for Leaders

The research on how the perceived and actual presence of AI affects behavior suggests that there are significant benefits, yet several potential disadvantages. The foundations for successful team performance are based upon the establishment of trust among team members. To be effective in the digital era, leaders will need to understand the impact of AI on individual behavior as well as on the development of team trust, team communication, and group dynamics.

Effective leaders may improve the development of trust, shared cognition, and performance by explicitly identifying elements of human cognition and performance. One way of doing this would be the co-development of a HAT (Human–AI Team) charter. For example, *co-creative systems* involve the development of a collaborative partnership understanding between humans and AI entities (Rezwana & Maher, 2023). A key quality of effective leadership will be leaders' willingness to give feedback to both humans and AI entities. This involves the skill of *human–AI tuning*, or adjusting an AI algorithm to complement human users' strengths and weaknesses (Inkpen et al., 2023). For example, in one investigation, human users were better at detecting flowing blood vessels when the AI algorithm was tuned to reduce false negatives (at the expense of increasing false positives), allowing humans to reject those recommendations more efficiently and improve accuracy.

Summary and Future Directions

It is undeniable that AI is already an inextricable part of the leadership repertoire and organizational strategy. Ideally, leaders and teams will embrace generative AI and thoughtfully integrate it into key organizational goals and strategy. However, it is clear that the mere use of AI does not ensure that leaders will make optimal decisions and enact effective strategies.

Thriving Versus Surviving

The ARLF distinguishes "thriving" from merely "surviving" in an AI-based, digital organization. Our concept of thriving versus surviving is conceptually similar to Higgins' (1998) concept of Promotion versus Prevention in terms of goal orientation.

According to Higgins (1998), people who have *promotion* goals focus on moving toward and embracing outcomes and events that will result in goal satisfaction – a type of thriving. Conversely, people who have a *prevention* focus expend energy trying to avoid negative outcomes. For leaders and their teams to thrive in the digital AI era, they must position themselves and their teams to work toward promotion goals. This is challenging, particularly because AI stirs anxiety and other negative emotions.

AI Acceptance

Yes, AI is "here" but it may not be in active use in organizations. Assuming that leaders desire their direct reports and teams to embrace AI, the question becomes how to increase usage. A study of the AI acceptance model revealed that perceived usefulness and ease of use were the most predictive factors in attitudes toward AI; perceived usefulness, and knowledge were the most predictive factors in the actual intention to use AI. This research suggests that leaders must address two factors in their pursuit of the behavioral adoption of AI: perceived usefulness and ease of use.

AI-Oriented Change Behavior

AI-Oriented change behavior refers to the ability of leaders to influence their direct reports and teams to use AI. One team of researchers developed a 6-item scale for assessing a leader's effectiveness in persuading their direct reports to use AI (e.g., "my supervisor often makes constructive suggestions on how AI technologies can improve organizational operations; my supervisor often adopts AI technologies for his or her own job, etc." (He et al., 2023, p. 9)). Leaders' AI-oriented change behavior is positively associated with their employees' performance orientation, which has the effect of increasing both employee job performance and also unethical behaviors. In addition, employee trait competitiveness exacerbates this effect, thereby leading direct reports to perform more effectively, but also engage in more unethical behavior. This double-edged sword represents an ethical challenge for leaders.

References

Agrawal, A. K., Gans, J. S., & Goldfarb, A. (2018). *Exploring the impact of artificial intelligence: Prediction versus judgment* (NBER Working Paper Series, 24626). https://doi.org/10.3386/w24626

Alblooshi, M. A. J. A., Mohamed, A. M., & Yusr, M. M. (2023). Moderating role of artificial intelligence between leadership skills and business continuity. *International Journal of Professional Business Review, 8*(6), e03225. https://doi.org/10.26668/businessreview/2023.v8i6.3225

Anderson, C., & Thompson, L. L. (2004). Affect from the top down: How powerful individuals' positive affect shapes negotiations. *Organizational Behavior and Human Decision Processes, 95*(2), 125–139. https://doi.org/10.1016/j.obhdp.2004.05.002

Banks, G. C., Dionne, S. D., Mast, M. S., & Sayama, H. (2022). Leadership in the digital era: A review of who, what, when, where, and why. *The Leadership Quarterly, 33*(5), 101634. https://doi.org/10.1016/j.leaqua.2022.101634

Bansal, G., Wu, T., Zhou, J., Fok, R., Nushi, B., Kamar, E., Ribeiro, M. T., & Weld, D. S. (2021). Does the whole exceed its parts? The effect of AI explanations on complementary team performance. *ArXiv (Cornell University).* https://doi.org/10.48550/arxiv.2006.14779

Bastardoz, N., & Van Vugt, M. (2019). The nature of followership: Evolutionary analysis and review. *The Leadership Quarterly, 30*(1), 81–95. https://doi.org/10.1016/j.leaqua.2018.09.004

Bigman, Y. E., Wilson, D., Arnestad, M. N., Waytz, A., & Gray, K. (2023). Algorithmic discrimination causes less moral outrage than human discrimination. *Journal of Experimental Psychology. General, 152*(1), 4–27. https://doi.org/10.1037/xge0001250

Bond, C. F., & Titus, L. J. (1983). Social facilitation: A meta-analysis of 241 studies. *Psychological Bulletin, 94*(2), 265–292. https://doi.org/10.1037/0033-2909.94.2.265

Bostrom, N. (2014). *Superintelligence: Paths, dangers, strategies.* Oxford University Press.

Brock, D. C., & Moore, G. E. (2006). *Understanding Moore's law: Four decades of innovation.* Chemical Heritage Foundation

Bughin, J., Hazan, E., Lund, S., Dahlström, P., Wiesinger, A., & Subramaniam, A. (2018). Skill shift: Automation and the future of the workforce. *McKinsey Global Institute, 1*, 3–84. https://www.mckinsey.com/featured-insights/future-of-work/skill-shift-automation-and-the-future-of-the-workforce

Cialdini, R. B. (2009). *Influence: Science and practice.* Pearson Education.

Cottrell, N. B., Wack, D. L., Sekerak, G. J., & Rittle, R. H. (1968). Social facilitation of dominant responses by the presence of an audience and the mere presence of others. *Journal of Personality and Social Psychology, 9*(3), 245–250

Crockett, M. J. (2017). Moral outrage in the digital age. *Nature Human Behaviour, 1*(11), 769–771. https://doi.org/10.1038/s41562-017-0213-3

Darley, J. M., & Latané, B. (1968). Bystander intervention in emergencies: Diffusion of responsibility. *Journal of Personality and Social Psychology, 8*(4), 377–383. https://doi.org/10.1037/h0025589

De Freitas, J., & Cikara, M. (2021). Deliberately prejudiced self-driving vehicles elicit the most outrage. *Cognition, 208*, 104555–104555. https://doi.org/10.1016/j.cognition.2020.104555

Dennis, A. R., Lakhiwal, A., & Sachdeva, A. (2023). AI agents as team members: Effects on satisfaction, conflict, trustworthiness, and willingness to work with. *Journal of Management Information Systems, 40*(2), 307–337. https://doi.org/10.1080/07421222.2023.2196773

Eulerich, M., Sanatizadeh, A., Vakilzadeh, H., & Wood, D. A. (2023). Is it all hype? ChatGPT's performance and disruptive potential in the accounting and auditing industries. *SSRN Electronic Journal.* http://dx.doi.org/10.2139/ssrn.4452175

The European Commission's High-Level Expert Group on Artificial Intelligence: A Definition of AI: Main Capabilities and Scientific Disciplines, Brussels. (2018). https://ec.europa.eu/futurium/en/system/files/ged/ai_hleg_definition_of_ai_18_december_1.pdf

Fast, N. J., & Schroeder, J. (2020). Power and decision making: New directions for research in the age of artificial intelligence. *Current Opinion in Psychology, 33*, 172–176. https://doi.org/10.1016/j.copsyc.2019.07.039

Fraune, M. R., Šabanović, S., & Kanda, T. (2019). Human group presence, group characteristics, and group norms affect human-robot interaction in naturalistic settings. *Frontiers in Robotics and AI, 6*, 48–48. https://www.frontiersin.org/articles/10.3389/frobt.2019.00048/full

Giroux, M., Kim, J., Lee, J. C., & Park, J. (2022). Artificial intelligence and declined guilt: Retailing morality comparison between human and AI. *Journal of Business Ethics, 178*(4), 1027–1041. https://doi.org/10.1007/s10551-022-05056-7

Graham, J., Haidt, J., & Nosek, B. A. (2009). Liberals and conservatives rely on different sets of moral foundations. *Journal of Personality and Social Psychology, 96*(5), 1029–1046. https://doi.org/10.1037/a0015141

Haidt, J. (2012). *The righteous mind: Why good people are divided by politics and religion.* Pantheon/Random House.

Harré, M. S. (2021). Information theory for agents in artificial intelligence, psychology, and economics. *Entropy (Basel, Switzerland), 23*(3), 310. https://doi.org/10.3390/e23030310

Harris-Watson, A. M., Larson, L. E., Lauharatanahirun, N., DeChurch, L. A., & Contractor, N. S. (2023). Social perception in human-AI teams: Warmth and competence predict receptivity to AI teammates. *Computers in Human Behavior, 145*, 107765. https://doi.org/10.1016/j.chb.2023.107765

He, G., Zheng, X., Li, W., Tan, L., Chen, S., & He, Y. (2023). The mixed blessing of leaders' artificial intelligence (AI)-oriented change behavior: Implications for employee job performance and unethical behavior. *Applied Research in Quality of Life.* https://doi.org/10.1007/s11482-023-10250-4

Higgins, E. T. (1998). Promotion and prevention: Regulatory focus as a motivational principle. In *Advances in experimental social psychology* (Vol. 30, pp. 1–46). Academic Press. https://doi.org/10.1016/S0065-2601(08)60381-0

Hohenstein, J., Kizilcec, R. F., DiFranzo, D., Aghajari, Z., Mieczkowski, H., Levy, K., Naaman, M., Hancock, J., & Jung, M. F. (2023). Artificial intelligence in communication impacts language and social relationships. *Scientific Reports, 13*(1), 5487–5487. https://doi.org/10.1038/s41598-023-30938-9

Inkpen, K., Chappidi, S., Mallari, K., Nushi, B., Ramesh, D., Michelucci, P., Mandava, V., Vepřek, L. H., & Quinn, G. (2023). Advancing human-AI complementarity: The impact of user expertise and algorithmic tuning on joint decision making. *ACM Transactions on Computer-Human Interaction, 30*(5), 1–29. https://doi.org/10.1145/3534561

Keating, J., & Nourbakhsh, I. (2018). Teaching artificial intelligence and humanity. In *Communications of the ACM* (Vol. 61, Issue 2, pp. 29–32). Association for Computing Machinery. https://doi.org/10.1145/3104986

Klichowski, M. (2020). People copy the actions of artificial intelligence. *Frontiers in Psychology, 11*, 1130–1130. https://doi.org/10.3389/fpsyg.2020.01130

Langer, E. J. (1992). Matters of mind: Mindfulness/mindlessness in perspective. *Consciousness and Cognition, 1*(3), 289–305. https://doi.org/10.1016/1053-8100(92)90066-J

Lemay, D. J., Basnet, R. B., & Doleck, T. (2020). Fearing the robot apocalypse: correlates of AI anxiety. *International Journal of Learning Analytics and Artificial Intelligence for Education (IJAI), 2*(2), 24. https://doi.org/10.3991/ijai.v2i2.16759

Li, J., & Huang, J. S. (2020). Dimensions of artificial intelligence anxiety based on the integrated fear acquisition theory. *Technology in Society, 63*, 101410. https://doi.org/10.1016/j.techsoc.2020.101410

Linegang, M. P., Stoner, H. A., Patterson, M. J., Seppelt, B. D., Hoffman, J. D., Crittendon, Z. B., & Lee, J. D. (2006). Human-automation collaboration in dynamic mission planning: A challenge requiring an ecological approach. *Proceedings of the Human Factors and Ergonomics Society Annual Meeting, 50*(23), 2482–2486. https://doi.org/10.1177/154193120605002304

Liu, B., Wei, L., Wu, M., & Luo, T. (2023). Speech production under uncertainty: How do job applicants experience and communicate with an AI interviewer? *Journal of Computer-Mediated Communication, 28*(4). https://doi.org/10.1093/jcmc/zmad028

March, C. (2021). Strategic interactions between humans and artificial intelligence: Lessons from experiments with computer players. *Journal of Economic Psychology, 87*, 102426. https://doi.org/10.1016/j.joep.2021.102426

McNeese, N. J., Schelble, B. G., Canonico, L. B., & Demir, M. (2021). Who/What is my teammate? Team composition considerations in human-AI teaming. *IEEE Transactions on Human-Machine Systems, 51*(4), 288–299. https://doi.org/10.1109/THMS.2021.3086018

Milella, F., Natali, C., Scantamburlo, T., Campagner, A., Cabitza, F. (2023). The impact of gender and personality in human-AI teaming: The case of collaborative question answering. In J. Abdelnour Nocera, M. Kristín Lárusdóttir, H. Petrie, A. Piccinno, & M. Winckler (Eds.) , *Human-computer interaction – Interact 2023. Interact 2023. Lecture notes in computer science* (Vol. 14143). Springer. https://doi.org/10.1007/978-3-031-42283-6_19

Miller, T. (2019). Explanation in artificial intelligence: Insights from the social sciences. *Artificial Intelligence, 267*, 1–38. https://doi.org/10.1016/j.artint.2018.07.007

Odeh, M. (2023). *Games and AI: How did game engines become unbeatable and does AI dominance entail any risks.* https://documentserver.uhasselt.be/bitstream/1942/41159/1/fe3737c8-5b98-4e08-b964-7f72ca262eaf.pdf

Park, J., & Woo, S.E. (2022). Who likes artificial intelligence? Personality predictors of attitudes toward artificial intelligence. *The Journal of Psychology, 156*(1), 68–94. https://doi.org/10.1080/00223980.2021.2012109

Peifer Y., Jeske T., Hille S. (2022). Artificial intelligence and its impact on leaders and leadership. *Procedia Computer Science, 200*, 1024–1030. https://doi.org/10.1016/j.procs.2022.01.301

Pratkanis, A. R. (2007). Social influence analysis: An index of tactics. In *The science of social influence: Advances and future progress* (pp. 17–82). Psychology Press.

PwC. (2024, January 15). *Economic optimism doubles, yet almost half of CEOs do not believe their businesses will be viable in a decade as tech and climate pressures accelerate: PwC global CEO survey* (Press release). https://www.pwc.com/bm/en/press-releases/27th-annual-global-ceo-survey.html

Rezwana, J., & Maher, M. L. (2023). Designing creative AI partners with COFI: A framework for modeling interaction in human-AI co-creative systems. *ACM Transactions on Computer-Human Interaction, 30*(5), 1–28. https://doi.org/10.1145/3519026

Roose, K., (2023, February 3). How ChapGPT kicked off an A.I. Arms race. *New York Times.* https://www.nytimes.com/2023/02/03/technology/chatgpt-openai-artificial-intelligence.html

Schelble, B. G., Flathmann, C., McNeese, N. J., Freeman, G., & Mallick, R. (2022). Let's think together! Assessing shared mental models, performance, and trust in human-agent teams. *Proceedings of the ACM on Human-Computer Interaction, 6*(GROUP), 1–29. https://doi.org/10.1145/3492832

Schur, M. (Writer), Zisk, C. (Director), (2007, October 4). Dunder mifflin infinity (Season 4, Episode 56 & 57) (TV series episode). In G. Daniels (Ed.), (Executive Producer), *The office.* NBC; NBCUniversal Media, LLC.

Shank, D. B., & DeSanti, A. (2018). Attributions of morality and mind to artificial intelligence after real-world moral violations. *Computers in Human Behavior, 86*, 401–411. https://doi.org/10.1016/j.chb.2018.05.014

Siau, K., & Wang, W. (2018). Building trust in artificial intelligence, machine learning, and robotics. *Cutter Business Technology Journal, 31*(2), 47–53. https://www.cutter.com/article/building-trust-artificial-intelligence-machine-learning-and-robotics-498981

Siemon, D. (2022). Elaborating team roles for artificial intelligence-based teammates in human-AI collaboration. *Group Decision and Negotiation, 31*(5), 871–912. https://doi.org/10.1007/s10726-022-09792-z

Spatola, N., & Urbanska, K. (2020). God-like robots: The semantic overlap between representation of divine and artificial entities. *AI & Society, 35*(2), 329–341. https://doi.org/10.1007/s00146-019-00902-1

Stubbs, K., Wettergreen, D., & Hinds, P. J. (2007). Autonomy and common ground in human-robot interaction: A field study. *IEEE Intelligent Systems, 22*(2), 42–50. https://doi.org/10.1109/MIS.2007.21

Sutskova, O. (2023). *Cognitive impacts of social virtual reality: Disentangling the virtual mere presence and audience effect.* Birkbeck, University of London. https://doi.org/10.18743/PUB.00051420

Sutskova, O., Senju, A., & Smith, T. J. (2023). Cognitive impact of social virtual reality: Audience and mere presence effect of virtual companions. *Human Behavior and Emerging Technologies, 2023,* 1–19. https://doi.org/10.1155/2023/6677789

Tur, B., Harstad, J., & Antonakis, J. (2022). Effect of charismatic signaling in social media settings: Evidence from TED and Twitter. *The Leadership Quarterly, 33*(5), 101476. https://doi.org/10.1016/j.leaqua.2020.101476

Tzafestas, S. G. (2018). Mobile robot control and navigation: A global overview. *Journal of Intelligent & Robotic Systems, 91,* 35–58. https://doi.org/10.1007/s10846-018-0805-9

Vilhekar, R. S., & Rawekar, A. (2024). Artificial intelligence in genetics. *Curēus (Palo Alto, CA).* https://doi.org/10.7759/cureus.52035

Vocke, C., Constantinescu, C., & Popescu, D. (2019). Application potentials of artificial intelligence for the design of innovation processes. *Procedia CIRP, 84,* 810–813. https://doi.org/10.1016/j.procir.2019.04.230

Vollmuth, P., Foltyn, M., Huang, R. Y., Galldiks, N., Petersen, J., Isensee, F., van den Bent, M. J., Barkhof, F., Park, J. E., Park, Y. W., Ahn, S. S., Brugnara, G., Meredig, H., Jain, R., Smits, M., Pope, W. B., Maier-Hein, K., Weller, M., Wen, P. Y., ... Bendszus, M. (2023). Artificial intelligence (AI)-based decision support improves reproducibility of tumor response assessment in neuro-oncology: An international multi-reader study. *Neuro-Oncology (Charlottesville, Va.), 25*(3), 533–543. https://doi.org/10.1093/neuonc/noac189

Ward, A. F., Duke, K., Gneezy, A., & Bos, M. W. (2017). Brain drain: The mere presence of one's own smartphone reduces available cognitive capacity. *Journal of the Association for Consumer Research, 2*(2), 140–154. https://doi.org/10.1086/691462

Zajonc, R. B. (1965). Social facilitation: A solution is suggested for an old unresolved social psychological problem. *Science, 149*(3681), 269–274. https://doi.org/10.1126/science.149.3681.269

BUSINESS INNOVATION

4

How Leaders Embrace Digital Transformation for Better Outcomes

Chapter 8

Driving Digital Transformation, Aligning Brand and Reputation

Rosilyn Sanders, Lara Bertola and Alan T. Belasen

Globalization has compelled businesses to adapt their processes and operations. The changing business environment creates an elevated level of uncertainty. Organizations must make changes to their processes and products to maintain or gain a competitive advantage in the face of disruptive technologies. The digital transformation presents key challenges and opportunities for organizations in hybrid workplaces such as healthcare (Burton-Jones et al., 2020; Hai et al., 2021). The global trend of mobile and social media has prompted several businesses to strive to create and maintain an online presence for their brands. Increasingly, retail and service businesses pay more attention to providing digital customer experiences.

The value creation, value delivery, and value capture systems of businesses around the globe have experienced the need to navigate transitions due to the introduction of digital technologies, including the Internet of Things (IoT), cloud computing, big data, and blockchain, among others (Ancillai et al., 2023). Companies embed digital technologies across their operations to drive fundamental change in business strategy, innovation, and, invariably, business performance (Tsou & Chen, 2023). This implies that it also has a role to play in building or maintaining the brand or reputation of the business.

DOI: 10.4324/9781003495307-12

Digital Technology

Using digital technologies in business and management has implications for the brand and reputation. Several studies have addressed digital technologies, digital transformation, and their disruptive effects on businesses and brands (Rautenbach et al., 2019Schneider & Kokshagina, 2021; Yeow et al. 2018) highlighting the importance of aligning resources and digital transformation strategy with business strategy.

Digital Transformation

Business owners and managers must align their brand and reputation with their overall strategy. It is easy to misinterpret the concept of digital transformation as simply a change in technology. Studies have shown that digital transformation goes beyond merely switching from paper-based to computer-based systems. Digital transformation involves a deep and coordinated cultural, workforce, and technological shifts that transform business models, strategic directions, and value propositions(Vial, 2019).

Scholars (e.g., Hinings et al., 2018) defined digital transformation as the process by which new technologies are integrated to create new roles, structures, practices, values, and beliefs that change, threaten, replace, or add to how businesses, ecosystems, industries, or fields operate (Hinings et al., 2018). It is a process that uses digital technologies to create disruptions that elicit strategic responses from organizations seeking to implement innovative value-creation methods while managing structural changes and overcoming organizational barriers that influence business outcomes.

The European Commission (2018) defines digital transformation as "characterized by the fusion of advanced technologies and the integration of physical and digital systems, the dominance of innovative business models and new processes, and the development of smart products and services" (p. 10).

These definitions imply a technological change and a significant shift in a company's central processes and operations. Digital transformation entails incorporating various forms of technology into every aspect of a workplace (Kim et al., 2021). Other studies support the idea that the concept of digital transformation exceeds a mere change in digital technology as digital transformation is not just about digital technology customers (Bloomberg 2018).Transformation entails a fundamental organizational change, so it goes beyond just a change in digital technology and the results produced to satisfy customers' needs. Bloomberg's conceptualization of digital transformation relates more to the business environment context. It implies business innovations to improve value creation and achieve greater customer satisfaction.

The process of digital transformation is far-reaching, as it is a transition that affects customer relations, internal processes, and value creation (Zaoui & Souissi, 2020). It is an evolving process rather than a one-off process that can be completed over a set period (Engesmo & Pantelli, 2020). This means that digital transformation continues even after the effects of the changes begin to show. Within this milieu, the dynamic interplay between human factors and technology becomes a driving force in reshaping organizational structure.

Digital transformation changes business models, structures, and organizational cultures. Therefore, it is pertinent that the digital transformation strategy aligns with organizational goals. Chanais et al. (2019) investigated how a digital transformation strategy is made from the point of view of an activity or process leading them to conclude that it was enacted through a bottom-up process, starting with new strategic activities, and working their way up to the top.

In today's business world, where digital transformations disrupt traditional workflows across diverse industries, the role of leadership in aligning the digital transformation strategy with organizational goals becomes even more critical (Oke et al., 2009). As organizations navigate through these dynamic changes, leaders are confronted with the urgent need to invest in enhancing requisite skills and competencies of their workforce.

Brilliantleaders are well suited for this new transformation. They are authentic and inspirational. They engage individuals and teams in innovation implementation, and foster learning and development (Watkins, 2013). Brilliant leaders dedicate themselves to effecting meaningful outcomes and driving positive change over time, —not only as an isolated undertaking (Cortellazzo et al., 2019). It is important to note that leading digital transformations in pre-digital or traditional organizations is quite challenging especially due to entrenched business models and organizational inertia (Chanais et al., 2019). Like in entrepreneurial organizations, this challenge punctuates the critical role of brilliant leaders in coping with stressful transitions. (Tumbas et al., 2017).

Studies like Vom Brocke et al. (2017) discuss the occurrence of digital transformation in companies with already-established digitization. This brings one to consider if the digital transformation process in these organizations is a process that began a long time ago (before the first introduction of digital technology) or if the digital transformation process occurs by introducing modern technology to already automated processes.

The digital transformation is about evolving the business—a continuous process occurring over time (Janowski, 2015; Loebbecke & Picot, 2015; Wang et al., 2020). In the past, digital transformation entailed introducing computer-based systems and automating processes; it is now more concerned with "the adoption and use of emerging technologies, which are in their nature evolving" (Morakanyane et al., 2017, p. 426).

How Leaders Embrace Digital Transformation for Better Outcomes

In today's modern business world, it is no longer just a passing trend for leaders to embrace digital transformation. It has become crucial for achieving better results and effectively guiding their organization's direction (Keating et al., 2023). This significant change requires leaders to react to technological advancements and take proactive steps to effectively utilize digital technologies, seizing meaningful opportunities and addressing potential risks. At the core of this transformation is the need to cultivate a company culture that not only accepts but also promotes digital transformation, encourages its implementation, and integrates it into the organization's fabric (Abdallah, et al., 2021).

However, the consequences of inertia might prove even graver, given historical precedents illustrating how failure to adapt to digital innovations can lead to the downfall of industry titans based on a lack of awareness regarding the diverse options and factors they should consider before immersing themselves in digital transformation endeavors (Matt et al., 2015). As the demand for new technologies persist, traditional management practices and organizational structures are becoming outdated. Leaders have been faced with new challenges, experimenting with new modes of thinking and doing, and taking their organizations through cycles of adaptation and renewal (Belasen, 2000).

Digital technologies are central to these changes, enabling connections between various industries and markets and overcoming geographical barriers. As a result, previously vertically integrated businesses are now intertwined in a value chain and dependent on each other. The connectivity and interdependence brought about by digitization are transforming the dynamics of value chains. With industrial networks intersecting through digitization, it becomes necessary to recognize and adapt to new relationships and modify external channels of communication, In this evolving scenario, the importance of skilled leaders becomes evident. These leaders promote cooperation among companies and navigate the intricate relationships in this interconnected setting, prompting the emergence of new market scenarios. This highlights the need for leaders to shift their focus towards harnessing digital technologies to establish unique market positions and stay ahead of rivals. As such, digital transformation becomes a differentiator in creating and sustaining competitive advantage.

According to Fahy (2000), strategic planning is crucial in guiding organizations through digital transformation. It is essential for leaders to effectively incorporate digital priorities into their overall strategic approach to navigating constantly changing market conditions, which involves more than just using digital tools; it also requires fostering an environment that values creativity and the ability to adapt to new technologies. Leaders must ensure that their organizations are well-prepared to address the challenges and opportunities the digital landscape presents. This means establishing processes and systems that can easily incorporate digital innovations and respond quickly to changes in the market.

Organizations need a culture that values innovation and adaptability to thrive in the digital landscape. Leaders must proactively identify areas where digital technologies can enhance operations and adjust their strategic frameworks accordingly. This proactive approach goes beyond reacting to technological advancements; it requires embracing change and consistently seeking opportunities to drive innovation through digital tools. Prioritizing the integration of digital strategies allows organizations to establish themselves as industry leaders while staying at the forefront of developments. Furthermore, businesses in different sectors encounter difficulties as they strive to keep up with a rapidly changing environment, and even though technological progress has transformed the way we work, achieving successful digital transformation relies on fundamental human interactions and tech skills to ensure efficient implementation (Bhens et al., 2016).

At the organizational level, one of the challenges of digital transformation is the need to develop a wide range of skills that are essential for adapting to technological trends (Val, 2019). In this sense, the labor market needs to adapt to the related demands (Caliano et al., 2019) because the increase in intelligence in the technological system and the generation of complex data require more qualified workers to make decisions in various areas of work (Holzmann & Gregori, 2023).

The significance of brilliant leadership in managing disruptive innovation cannot be emphasized enough. Leaders must now prioritize talent management, technological proficiency, and competency development to meet the demands of the digital era. They must also recognize that employees now have increased influence through knowledge and access to networks of communication and are more active in decision-making processes (Klus & Müller, 2021). Managing essential changes like digital transformation necessitates more than anticipation—it also requires creativity. Successful digital evolution requires leaders to cultivate an environment that encourages and recognizes innovative thinking in the digital realm.

Efficient communication pathways for sharing information about digital initiatives throughout the organization are essential. Embracing digital transformation empowers leaders to guide their organizations toward improved results by establishing a culture that embraces change, remains adaptable, and is receptive to new ideas, technologies, and methods to enhance company productivity, customer satisfaction, and operational effectiveness.

Furthermore, influential brilliant leaders understand the importance of collaboration and networking (Cortellazzo et al., 2019). Understanding the integration and expansion of technology entails recognizing its non-linear trajectory, which is influenced by various factors such as the type of technology, its contextual application, and the core values of the organization. . The convergence of leadership and digital transformation emerges as a compelling practice area, demanding a nuanced comprehension of the intricate dynamics shaping organizational change in the digital era. Leonardi (2020) outlines the digital transformation process as a series of interconnected phases, necessitating agile adaptation facilitated by collaborative teamwork. This transformative journey encompasses critical stages, including securing leadership endorsement, involving employees, leveraging technology, promoting data-driven behavioral shifts, enhancing local operational efficiency, and aligning efforts with overarching corporate goals.

Leadership Paradigms

As organizations navigate the complexities of digital transformation, leadership paradigms necessitate a recalibration to accommodate the evolving business goals and strategies (Kraus et al., 2022; Schwarzmüller et al., 2018). This recalibration demands an augmented focus on talent management, technological literacy, competency development, and the need to shift away from conventional leadership modalities (Cortellazzo et al., 2019). The burgeoning influence of digital technologies fundamentally alters power dynamics within organizations, instigating a reevaluation of communication methodologies (Hanelt et al., 2021).

In the fast-paced and ever-evolving digital transformation, leadership's role cannot be understated. To effectively navigate the complexities of this era, leaders must embody qualities that inspire innovation, drive change, and foster a culture of adaptability within their organizations. These leaders must possess a vision for the future backed by a deep understanding of digital technologies' potential impact on their industry and business operations. Additionally, leaders must be agile and willing to embrace change themselves (Cortellazzo et al., 2019).

The proliferation of digital technologies introduces myriad paradoxes that underscore contemporary leadership's complexity (Schiuma et al., 2022). Digitalization facilitates both centralization and decentralization of decision making authority, necessitating a nuanced approach to leadership and allowing for quicker and more accurate processes and improved communication transparency (Pflaeging, 2014). The increased transparency and the abundance of information requires leaders to explore new ways to influence and inspire others (Westerman et al., 2014).

Transformational leaders must maintain their role as motivational inspirers by promoting team cohesion, using open communication to clarify the mission, and fostering a culture of learning, experimentation, and adaptation. This involves implementing digital tools and processes, integrating virtual work environments, and managing the transition from traditional to digital working. As a result, it broadens the range of tools available to leaders, allowing them to utilize technology to enhance their messages. These tools simplify the communication of overarching goals and the process of strategic renewal (Warner & Wäger, 2019). Further, the advent of digital technologies augments labor market flexibility, challenging conventional notions of stability and requiring the reevaluation of long-term competence development strategies.

In addition, it is essential to emphasize the deployment of diverse management styles to reconcile the conflicting demands inherent in digital transformationsand foster a culture of collaborative innovation. Embracing the paradoxes inherent in digital environments and deploying diverse management styles are critical for learning and leadership development (Gregory et al., 2015). Brilliant leaders in the dynamic digital transformation landscape are committed to continuous learning. They prioritize staying abreast of emerging technologies and best practices while fostering a culture of ongoing development and skill training within their organizations.

Remaining attentive to these changes is crucial for sustaining success as technology continues to evolve at an unprecedented pace. In doing so, brilliant leaders can position their organizations at the forefront of digital transformation, playing a pivotal role by ensuring organizational readiness to confront the dynamic challenges and opportunities in this thriving landscape. To achieve this goal effectively, brilliant leaders institute robust processes and adaptable systems capable of integrating smoothly with digital innovation, paving the way for sustainable growth throughout the organization.

Understanding the Qualities of Brilliant Leadership

Brilliant leadership is a quality that is highly sought-after today. Leadership plays a significant role in the success and progress of organizations, communities, and even nations. Influential leaders can inspire and influence others toward achieving predetermined goals. They possess qualities that make them stand out and can flex their influence while communicating and delegating effectively. These essential leadership qualities can be learned and improved at all levels of an organization, making it possible for aspiring leaders to become brilliant leaders. Leadership is not just about having a position of authority or holding a title; it is about the ability to guide and empower others. The influence of leadership goes beyond just achieving goals. Above all, leadership influences goal achievement. It empowers people to act and work towards attaining specific goals.

Brilliant leaders can think and act on their own and their followers' values and interests. They understand leaders' and followers' needs and aspirations and can align them toward a common purpose (Geoghegan & Dulewicz, 2008). While society can quickly identifies a lousy leader, discovering a good leader is often more challenging. Good leaders possess certain qualities that set them apart from others. Trustworthiness is undeniably at the top of the list of qualities required by any leader, and it is the foundation upon which successful relationships and effective teams are built (Belasen & Eisenberg, 2023).

When individuals within an organization are consistently exposed to trustworthy leaders, particularly those who exhibit a strong sense of ethical behavior, they tend to assimilate and replicate these behaviors. This phenomenon not only underscores the importance of trust in leadership but also highlights the influence leaders can have on shaping the conduct and culture of their teams or organizations. Moreover, it suggests that cultivating trust and promoting regulatory behavior among leaders can yield cascading benefits throughout the entire organizational structure, fostering a more inclusive and ethical working environment (Belasen & Toma, 2015).

Brilliant leaders, however, possess certain qualities that set them apart. Brilliant leaders maintain their role as motivational inspirers, promoting team cohesion and using transparent communication to clarify the mission and foster a culture of learning, experimentation, and adaptation. This involves implementing digital tools and processes, integrating virtual work environments, and managing the transition from traditional to digital workplaces.

Despite how the digital transformation revolutionize industries and markets as well as how businesses operate (Nikmehr et al., 2021), leaders must craft a clear and compelling vision for their organizations. This vision should encompass the organization's goals, strategies, and values, leveraging digital technologies to drive innovation and growth (Nikmehr et al., 2021). A strong leadership vision will guide the organization in navigating the complexities of digital transformation while inspiring and motivating employees to embrace change and use their social networks to promote the reputational assets of the organization. Externally, managing a corporate reputation via social media is essential for building long-term relationships with consumers, especially during disruptions (Belasen & Belasen, 2019).

Brilliant leaders are committed to continuous learning. They prioritize staying abreast of emerging technologies and best practices while fostering a culture of ongoing education and skill development within their organizations. Remaining attentive to these changes is crucial for sustaining success as technology continues to evolve at an unprecedented pace. In doing so, brilliant leaders can position their organizations at the forefront of digital transformation, playing a pivotal role by ensuring organizational readiness to confront the dynamic challenges and opportunities in this thriving landscape. To achieve this goal effectively, they institute robust processes and adaptable systems capable of integrating seamlessly with digital innovation, paving the way for sustainable growth throughout the organization.

The wide range of characteristics and abilities provides numerous possible choices for design. However, at the core of every successful leader is a successful individual, regardless of the specific combination of abilities and traits they may possess (Bregman, 2022). The successful individual can be viewed from two perspectives: internal and external; it pertains to your personal qualities and extends beyond yourself. Chapter 10 elaborates on these qualities.

Internally, successful individuals may have a strong CORE™—confidence, optimism, resilience, and engagement—qualities that, when combined, enhance success in any scenario (see, Middlebrooks et al., 2018). Confidence results in a favorable perspective on the world and one's achievements (Schutte, 2014), which nurtures the capacity to bounce back quickly from challenges (Nguyen, 2016). As resilience develops, every display of determination contributes to heightened confidence (Ackerman, 2021). Resilience is about gaining critical competencies for navigating major disruptions. Resilient leaders focus on strategies for building a culture of trust, foster teamwork, promote interprofessional cooperation, and improve business outcomes (Belasen, 2022).

At the core of this process is positive involvement, driving progress by enriching experiences, knowledge acquisition, and the creation of new avenues for additional participation because emotions can initiate positive feedback loops, ultimately resulting in an overall improvement in well-being (Kanter, 2011). Externally, leaders' effectiveness is determined by how others perceive them to be (Fredrickson & Joiner, 2018). For some individuals, this effectiveness initially stems from charisma. In general terms, however, the perception of leaders' effectiveness reflects their personal stregths, credibility, and reputation.

Kouzes and Posner (2006) emphasize the significance of credibility as the cornerstone of leadership, stating that without belief in the messenger, there can be no belief in the message. Credibility is essential for establishing a positive rapport with followers, enabling positive influence. Employees are more likely to exhibit pride in their organization, experience a strong sense of unity within their team, align their values with organizational values, feel connected and committed to the organization, and take ownership when they perceive high credibility in their immediate manager.

Goffee and Jones (2005) highlighted four qualities effective leaders employ: showing their humanity, intuitively sensing timing and actions, managing with empathy, and capitalizing on their uniqueness as leaders. They view leadership as a process of influence consisting of a series of steps or activities over time which open many possibilities for further explorations. The positional leader shifts to becoming a facilitator of the process rather than the sole person in charge. This perspective recognizes that guiding individuals and organizations toward a goal is a dynamic, situational, and context-dependent journey.

Brand Positioning and Reputation

Brand in business refers to customers' perception of that business and its product. Businesses build their brands by creating and projecting unique attributes and a sustainable trademark image to their consumers and ensuring customer attachment is inclined to these attributes (Fayvishenko, 2018). The reputation of a business largely relies on its corporate credibility and entails the evaluation by consumers of the honesty and expertise of that business (Goldsmith et al., 2000). Trust is essential in the relationship between buyers and sellers or businesses and their customers (Ebert, 2009; Schoorman et al., 2015). Purchase decisions are influenced by trust, and beyond that, customers tend to develop brand loyalty when they can trust the honesty and expertise of the business. Business reputation influences the trust level and consumer purchase decisions (Lassoued & Hobbs, 2015). Elevating brand and reputation to a strategic priority is necessary for crafting corporate messages and communicating these messages to diverse stakeholders coherently and ethically. Stakeholders may interpret the same messages divergently in their own ways, and these interpretations affect their attitudes and preferences. When the lines of communication are clear, the credibility of the communication increases. Knowing that leaders at all levels of the organization use common language for sharing expectations with internal and external stakeholders helps reduce the potential for miscommunication in the workplace as well as reduce linguistic ambiguity in strategic communications, thus increasing the reputational assets of the organization (Belasen & Belasen, 2019).

Based on signaling theory, businesses can obviate information asymmetry and influence consumer purchase intention by projecting a positive brand image (Yasar et al., 2020). Bhandari and Rodgers (2017) confirm that electronic word of mouth can influence a business's brand and reputation. According to them, digitally communicated brand feedback had a simultaneous positive and negative effect on purchase intentions, and brand trust mediated the positive effect.

Conclusion

The business, the commitment of its leadership or management, and the strategy applied can strongly influence digital innovations (Ko et al., 2022). Despite the opportunities offered by digital transformation, businesses often need help integrating and exploiting digital technology (Heavin & Power 2018). Business leaders can either make plans that are oriented and targeted at using the opportunities created by digital transformation or formulate emergent strategies based on industry dynamics or consumer preferences. In the words of Mintzberg (1994, p. 111), "all viable strategies have emergent and deliberate [i.e., planned] qualities" aligned with the following:

■ **Objectives**: The digital strategy needs to align with organizational goals. It should reinforce the existing business growth strategy, market expansion, and operational efficiency so that all stakeholders involved in implementing the digital transformation process remain in line with building and sustaining the business brand.

▪ **Agility**: A consequential attribute required to ensure alignment of digital transformation strategy and resources is "agility" (Troise et al., 2022). This agility involves sensing and responding to opportunities in emerging business needs, market changes, and new technologies (Leonhardt et al., 2017). Agility entails business flexibility such that business leaders can adjust activities to suit unpredictability in the competitive business environment and ensure the sustainability of their brand.

Digital transformation involves automated processes, innovative technology, and changes in organizational strategies, which are translated to improved operating efficiency, better customer experience, and positive brand image.Business leaders who aim to survive in a competitive market must take advantage of digital transformation to drive innovations that improve their reputational assets and branding capabilities (Handini & Pangestuti, 2021; Hoffmann & Weithaler, 2015).

References

Abdallah, Y. O., Shehab, E., & Al–AshaabAl–Ashaab, A. (2021). Understanding digital transformation in the manufacturing industry: A systematic literature review and future trends. *Product: Management and Development, 19*(1).

Ackerman, C. E. (2021, February 12). What is self-confidence? + 9 ways to increase it. *PositivePsychology.com*. https://positivepsychology.com/self-confidence/

Ancillai, C., Sabatini, A., Gatti, M., & Perna, A. (2023). Digital technology and business model innovation: A systematic literature review and future research agenda. *Technological Forecasting and Social Change, 188*, 122307.

Belasen, A. T. (2000). *Leading the learning organization: Communication and competencies for managing change*. State University of New York Press.

Belasen, A. T., & Toma, R. (Eds.). (2015). *Confronting corruption in business: Trusted leadership, civic engagement*. Routledge.

Belasen, A.T., & Belasen, A. R. (2019). The strategic value of integrated corporate communication: Functions, social media, stakeholders, *International Journal of Strategic Communication, 13*(4), https://doi.org/10.1080/1553118X.2019.1661842

Belasen, A. T. (2022). *Resilience in Healthcare Leadership: Practical Strategies and Self-Assessment Tools*, New York, NY, Routledge.

Belasen, A. T. & Eisenberg, B. (2023). Building Trust for Better Crisis Communication: Lessons for Leadership Development, Chapter 7 in Nicole Pfeffermann & Monika Schaller, Editors, *New Leadership Communication - Inspire Your Horizon*, pp.93–110, Switzerland, Springer. https://doi.org/10.1007/978-3-031-34314-8_

Bhandari, M., & Rodgers, S. (2017). What does the brand say? Effects of brand feedback to negative eWOM on brand trust and purchase intentions.*International Journal of Advertising 37*(1). 125–141 .https://doi.org/10.1080/02650487.2017.1349030

Bhens, S., Lau, L., & Sarrazin, H. (2016, September). *You need the new tech talent to succeed in digital*. Digital McKinsey.

Bloomberg, J. (2018). Digitization, digitalization, and digital transformation: confuse them at your peril. *Forbes*. August, 28(2019), 1–6.

Bregman, P. (2022). *Great leaders are confident, connected, committed, and courageous* (pp. 3–5). Coach Me! Your Board of Directors: Leadership advice from the world's greatest coaches.

Burton–Jones, A., Akhlaghpour, S., Ayre, S., Barde, P., Staib, A., & Sullivan, C. (2020). Changing the conversation on evaluating digital transformation in healthcare: insights from an institutional analysis. *Information and Organization, 30*(1), 100255

Cagliano, R., Canterino, F., Longoni, A., & Bartezzaghi, E. (2019). The interplay between brilliant manufacturing technologies and work organization: The role of technological complexity. *International Journal of Operations & Production Management, 39*(6/7/8), 913–934.

Chanais, S., Myers, M. D., & Hess, T. (2019). Digital transformation strategy making in pre-digital organizations: The case of a financial service provider. *Journal of Strategic Information Systems, 28*(1), 03.

Cortellazzo, L., Bruni, E., & Zampieri, R. (2019). The role of leadership in a digitalized world: A review. *Frontiers in Psychology, 10*, 1938.

Ebert, T. (2009). *Trust as the key to loyalty in business-to-consumer exchanges* (Vol. 1). Springer Fachmedien.

Engesmo, J., & Panteli, N. (2020). *Digital transformation and its impact on IT structure and leadership.* Paper presented at Scandinavian Conference on Information Systems, Sweden.

European Commission, Digital Transformation Scoreboard. (2018, December). https://digital -strategy.ec.europa.eu/en/library/definition-artificial-intelligence-main-capabilities-and -scientific-disciplines

Fahy, J. (2000). The resource–based resource–based view of the firm: Some stumbling–blocks on the road to understanding sustainable competitive advantage. *Journal of European Industrial Training, 24*(2/3/4), 94–10.

Fayvishenko, D. (2018). Formation of brand positioning strategy. *Baltic Journal of Economic Studies, 4*(2), 245–248.

Fredrickson, B. L., & Joiner, T. (2018). Reflections on positive emotions and upward spirals. *Perspectives on Psychological Science, 13*(2), 194–199.

Geoghegan, L., & Dulewicz, V. (2008). Do project managers' leadership competencies con-tribute to project success? *Project Management Journal, 39*(4), 58–67.

Goffee, R., & Jones, G. (2005). Managing authenticity. *Harvard Business Review, 83*(12), 85–94.

Goldsmith, R. E., Lafferty, B. A., & Newell, S. J. (2000). The impact of corporate credibility and celebrity credibility on consumer reaction to advertisements and brands. *Journal of Advertising, 29*(3), 43–54.

Gregory, R. W., Keil, M., Muntermann, J., & Mähring, M. (2015). Paradoxes and the nature of ambidexterity in IT transformation programs. *Information Systems Research, 26*, 57–80.

Handini, Y. D., & Pangestuti, E. (2021, September). Branding capability, innovation and business performance. In *3rd Annual international conference on public and business administration (AICoBPA 2020)* (pp. 26–29). Atlantis Press.

Hanelt, A., Bohnsack, R., Marz, D., & Antunes Marante, C. (2021). A systematic review of the literature on digital transformation: Insights and implications for strategy and orga-nizational change. *Journal of Management Studies, 58*(5), 1159–1197.

Hai, T. N., Van, Q. N., & Thi Tuyet, M. N. (2021). Digital transformation: Opportunities and challenges for leaders in the emerging countries in response to COVID-19 pan-demic. *Emerging Science Journal, 5(1)*, 21–36.

Heavin, C., & Power, D. J. (2018). Challenges for digital transformation–towards a con-ceptual decision support guide for managers. *Journal of Decision Systems, 27*(Suppl. 1), 38–45.https://doi.org/10.1080/12460125.2018.1468697

Hinings, B., Gegenhuber, T., & Greenwood, R. (2018). Digital innovation and transformation: An institutional perspective. *Information and Organization, 28*(1), 52–61.

Hoffmann, C., & Weithaler, L. (2015). Building brand reputation in the digital age: Identifying effective brand. *Management Review, 44*(3), 72–86.

Holzmann, P., & Gregori, P. (2023). The promise of digital technologies for sustainable entrepreneurship: A systematic literature review and research agenda. *International Journal of Information Management, 68*, 102593.

Janowski, T. (2015). Digital government evolution: From transformation to contextualization. *Government Information Quarterly, 32*(3), 221–223.

Kanter, R. M. (2011). Cultivate a culture of confidence. *Harvard Business Review, 89*(4), 34.

Keating, D J., Cullen-Lester, K L., & Meuser, J D. (2023). Virtual work conditions impact negative work behaviors via ambiguity, anonymity, and (un)accountability: An integrative review. *Journal of Applied Psychology, 109*(2), 169–201.

Kim, S., Choi, B., & Lew, Y. K. (2021). Where is the age of digitalization heading? The meaning, characteristics, and implications of contemporary digital transformation *Sustainability,* 13(16), 8909.

Klus, M F., & Müller, J. (2021). The digital leader: what one needs to master today's organizational challenges. *Journal of Business Economics, 91*(8), 1189–1223. https://doi.org/10.1007/s11573–021–01040–1

Ko, A., Fehér, P., Kovacs, T., Mitev, A., & Szabó, Z. (2022). Influencing factors of digital transformation: Management or IT is the driving force?. *International Journal of Innovation Science, 14*(1), 1–20.

Kouzes, J. M., & Posner, B. Z. (2003). *The five practices of exemplary leadership.* Wiley.

Kouzes, J. M., & Posner, B. Z. (2006). *The leadership challenge* (Vol. 3). John Wiley & Sons.

Kraus, S., Durst, S., Ferreira, J. J., Veiga, P., Kailer, N., & Weinmann, A. (2022). Digital transformation in business and management research: An overview of the current status quo. *International Journal of Information Management, 63*, 102466.

Lassoued, R., & Hobbs, J. E. (2015). Consumer confidence in credence attributes: The role of brand trust. *Food Policy, 52*, 99–107.

Leonardi, P. (2020). You are going digital—Now what?*MIT Sloan Management Review, 61*(2), 28–35S.

Leonhardt, D., Haffke, I., Kranz, J., & Benlian, A. (2017). Reinventing the IT function: The role of IT agility and IT ambidexterity in supporting digital business transformation. 25th *European Conference on Information Systems* ,Vol. 63, pp. 968–984.

Loebbecke, C., & Picot, A. (2015). Reflections on societal and business model transformation Arising from digitization and big data analytics: A research agenda. *The Journal of Strategic Information Systems, 24*(3), 149–157.

Matt, C., Hess, T., & Benlian, A. (2015). Digital transformation strategies. *Business & Information Systems Engineering, 57*, 339–343.

Middlebrooks, A., Allen, S. J., McNutt, M. S., & Morrison, J. L. (2018). *Discovering leadership: Designing your success.* SAGE Publications.

Mintzberg, H. (1994). Rethinking strategic planning part I: Pitfalls and fallacies. *Long Range Planning, 27*(3), 12–21.

Morakanyane, R., Grace, A. A., & O'Reilly, P. (2017). *Conceptualizing digital transformation in business organizations: A systematic review of the literature.* Bled eConference.

Nguyen, Q. (2016). Employee resilience and leadership styles: The moderating role of proactive personality and optimism. *New Zealand Journal of Psychology* (Christchurch. 1983), *45*(2), 13–21.

Nikmehr, B., Hosseini, M. R., Martek, I., Zavadskas, E. K., & Antucheviciene, J. (2021). Digitalization as a strategic means of achieving sustainable efficiencies in construction management: A critical review. *Sustainability, 13*(9), 5040.

Oke, A., Munshi, N., & Walumbwa, F. O. (2009). The influence of leadership on innovation processes and activities. *Organizational Dynamics, 38*(1), 64–72.

Pflaeging, N. (2014). *Organize for complexity: How to get your life back into work and build a high-performance organization.* BetaCodex Publishing.

Rautenbach, W. J., de Kock, I., & Jooste, J. L. (2019, June). *The development of a conceptual model for enabling a value-adding digital transformation: A conceptual model that aids organisations in the digital transformation process.* In 2019 IEEE International Conference on Engineering, Technology and Innovation (ICE/ITMC) (pp. 1–10). IEEE.

Schiuma, G., Schettini, E., Santarsiero, F., & Carlucci, D. (2022). The transformative leadership compass: six competencies for digital transformation entrepreneurship. *International Journal of Entrepreneurial Behavior & Research, 28*(5), 1273–1291.

Schneider, S., & Kokshagina, O. (2021). Digital transformation: What we have learned (thus far) and what is next. *Creativity and Innovation Management, 30*(2), 384–411.

Schoorman, F. D., Wood, M. M., & Breuer, C. (2015). Would trust by any other name smell as sweet? Reflections on the meanings and uses of trust across disciplines and context. In B. H. Bornstein & A. J. Tomkins (Eds.), *Motivating cooperation and compliance with authority: The role of institutional trust,* (Vol. 62, pp. 13–35). Springer

Schwarzmüller, T., Brosi, P., Duman, D., & Welpe, I. M. (2018). How does the digital transformation affect organizations? Key themes of change in work design and leadership. *Management Revue, 29*(2), 114–138.

Schutte, N. S. (2014). The broaden and build process: Positive affect, ratio of positive to negative affect and general self-efficacy. The *Journal of Positive Psychology, 9*(1), 66–74. https://doi.org/10.1080/17439760.2013.841280

Troise, C., Corvello, V., Ghobadian, A., & O'Regan, N. (2022). How can SMEs successfully navigate VUCA environment: The role of agility in the digital transformation era. *Technological Forecasting and Social Change,* vol. *174(C).* doi: 10.1016/j.techfore.2021.121227

Tsou, H. T., & Chen, J. S. (2023). How does digital technology usage benefit firm performance? Digital transformation strategy and organizational innovation as mediators. *Technology Analysis & Strategic Management, 35*(9), 1114–1127.

Tumbas, S., Berente, N., & Vom Brocke, J. (2017). *Born digital: Growth trajectories of entrepreneurial organizations spanning institutional fields.* ICIS.

Vial, G. (2019). Understanding digital transformation: A review and a research agenda. *The Journal of Strategic Information Systems, 28*(2), 118–144.

Vom Brocke, J., Maaß, W., Buxmann, P., Maedche, A., Leimeister, J. M., & Pecht, G. (2018). Future work and enterprise systems. *Business & Information Systems Engineering, 60,* 357–366.

Wang, W. Y. C., & Wang, Y. (2020). Analytics in the era of big data: The digital transformations and value creation in industrial marketing. *Industrial Marketing Management, 86,* 12–15.

Warner, K. S., & Wäger, M. (2019). Building dynamic capabilities for digital transformation: An ongoing process of strategic renewal. *Long-range Planning, 52*(3), 326–349.

Watkins, A. (2013). *Coherence: The secret science of brilliant leadership.* Kogan Page Publishers.

Westerman, G., Bonnet, D., & McAfee, A. (2014). *Leading digital: Turning technology into business transformation.* Harvard Business Press.

Yasar, B., Martin, T., & Kiessling, T. (2020). An empirical test of signalling theory. *Management Research Review, 43*(11), 1309–1335.

Yeow, A., Sia, S. K., Soh, C., & Chua, C. (2018). Boundary organization practices for collaboration in enterprise integration. *Information Systems Research, 29*(1), 149–168.

Zaoui, F., & Souissi, N. (2020). Roadmap for digital transformation: A literature review. *Procedia Computer Science, 175,* 621–628.

Chapter 9

Increasing Value Proposition, Engaging Stakeholders for Innovation

Tim Mazzarol and Sophie Reboud

Introduction

Research literature recognizes the importance of a firm's ability to identify and develop a compelling customer value proposition (CVP) as the foundation of its business model (Miller & Swaddling, 2002). This requires the leadership of the firm to possess the 'soft skills' to engage with key stakeholders, develop trust, navigate risk and uncertainty within their task environment, and use knowledge management and organizational learning. Opportunity screening is also essential to successful commercialization, typically involving the leadership team possessing entrepreneurial cognition and the application of biases and heuristics to guide decision-making. This chapter examines the role of company leadership within innovative small firms (ISFs) in identifying and co-creating value with key stakeholders in the commercialization of innovations. Research literature is discussed, and survey data and case studies are used to provide context and relevant examples.

Screening Opportunities and the Decision-Making Process

Opportunity screening is an essential step in the commercialization of any innovation. It is a complex and iterative process involving stages of identification, analysis, and assessment, with continuous knowledge enhancement that stimulates better understanding, idea generation, and new insights (Koen et al., 2002).

DOI: 10.4324/9781003495307-13

Screening and Analysis

Identifying opportunities is a fundamental part of the entrepreneurial journey (Mazzarol & Reboud, 2020a). Entrepreneurial cognition is a process for acquiring, assimilating, transforming, and exploiting knowledge and information. It acts as an analytical filter and influences the decision to innovate and the identification of opportunities (Mitchell et al., 2002). It influences how the firm's management recognizes and selects opportunities (Shepherd & Patzelt, 2017). However, opportunity identification is only a part of the opportunity selection process, which requires the firm's leadership to navigate uncertainty and ambiguity. It serves to mitigate any lack of information and knowledge, facilitate the commercialization process, and optimize the use of the firm's resources, skills, and competencies (Timmons, 1999).

Entrepreneurs rely on prior knowledge, from experience or education, to screen and select opportunities (Shane, 2000). Successful ISF leaders consider opportunities where they have prior knowledge and experience, and where they can envision a pathway for a project to be successfully commercialized (Sharma, 2019). Multiple opportunities are usually presented that must be screened and assessed prior to a final decision. Selection processes rarely have clear best-worst options and are influenced by the context, capabilities, and prior experience of the decision-makers (Shepherd & Patzelt, 2018). Entrepreneurial alertness is a feature of entrepreneurial cognition and comprises the six dimensions listed in Table 9.1 (Sharma, 2019). It is a process that involves both inherent characteristics of the individual and outcomes from their interaction with the external environment.

Influences on the Decision-Making Process

Entrepreneurial decision-making involves at least five interconnected areas: (i) the decision to evaluate an opportunity; (ii) how the entrepreneur decides; (iii) how their decisions vary over time; (iv) their experience of the technology; and (v) the influence of non-economic considerations (Shepherd et al., 2015). This process is influenced by the entrepreneur's education, training, knowledge, and professional experience (Davidsson & Honig, 2003), as well as their propensity to deal with risk and uncertainty (Forlani & Mullins, 2000). This propensity for risk-taking may be influenced by their prior work experience (Elfenbein et al., 2010), and how they assess the *affordable loss* should the project fail (Sarasvathy, 2001).

Once the decision to proceed has been made, attention should be given to the implementation of a systematic new product development (NPD) process along with associated planning and business model development (Cooper, 2008, 2017, 2019; Blank & Dorf, 2012). However, most ISFs lack formalization in relation to NPD and commercialization systems, with most start-up ventures pursuing innovation opportunities, at least in their early stages, via informal approaches (Bhide, 1994; Brinckmann et al., 2010). The entrepreneur's decision to abandon the project should also be considered,

Table 9.1 Entrepreneurial Alertness Key Dimensions

EA dimensions	Application to entrepreneurial alertness
Sensing and search information	Entrepreneurial alertness is characterized by the ability of entrepreneurs to systematically sense and search for information, evaluate this information, and make decisions based on what they learn. This provides them with a process for screening opportunities
Cognitive ability	An important element in the process of entrepreneurial discovery is the ability to examine available information using a schema (e.g., rules, biases, heuristics) that the individual has developed to assist them in screening opportunities
Knowledge and experience	Also of importance to entrepreneurial discovery is the individual's own prior knowledge and experience, which they have accumulated through their past work environment, education, or social networks. This can include domain-specific knowledge (e.g., marketing, finance, engineering)
Personality factors	While there is little consensus as to what specific personality traits might be of value to entrepreneurial discovery, the role of creativity has been identified as playing an important role, along with achievement orientation, self-efficacy, and internal locus of control
Social networks	The value of social networks to entrepreneurial discovery is associated with their ability to generate a flow of information and advice that can overcome the problem of information asymmetry. Strong social capital is therefore a key factor in enhancing opportunity screening
Entrepreneurial environment	External environmental factors (e.g., political, economic, social, technological, legal, and environmental) influence the individual's entrepreneurial alertness. This takes the form of their assessment of the opportunities and threats they might face within a target market, and in turn, how this environment might be navigated to allow them to exploit an opportunity

Source: Adapted from Sharma (2019).

which is a feature of the NPD process (Cooper & Edgett, 2005). The decision-making process found within entrepreneurial cognition involves the use of biases and heuristics to guide the decision-maker (Busenitz & Barney, 1997; Shepherd et al., 2015).

These comprise idiosyncratic mental rubrics derived from the entrepreneurial leader's experience and learning. Within highly complex and uncertain environments, this type of decision-making based on entrepreneurial cognition may be more valuable than that based on managerial cognition (Uzkurt et al., 2012). For ISFs, a decision-making process based on these foundations is important (De Carolis & Saparito, 2006). However, the leadership team must also be committed to the project and must also possess the competencies to navigate regulatory issues likely to impact the project's progress (Cooper & Kleinschmidt, 1995; Zafar & Kantola, 2019). Key factors that are also influential include the leadership's entrepreneurial orientation (Lumpkin & Dess, 1996), personal networks (e.g., social capital) (Partanen et al., 2008), learning capacity (absorptive capacity) (Kim et al., 2018), and market orientation (Sedighadeli & Kachouie, 2013).

Influence of the Context

The task environment in which the decision-making is being made is also important. Here, the leadership team needs to be proactive, not reactive, to environmental opportunities and threats (Urbano et al., 2018). Consideration of market competition, collaboration and alliance formation opportunities, knowledge exchange, and regulatory change are all important (Aslan & Vatansever, 2018).

Business Model Theory and Commercialization

The value customers perceive in a new product or service is a trade-off of perceived costs and benefits. Proactive ISFs can shape these perceptions through communication and customer/stakeholder engagement (Mazzarol et al., 2022). The *business model* concept has been studied extensively (Massa et al., 2017). Despite some variations, a business model is defined as a mechanism through which value is identified, created, and delivered sustainably to customers (Osterwalder et al., 2005; Amit & Zott, 2012; Teece, 2010, 2018).

The Business Model Functions

A business model should articulate the CVP, identify the target market segments most likely to adopt the innovation, define how the firm's strategic network should be configured and where the firm is best located to create and capture value, how revenue and profit will be generated, and how it can work with its network to create cospecialized assets (Chesbrough, 2007). The articulation of the CVP is a crucial first step and must be developed from customers' perspective, not that of the firm (Amit & Zott, 2012). A business model's role is to identify how value can be sensed, seized, transformed, and exploited (Teece, 2010), while configuring the firm's resources and capabilities to sustainably deliver this value (Osterwalder et al., 2015).

Careful targeting of leading customers within worthwhile market segments is critical (Johnson et al., 2008). Identifying early adopters willing to co-create value within the commercialization process is important (Grupp & Maital, 2001), as is how the firm will leverage its value chain (e.g., key suppliers, leading customers, and complementary resource network actors) (de Figueirêdo et al., 2014). This should focus on the co-creation of value and cospecialized assets capable of generating isolating mechanisms to block out competitors (Kirchberger & Pohl, 2016; Teece, 2007, 2012).

The business model must also identify how financial value will be created through an analysis of the cost-profit-volume relationship (Chesbrough, 2007). Yet, attention should also be given to the development of 'soft systems' that can facilitate decision-making within highly uncertain environments. This is assisted by the engagement of the firm's strategic network, not just in the creation of economic capital, but also social capital (e.g., trust, reciprocity, and networks) (Jarillo, 1988; Ostgaard & Birley, 1994; Holmlund & Törnroos, 1997). The business model is therefore a multifaceted tool that considers the market opportunities and threats, and the firm's internal weaknesses and strengths, then reconfigures them via collaborative action within a strategic network to co-create and deliver a CVP and a competitive strategy (Teece, 1996; Mazzarol & Reboud, 2009; Duhamel et al., 2014).

The Business Model Elements

Since the mid-2000s, the business model has become a key operational and strategic tool for decision-making (Massa et al., 2017). This has been facilitated by the application of the business model canvas developed by Osterwalder (2005), comprising nine key elements (Osterwalder & Pigneur, 2010) as illustrated in Figure 9.1. This framework provides a valuable planning tool for managers and start-up entrepreneurs (Ebel et al., 2016).

As shown in Figure 9.1, the first and most important component is the CVP, which contains the elements discussed above in relation to this function. It is the primary driver of an effective business model. The second is the market-facing component, comprising the targeted customer/market segments, the relationships between the firm

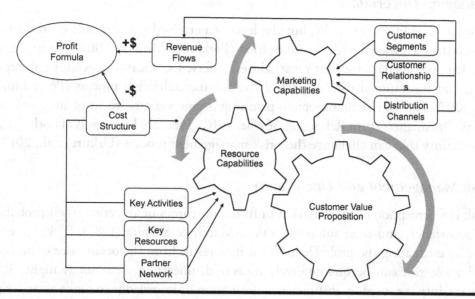

Figure 9.1 The Business Model Components and Their Relationships

and its target customers, and the most appropriate distribution channels for a given customer segment (Casadesus-Masanell & Ricart, 2011). The third is the resource capabilities encompassing the key activities, key resources, and key partner networks required to deliver the CVP in a sustainable competitive manner. As discussed above, this requires the co-creation of value and the development of cospecialized assets around which the firm can build its dynamic capabilities (see, Teece et al., 1997; Teece, 2007, 2012, 2014a, 2014b, 2016, 2018). The fourth component is the profit formula, which is an outcome of the firm's revenue flows and cost structure (e.g., expenditure) required. This cost-profit-volume analysis will determine the overall viability of the business model design.

The successful implementation of a business model requires the firm to align all nine elements across the four sections and ensure that they are informed by, and in turn inform, the firm's overall business strategy. Successful commercialization requires the firm to possess strong dynamic capabilities (e.g., the ability to sense, co-create, seize, and transform) via the configuration of its own and its strategic network partners' resources and capabilities (Teece, 2012, Teece 2014a; Teece 2014b, Teece 2018).

How an ISF uses its resources and reconfigures them into bundles of capabilities that can be applied to co-create value with both lead customers and key suppliers is important to successful commercialization (Olander et al., 2009; Teece, 2010; Mazzarol & Reboud, 2020b; Mazzarol et al., 2022). Strategic networks offer the firm access to resources and capabilities (Kotabe & Swan, 1995) and can be based on both formal and informal relationships (Tsai, 2009; West & Bogers, 2014). However, both parties need to realize the value from the partnership (Alvarez & Barney, 2001).

Managing Uncertainty

Innovation is inherently risky, but the level of perceived risk depends on the level of uncertainty associated with the innovation (Forlani & Mullins, 2000). Managing risk is a key managerial task that must address safety, technical, financial, legal, regulatory, and reputational risks as part of the commercialization process (Pérez-Luño et al., 2007). Formal risk management planning is now a central focus of large and small firms (Brustbauer, 2016; Reboud & Séville, 2016). ISFs face high levels of both risk and uncertainty that can challenge their risk management process (Uzkurt et al., 2012).

Risk Management and Uncertainty

Risk is a perception of the variation in future outcomes of an action, their probability of occurrence, and their subjective value (March & Shapira, 1987). Risk is measurable by estimating the probable loss that may result from the occurrence of an event, and while risk can be quantitatively measured, uncertainty cannot (Knight, 1933). Uncertainty is caused by insufficient information or knowledge to make accurate predictions about the likely outcome of an action or event. Although risk management is now integrated into the management of most large companies, it is less practiced by small firms (Falkner & Hiebl, 2015).

Risk management in ISFs is often assumed by the leadership team and is generally conducted intuitively and informally, without specific tools (Jayathilake, 2012). It is not usually addressed in the same systematic way as found in larger or less innovative firms, which face less uncertain task environments, and where it is applied, it is usually in relation to financial risk, particularly where venture capital has been invested (Reboud & Séville, 2016). However, as Table 9.2 shows, the key issues that emerge from the literature about risk management in ISFs focus on three main themes: (i) the risk behavior characteristics of the owner-managers of these companies; (ii) the risk management processes they follow; and (iii) the different types of risk they encounter.

ISFs engaged in commercialization face environments of high uncertainty that create high perceived market, technological, and financial risks. The leadership of such firms must apply entrepreneurial cognition and decision-making to develop appropriate business models facilitated by strategic alliances, knowledge sharing, and creation of cospecialized assets (Teece, 2014b; Echeverri-Carroll, 1999; Tsai, 2009; Laperche & Liu, 2013). This requires the leadership team to build strong social capital, absorptive capacity, and dynamic capabilities, using effective communication and engagement strategies. Further, leadership should engender trust, form common understandings, promote shared goals and obligations that can mitigate the risks of geographic distance, disparities in knowledge and skills, and a willingness collaborate (Gao et al., 2013).

Absorptive Capacity and the Management of Risk

Knowledge management and absorptive capacity play an important role in the decision of small, innovative companies to innovate (Cerchione et al., 2016). *Absorptive capacity* is the process of acquisition, assimilation, transformation, and exploitation of knowledge (Cohen & Levinthal, 1990; Zahra & George, 2002). It is an essential process within organizational learning and knowledge management, facilitated by communication exchanges both within and outside the innovator firm (Sher & Lee, 2004). By enhancing knowledge within the firm's leadership and project management teams, it serves to reduce uncertainty and mitigate risks encountered during the commercialization process (Lee et al., 2013). Effective engagement of all stakeholders within the firm's network (e.g., leading customers, key suppliers, and complementary actors) is important (Rothaermel & Deeds, 2004).

Commercialization requires both entrepreneurship and innovation management skills to be applied. However, while innovation is a key component of entrepreneurship, these two areas have tended to be examined separately in academic literature (Shepherd & Patzelt, 2017). Yet, it is important to understand how the intersection of the two 'cornerstones', *absorptive capacity* and systematic *innovation management*, is essential to NPD and commercialization success.

Table 9.2   Risk Management in SMEs, Summary of Findings from a Literature Review

Themes	Main findings
SME owner and firm characteristics influence over risk behavior	Better-educated SME owners show higher adoption of risk mitigation strategies. Younger owners are less risk-averse than older ones. Male owners show a greater risk appetite than female owners
	Owners of smaller firms have lower risk tolerance than those in larger firms
Common characteristics of the risk management process in SMEs	Risk identification should be undertaken continuously and systematically using methods and tools to facilitate the process (e.g., risk management planning). Strategic project risks should be avoided, while operational project risks should be identified and managed
	Due to limited resources, SMEs typically only address the most serious risks identified. A simplified risk analysis process is desirable. Employees with limited knowledge of risk management can hinder risk identification and mitigation
	A range of risk management tools and techniques exist within the extant literature
	All employees should be informed of the firm's risk management goals
	SMEs should define performance standards or criteria to monitor the risk management process
Common types of risk that SMEs face	SMEs can face risks from fluctuations in bank interest rates, as well as rising costs of raw materials that cannot be passed on to customers. Cybersecurity threats and rapid technological change, plus overdependence on key suppliers, create major risks
	Business growth is a risk to SMEs, and owners with higher risk propensity will seek to expand into new markets with new product technologies
	Knowledge should be protected within SMEs, but the loss of long-term employees and managers poses a major risk to SMEs due to the loss of knowledge and expertise. Informal knowledge management processes can hinder risk management within SMEs, and firms rarely offer employee training programs

Source: Adapted from Falkner and Hiebl (2015).

Methodology

A sample of 567 ISFs from 11 OECD countries were surveyed to assess their readiness for the commercialization of an innovation (Mazzarol & Reboud, 2011; Mazzarol et al., 2022). Table 9.3 summarizes the characteristics of these firms where it can be seen that they originated from a range of countries representing all sizes and a range of industries. The people interviewed were predominantly men and were either start-up founders or CEO managers. The majority (93.4%) of firms had past commercialization experience, and 43% had successfully commercialized over six innovations in the

Table 9.3 Sample Characteristics of Innovative Small Firms

Characteristics	Description
Number of firms	567
Countries of origin	Australia, Austria, Belgium, Canada, France, Germany, Italy, New Zealand, Spain, Switzerland, and the United States
Firm size	Micro-businesses (>9 employees) = 33%. Small businesses (10–49 employees) = 29%. Medium-sized businesses (50–249 employees) = 32%. Large businesses (>250 employees) = 6%
Industry sectors	Manufacturing = 34.9%. Services and retailing = 29%. Others (e.g., agribusiness, software, ICT) = 36.1%.
Growth rates three year (average)	Employees = 13 people. Turnover = €3.5 million
Respondent profile	Males = 89% with ages primarily from 20 to 65 years. Females = 11% primarily within the range of 20 to 29 years. Primarily CEO managers or entrepreneurial start-up founders
Profile of ISFs	Average firm had been in operation for 24 years, employed 70 people, with an annual turnover of €15.7 million
Successful new product development (NPD) over the past three years	NPD NIL = 6.4% NPD 1–5 = 50.6%. NPD 6–10 = 20%. NPD >10 = 23%
Innovation intensity	Average annual investment of 22% of turnover into R&D and NPD
Type of innovation commercialized	Product and service innovations = 72%. Process innovations = 16%. Market development innovations = 6%. Marketing innovations = 3%. Administrative innovations = 2.8%

Source: Adapted from Mazzarol and Reboud (2011); Mazzarol et al. (2022).

previous three years. Growth rates within these firms were also high, and their average investment of 22% annual turnover into R&D showed them to be highly innovation-intensive compared to the OECD average (Hirsch-Kreinsen et al. (2008).

All data were collected face-to-face with respondents, which assisted in the validation and reliability of the survey. The questionnaire assessed the firms' performances using 5-point Likert-type rating scales that ranged from 1 = not at all to 5 = totally, in relation to whether the firm possessed a particular capability or conducted a specific activity. On a 40-item scale, the key capabilities and activities were examined across four key areas: (i) marketing and sales, (ii) innovation management, (iii) resource availability, and (iv) strategic management. Each area contained ten items. Commercialization success was measured using a 4-point categorical scale assessing how many innovations had been successfully launched over the previous three years (e.g., NIL, 1–5, 6–10, and >10).

The relationships between the capabilities and activities database and the four categories of successful commercialization were examined using an analysis of variance (ANOVA) technique. Specific case studies were identified and selected from within the database for more in-depth analysis and examined using quantitative data techniques (Yin, 2014). These are used in subsequent sections of this chapter to provide illustrative examples of the role played by the firms' leaders in engaging key stakeholders and co-creating value.

Key Findings from the Survey

As shown in Table 9.4, from a *marketing and sales* perspective, success was associated with collaboration with customers in the commercialization process, which most research shows to be critical to successful NPD and commercialization (Farrell, 1994; Griffin & Hauser, 1993). Successful ISFs were also more likely to have researched customer ability to trial and test the innovation prior to adoption, which is important to innovation adoption and diffusion (Rogers, 1976, 1995). They were also more likely to have developed a good understanding of customer price sensitivity (a proxy for perceived value). Such customer engagement features in most NPD systems (Koen et al., 2002; Blank & Dorf, 2012; York & Danes, 2014).

Five factors were identified in relation to *innovation management*. The first was the importance of collaborating with customers to cocreate value within the NPD process. The other three factors related to the firms having developed formal NPD systems, capabilities to develop prototypes without outside assistance, and being strategically focused on innovation. Active engagement with customers in a cocreation process is well-recognized in the literature as important to commercialization (Appiah-Adu & Singh, 1998; Huang et al., 2002; Holger, 2002; Fernades & Remelhe, 2016).

Table 9.4   Key Success Factors in Commercialization among Innovative Small Firms

Area of activity	Capabilities and activities question item (NPD ANOVA mean $p < .05$)	Implication of findings
Marketing and sales	Previous collaboration with customers over innovations. (NPD >10 μ = 4.02; NPD 6–10 μ = 3.85; NPD 1–5 μ = 3.68; NPD NIL μ = 2.90)	Increased collaboration with customers is associated with increased NPD success
	Having researched how easily customers will be able to test or trial the innovation prior to adoption. (NPD >10 μ = 3.82; NPD NIL μ = 3.30)	Research into customer pre-adoption trials is found more among firms with greater NPD success and experience
	Having fully explored the most appropriate pricing strategy for the innovation. (NPD >10 μ = 3.82; NPD NIL μ = 3.30)	Firms with most NPD success more likely than those with none to have a clear pricing strategy
Innovation management	Actively involving customers in the development of innovations. (NPD >10 μ = 3.98; NPD 6–10 μ = 3.90; NPD NIL μ = 3.40).	Increased cocreation with customers is associated with increased NPD success
	Having previous experience in NPD commercialization. (NPD >10 μ = 4.48; NPD 6–10 μ = 4.32; NPD 1–5 μ = 3.78; NPD NIL μ = 2.85)	Increased commercialization experience is associated with increased NPD success
	Having the ability to fully develop a prototype technically without outside assistance. (NPD >10 μ = 3.76; NPD NIL μ = 3.20)	The ability to fully develop a prototype without outside technical assistance is a sign of increasing capabilities in commercialisation
	Feeling that the generation of new innovations is a major focus of the business. (NPD >10 μ = 4.45; NPD 1–5 μ = 3.94)	Being focused on innovation as the key strategic goal of a firm is a measure of success in commercialisation
	Having a formal process for NPD. (NPD >10 μ = 3.94; NPD 6–10 μ = 3.70; NPD 1–5 μ = 3.14)	There is a positive relationship between NPD success and formalization of the NPD and commercialisation process

(Continued)

Table 9.4 (Continued)   Key Success Factors in Commercialization among Innovative Small Firms

Area of activity	Capabilities and activities question item (NPD ANOVA mean $p < .05$)	Implication of findings
Resource availability	Whether the firm had identified sources of venture capital financing for the innovation. (NPD NIL $\mu = 2.88$; NPD 6–10 $\mu = 2.18$)	Firms with no NPD success are more likely to seek VC funds. However, VC funding is not easily secured for early-stage ventures
	Whether the firm had explored government assistance programs for small innovative firms. (NPD NIL $\mu = 3.63$; NPD 1–5 $\mu = 2.93$; NPD 6–10 $\mu = 2.81$)	Firms with no NPD success are more likely to seek support from government assistance programs than their more successful counterparts. This may reflect their lack of expertise in NPD and commercialisation
	Whether the firm's financial resources were adequate for the future commercialization. (NPD >10 $\mu = 3.80$; NPD 6–10 $\mu = 3.80$; NPD 1–5 $\mu = 3.37$; NPD NIL $\mu = 2.83$)	Firms with more success in NPD are more likely to have sufficient financial resources to commercialize their innovation. In turn, they will be less likely to seek VC funding
	Whether the firm's physical resources were adequate for the future commercialization. (NPD >10 $\mu = 4.31$: NPD 6–10 $\mu = 3.95$; NPD 1–5 $\mu = 3.69$; NPD NIL $\mu = 3.37$)	Firms with more success in NPD are also more likely to have sufficient physical resources to commercialize their innovation
	Whether the firm had an experienced project management team to work on the idea. (NPD 6–10 $\mu = 4.06$; NPD NIL $\mu = 3.56$)	Firms with little or no NPD success are less likely to have an experienced project management team than those with more success
	Whether the firm had the competencies to fully commercialize the project alone. (NPD >10 $\mu = 4.05$; NPD 6–10 $\mu = 3.92$; NPD NIL $\mu = 3.39$)	There is a positive relationship between NPD success and the possession of competencies to manage the commercialisation process
	Whether the firm had the technological resources to create a prototype. (NPD >10 $\mu = 4.41$; NPD 6–10 $\mu = 4.25$; NPD NIL $\mu = 3.85$)	There is a positive relationship between NPD success and the possession of the technological resources to manage the commercialisation process

(Continued)

Table 9.4 (Continued)   Key Success Factors in Commercialization among Innovative Small Firms

Area of activity	Capabilities and activities question item (NPD ANOVA mean ρ < .05)	Implication of findings
Strategic management	Having secured all necessary compliances and authorizations. (NPD >10 μ = 4.21; NPD NIL μ = 3.56)	Firms with significant NPD success are more likely than those with no NPD success to have secured all compliances and authorisations
	Having a formal written business plan for the innovation. (NPD NIL μ = 3.93; NPD 1–5 μ = 3.24)	Firms with no prior NPD success are more likely to have prepared a formal business plan for their innovation than firms with some success

Source: Adapted from Mazzarol et al. (2022).

Seven factors were identified within the area of *resource availability*, which reflects the common challenge of resource scarcity facing most ISFs (Rosenbusch et al., 2011). These showed differences between experienced and inexperienced ISFs. Firms with greater success in commercialization were more likely to possess the competencies and the financial, physical, and technological resources needed for their projects. The novice or less-experienced firms were more likely to be seeking venture capital (VC) funding and government assistance. These firms also lacked experienced NPD project teams. This focus on VC funding potentially indicates both a lack of financial resources and naivety about VC investment (Meglio et al., 2017).

Within the *strategic management* area, differences were found between experienced and inexperienced firms, with the former being more likely to have secured any compliances and authorizations, while the latter were more likely to have prepared a formal written business plan. Although formal planning is valuable, it is potentially less useful to firms engaged in highly uncertain and dynamic business environments than those in more stable and certain ones (Brinckmann et al., 2010). The less experienced firms' greater propensity to seek government assistance may also reflect their lack of experienced NPD project teams. Overall, these findings highlight the importance of customer engagement, knowledge management, and capacity building around capabilities for successful commercialization.

Case Studies of Commercialization Leadership

In this section, we examine three case studies of ISFs that have demonstrated brilliant leadership in increasing the value proposition through engagement with key stakeholders. These cases are drawn from the recent research undertaken into the commercialization practices of ISFs (Mazzarol et al., 2022).

Case Study 1 – Ethique, Environmentally Sustainable Beauty Products

Ethique is a New Zealand-based company founded in 2012 by Brianne West, a science graduate from the University of Canterbury, Christchurch. Its strategic purpose is to provide eco-friendly skincare and haircare products (e.g., face washes, hair shampoo) that are supplied in solid bar form rather than liquid to remove the need for plastic bottles and water use. For example, each shampoo bar saves the need for three 350 ml plastic bottles and 2.7 l of water. Using crowdfunding to raise the necessary start-up capital in 2015, Ethique was generating international sales by the end of the following year. Further crowdfunding was undertaken in 2017. By 2020, Ethique was producing over 60 separate solid bar beauty products that were being distributed internationally in Australia, the United States, Britain, Asia, and the European Union (EU).

From a business model perspective, Ethique has driven its growth predominantly via online marketing and sales. Its CVP focuses on eco-friendly, zero plastic, and low water use benefits without compromising the quality of personal skin and hair care products. This has been reinforced with certification as a B-Corp enterprise, with all suppliers meeting environmental (e.g., zero palm oil) and social performance standards (e.g., anti-slavery). It also donates 20% of its profits to charities and carbon offset projects. However, the company has specifically targeted end-user consumers who are most likely to be attracted to this CVP.

Commencing with online marketing and sales platforms, Ethique widened its sales distribution to include pharmacies, beauty and healthcare boutiques, department stores, and supermarkets. This involved the founder forging strategic alliances with large eCommerce platforms, online pharmacies, and major pharmacy and retail chains. By 2020, the company had its products sold via 2600 retail stores across 16 countries, a network that expanded to over 22 countries by 2024. To engage with its customers, Ethique has made significant use of direct contact supported by e-newsletters, blogs, and social media. This includes not just direct sales via its website but also customized advice for each customer, assisting them in choosing the most appropriate products for their individual skin or hair type. In addition, customers can earn points that offer discounts for future purchases, and a full refund within 14 days is offered to any customer who is unhappy with the product.

Ethique also enhances its CVP by developing close relationships with manufacturers, distributors, and retailers around the world, as well as suppliers of ingredients from Africa, South America, and the South Pacific, including cooperatives that provide employment and wealth creation within a fair-trade framework. These relationships require significant social capital formation and the creation of trust and co-creation of value across the supply chain. For customers who are attracted by both the quality and the eco-friendly nature of the products supplied by Ethique, it is important from the CVP perspective that they know where these ingredients are sourced, and the social and environmental concerns shown by the company in the management of its suppliers and distributors.

Case Study 2 – Memphasys Ltd., Biotechnology Brilliance

Memphasys Ltd. (MEM) is a small, publicly listed biotechnology firm from Australia involved in the commercialization of a proprietary technology that forms part of a medical device, 'Felix', that can separate sperm in order to facilitate successful in vitro fertilization (IVF). The technology is based on a patented cell-membrane (CS10) that uses electrophoresis technology to separate cells and protein to successfully separate the higher quality sperm able to enhance the likelihood of fertilization. The company's origins trace back to 2004 when the firm Life Therapeutics Ltd. was spun off from the parent company Granipore Ltd., a specialist in electrophoresis technology. The following year, NuSep Ltd. was spun off from Life Therapeutics, taking with it sperm-cell separation technology.

NuSep Ltd. was publicly listed on the Australian Stock Exchange (ASX) in March 2010, raising $5 million for the commercialization of its sperm separation technology. That same year, the company was renamed NuSep Holdings Ltd., and in 2012 it announced major plans for expansion into Asia via a therapeutic plasma business, PrIME Biologics. During 2013, Alison Coutts joined the board of NuSep with the specific task of commercializing sperm cell separation technology. Alison graduated from Melbourne University with a degree in chemical engineering, a graduate diploma in biotechnology, and an MBA with distinction. Prior to joining NuSep, she had extensive experience in engineering project management and strategy with major firms like Bechtel Corporation and the Boston Consulting Group. She had also been involved in co-founding ASX-listed technology companies. Following a restructuring of the NuSep board and senior management, Alison was appointed as the Executive Chair of the company in 2014. In 2016, the company changed its name to Memphasys Ltd. (MEM).

Since its foundation, MEM has grown steadily with strong collaborative alliances with academic researchers working within universities and commercial partnerships with other companies that acquired shares in the firm, as well as national and international partnerships with organizations that are able to assist with the commercialization process through sub-contracted production of components, or marketing and distribution. However, this process has not always been smooth, and it has required CEO Alison Coutts' skills in leadership, networking, and negotiation to generate the desired results.

Alison's success within MEM has been based on her social capital building and strong strategic networking. This includes close alliances with world-renowned reproductive biologist Professor John Aitken from Australia's University of Newcastle (UON) and the creation of a network of key suppliers, leading customers, and complementors such as universities. This includes key supplier Hydrix Ltd., a medical device manufacturer that designes and supplies the cartridge systems for 'Felix' device and became a shareholder in 2017, and W&S Plastics, one of Australia's largest plastics manufacturers that supplies all 'Felix' devices.

On the market side, there was a Swedish firm ANOVA Karolinska, which conducted field trials of 'Felix' and served as a key opinion leader (KOL) promoting the product. MEM has developed a global network of KOL alliance partners throughout Europe, Australia, Canada, China, Japan, India, Iran, and the United States, which enhances its marketing and sales efforts. Within the complementors' network, MEM has secured agreements with universities for both research and source of graduates to enhance their workforce.

According to Alison Coutts, her approach to developing these networks is one of a 'targeted search approach' that looks for the people needed to join the project team, and a word-of-mouth 'snowball technique' follows that generates the right contacts and leads to the best candidates and alliance partners. This process of building up the company's human resources while simultaneously developing its network of suppliers, research partners, and distributors required strong skills and capabilities in social capital building, leadership, and communication. It also required concurrent management of the firm's shareholders, R&D project teams, and end-user consumers co-creating value across all stakeholders through knowledge sharing and organizational learning, focusing on process, reliable data, and continuous problem-solving.

Coutt's approach to this process drew upon her background as an engineer and scientist, addressing problems as part of a project management challenge, looking at each problem in terms of how it could be solved, and remaining professional. She also applied it to the firm's marketing and sales, with the KOL network being an example. The KOL network comprises 'opinion leaders' within key organizations who provide word-of-mouth (WOM) support for the adoption of the new technology. This includes medical personnel operating IVF centers with whom MEM develops good direct relationships and regularly engages at conferences and other events. This builds trust, and the knowledge exchange between them enhances MEM's capabilities, leads to product development, and facilitates positive WOM for their 'Felix' product. Creating the KOL network required the development of close working relationships with these alliance partners, engaging them in a continuous process of knowledge exchange and co-creation of value.

Case Study 3 – ThinkSmart

ThinkSmart was an Australian firm that pioneered the leasing and financing of office technology and computer equipment to small businesses. The company was founded in 1996 by Ned Montarello, the son of Italian migrants who became an insurance agent after finishing high school and through that experience developed skills in sales, marketing, and financial management. He possessed strong negotiation and communication skills, as well as a good understanding of the financial sector. The leadership team of ThinkSmart was a board of directors comprising Ned Montarello as founder, along with Steven Penglis, David Griffith, and Peter Mansell, who provided expertise in legal, financial, and merchant banking areas. This leadership team provided Montarello with the expertise and advice that he lacked from his own prior experience.

From its establishment to the end of the 1990s, Montarello expanded ThinkSmart across Australia. This required negotiations with both major office technology retailers and the major banks. The ThinkSmart business model's CVP was that it offered an efficient and cost-effective way to bridge the gap between the retailers and the banks, while providing reliable credit to small business customers. The ThinkSmart system offered a plug-in point of sale (POS) system with credit checks and fast, on-the-spot financing for the customers. This product was called RentSmart, and the software system supporting it was CheckSmart. The CVP offered to small businesses was strong, but also to the banks and retailers.

In 1999, Montarello negotiated a joint venture agreement with Dixons, the largest computer and office equipment company in the United Kingdom. His decision to form a joint venture rather than a standalone business was due to the commercial risk of moving ThinkSmart into such a large market. However, by working with Dixons, the risk could be mitigated even if the returns would be shared. Nevertheless, to secure the deal, Montarello had to win the trust of the owner of Dixons and negotiate a deal that would be to both parties' mutual benefit. Drawing upon his sales skills and expertise in negotiation, Ned focused on making a direct pitch to the owner, a person with whom he had no prior contact. He called him from Australia, introduced himself, explained briefly what his visit to the UK was about, and secured 20 minutes of the owner of Dixons' time to present his proposal. The meeting was accepted, and after some lengthy discussions, it led to the joint venture with ThinkSmart being a minor shareholder emerging in 2002.

Montarello was happy with the outcome because, despite the minor shareholding, the size of the UK market was so large that it eventually dwarfed that of Australia. In 2003, ThinkSmart was established in Spain, and the company was publicly listed in 2007 on the Australian Stock Exchange (ASX), raising $204 million. In 2016, the listing was migrated to the UK, and in 2018, 90% of its shares were sold to US firm Afterpay Ltd., with the later conversion of the remaining 10% capital into Afterpay shares. These were exchanged for US shares in Block Inc., which acquired Afterpay in 2022 (Tuscan Equity, 2023; Lanyon, 2022).

According to Montarello, his success was based on surrounding himself with a strong advisory team and building trusted relationships with his key suppliers and leading customers. His opportunity screening was also important. When assessing a potential market or country to target for expansion, he used a 'biases and heuristics' framework to guide his decision. This focused on four key questions to assess risk. First, did the country have a similar taxation system to Australia or Britain? Second, did it have a large small business sector? Third, was there a high degree of technological change in the country to justify leasing, not buying? Fourth, was there a centralized credit bureau that could supply reliable credit-risk data on customers? He knew his product worked, but if any of the four questions was a 'no,' he would not proceed.

Conclusion

The findings from the global survey of ISFs and the three case studies discussed above highlight the importance of customer engagement and cocreation of value through stakeholder engagement in the commercialization process. This requires formal NPD systems, networking with potential sources of expert advice and financing (e.g., government support agencies and venture capital firms). Through these networks, the firm can access resources and capabilities. However, the firm should possess a clear strategic commercialization plan for the innovation and address compliance and authorizations required (e.g., patents, design registrations, industry standards, safety, therapeutic, and drug approvals).

All three case studies demonstrate the importance of entrepreneurial cognition and the leveraging of prior experience, social capital building, knowledge management, absorptive capacity, and dynamic capabilities in the success of their commercialization. Each of the three company leaders had different backgrounds, yet they all navigated environmental uncertainty and potential risk by relying on their prior experience, education, and application of biases and heuristics to effectuate a pathway. They worked rapidly through the absorptive capacity loop of knowledge acquisition, assimilation, transformation, and exploitation at the team level, while concurrently moving the firm through the dynamic capabilities loop of sensing, co-creating, seizing, and transforming their CVP and its business model.

For example, Brianne West focused strongly on her desire to create eco-friendly beauty products, leveraging her science education to help her develop products and form alliances with industrial chemists, packaging firms, key suppliers, and online marketing companies to enable her to develop products and deliver them to customers. She also actively engaged with her early adopters and built sustainable relationships with her customers via the firm's online platforms that provided two-way communication to gather voice-of-customer feedback and provide end-users with knowledge and information about the firm's products, how best to use them, and their impact on the environment.

MEM CEO and Executive Chair Alison Coutts successfully grew the company from a start-up to a global leader in IVF technology, leveraging her own engineering and management education, prior experience working within large firms, and other start-ups. Her ability to forge long-term relationships with key experts such as Professor John Aitken enabled MEM to gain the trust of significant KOL partners around the world, willing to undertake trials and provide a source of word-of-mouth promotion of the 'Felix' technology. Her own sense of integrity and humility as a leader served MEM well in its development of a key supplier network, such as Hydrix Ltd. and W&S Plastics, and research collaborations with universities.

Ned Montarello built ThinkSmart from an initial idea of how to solve a gap in the market for easy-to-use equipment rentals for small businesses, leveraging the knowledge and expertise of a board of directors who offered complementary knowledge and skills to his own. He also created a CVP that appealed not only to the small business customers but to both the banks and major retailers. This required a significant amount of personal skill in negotiation, trust building, and stakeholder management, which Montarello demonstrated.

His strategic growth of the company was guided by his use of biases and heuristics within his own entrepreneurial cognition, using a simple screening test (e.g., large small-business population, reliable banking credit system, appropriate taxation codes, rapid technology change) to decide whether a particular target market was worthwhile. Furthermore, he demonstrated that he could apply his interpersonal communication skills to form a durable joint-venture partnership with the owner of Dixon's in the UK, a deal that was to yield significant returns over the long term.

While having a good product or breakthrough innovation can be important, the key to successful commercialization, particularly for ISFs, requires the firm's leadership team to be adept in social capital building, entrepreneurial cognition, knowledge management, absorptive capacity, dynamic capabilities, and business model design and development.

References

Alvarez, S. A., & Barney, J. B. (2001). How can entrepreneurial firms really benefit from alliances with large firms? *Academy of Management Executive, 15*(1), 139–148. https://doi.org/10.5465/ame.2001.4251563

Amit, R., & Zott, C. (2012). Creating value through business model innovation. *Mit Sloan Management Review, 53*(3), 41–49. https://sloanreview.mit.edu/article/creating-value-through-business-model-innovation/

Appiah-Adu, K., & Singh, S. (1998). Customer orientation and performance: A study of SMEs. *Management Decision, 36*(6), 385–394

Aslan, H., & Vatansever, B. (2018). Efficiency of knowledge inflow structures: The mediation effect of task environment analysis. *International Journal of Research in Business and Social Science, 7*(4), 30–43. https://doi.org/10.20525/ijrbs.v7i4.905

Bhide, A. (1994). How entrepreneurs craft strategies that work. *Harvard Business Review, 74*(2), 150–161. https://hbr.org/1994/03/how-entrepreneurs-craft-strategies-that-work

Blank, S., & Dorf, B. (2012). *The startup owner's manual: The step-by-step guide for building a great company*. K&S Ranch Publishing.

Brinckmann, J., Grichnik, D., & Kapsa, D. (2010). Should entrepreneurs plan or just storm the castle? A meta-analysis on contextual factors impacting the business planning-performance relationship in small firms. *Journal of Business Venturing, 25*(1), 24–40. https://doi.org/10.1016/j.jbusvent.2008.10.007

Brustbauer, J. (2016). Enterprise risk management in SMEs: Towards a structural model. *International Small Business Journal*, *34*(1), 70–85. https://doi.org/10.1177/0266242614542853

Busenitz, L., & Barney, J. B. (1997). Differences between entrepreneurs and managers in large organisations: Biases and heuristics in strategic decision-making. *Journal of Business Venturing*, *12*(1), 9–30. https://doi.org/10.1016/S0883-9026(96)00003-1

Casadesus-Masanell, R., & Ricart, J. E. (2011). How to design a winning business model. *Harvard Business Review*, *89*(1/2), 100–108.

Cerchione, R., Esposito, E., & Spadaro, M. (2016). A literature review on knowledge management in SMEs. *Knowledge Management Research & Practice*, *14*(2), 169–177. https://doi.org/10.1057/kmrp.2015.12

Chesbrough, H. W. (2007). Business model innovation: it's not just about technology anymore. *Strategy & Leadership*, *35*(6), 12–17. http://dx.doi.org/10.1108/10878570710833714

Cohen, W., & Levinthal, D. (1990). Absorptive capacity: A new perspective on learning and innovation. *Administrative Science Quarterly*, *35*(1), 128–152. https://doi.org/10.2307/2393553

Cooper, R. G. (2008). The StageGate idea-to-launch process update, what's new and NexGen systems. *Journal of Product Innovation Management*, *25*(3), 213–232. https://doi.org/10.1111/j.1540-5885.2008.00296.x

Cooper, R. G. (2017). Idea-to-launch gating systems: Better, faster and more agile. *Research Technology Management*, *60*(1), 48–52. https://doi.org/10.1080/08956308.2017.1255057

Cooper, R. G. (2019). The drivers of success in new-product development. *Industrial Marketing Management*, *76*(1), 36–47. https://doi.org/10.1016/j.indmarman.2018.07.005

Cooper, R. G., & Edgett, S. J. (2005). *Lean, rapid and profitable new product development*. Product Development Institute.

Cooper, R. G., & Kleinschmidt, E. J. (1995). Benchmarking the firm's critical success factors in new product development. *Journal of Product Innovation Management*, *12*(5), 374–391. https://doi.org/10.1016/0737-6782(95)00059-3

Davidsson, P., & Honig, B. (2003). The role of social and human capital among nascent entrepreneurs. *Journal of Business Venturing*, *18*(3), 301–331. https://doi.org/10.1016/S0883-9026(02)00097-6

De Carolis, D. M., & Saparito, P. (2006). Social capital, cognition, and entrepreneurial opportunities: A theoretical framework. *Entrepreneurship Theory and Practice*, *30*(1), 41–56. https://doi.org/10.1111/j.1540-6520.2006.00109.x

de Figueirêdo, J. H., Meuwissen, M., & Oude Lansink, A. (2014). Integrating structure, conduct and performance into value chain analysis. *Journal of Chain and Network Science*, *14*(1), 21–30. https://doi.org/10.3920/JCNS2014.0231

Duhamel, F., Reboud, S., & Santi, M. (2014). Capturing value from innovations: The importance of rent configurations. *Management Decision*, *52*(1), 122–143. https://doi.org/10.1108/MD-03-2013-0169

Ebel, P., Bretschneider, U., & Leimeister, J. M. (2016). Leveraging virtual business model innovation: A framework for designing business model development tools. *Information Systems Journal*, *26*(5), 519–550. https://doi.org/10.1111/isj.12103

Echeverri-Carroll, E. L. (1999). Knowledge flows in innovation networks: A comparative analysis of Japanese and US high-technology firms. *Journal of Knowledge Management*, *3*(4), 296–303.

Elfenbein, D. W., Hamilton, B. H., & Zenger, T. R. (2010). The small firm effect and the entrepreneurial spawning of scientists and engineers. *Management Science*, *56*(4), 659–681. https://doi.org/10.1287/mnsc.1090.1130

Falkner, E. M., & Hiebl, M. R. W. (2015). Risk management in SMEs: A systematic review of available evidence. *The Journal of Risk Finance*, *16*(2), 122–144. https://doi.org/10.1108/JRF-06-2014-0079

Farrell, R. (1994). Quality function deployment: Helping business identify and integrate the voice of the customer. *Industrial Engineering, 26*(10), 45–45.

Fernandes, T., & Remelhe, P. (2016). How to engage customers in co-creation: Customers' motivations for collaborative innovation. *Journal of Strategic Marketing, 24*(3/4), 311–326. https://doi.org/10.1080/0965254X.2015.1095220

Forlani, D., & Mullins, J. W. (2000). Perceived risks and choices in entrepreneurs' new venture decisions. *Journal of Business Venturing, 15*(4), 305–322. https://doi.org/10.1016/S0883-9026(98)00017-2

Gao, S. S., Sung, M. C., & Zhang, J. (2013). Risk management capability building in SMEs: A social capital perspective. *International Small Business Journal, 31*(6), 677–700. https://doi.org/10.1177/0266242611431094

Griffin, A., & Hauser, J.R. (1993). The voice of the customer. *Marketing Science, 12*(1), 1–27.

Grupp, H., & Maital, S. (2001). *Managing new product development and innovation: A microeconomic toolbox.* Edward Elgar.

Hirsch-Kreinsen, H., Hahn, K., & Jacobsen, D. (2008). The low-tech issue. In H. Hirsch-Kreinsen & D. Jacobsen (Eds.), *Innovation in low-tech firms and industries* (pp. 3–24). Edward Elgar.

Holger, E. (2002). Success factors of new product development: A review of the empirical literature. *International Journal of Management Reviews, 4*(1), 1–40.

Holmlund, M., & Tornroos, J-A. (1997). What are relationships in business networks? *Management Decision, 35*(4), 304–309. https://doi.org/10.1108/00251749710169693

Huang, X., Soutar, G.N., & Brown, A. (2002). New product development processes in small to medium-sized enterprises: Some Australian evidence. *Journal of Small Business Management, 40*(1), 27–42.

Jarillo, J. C. (1988). On strategic networks. *Strategic Management Journal, 9*(1), 31–41. https://doi.org/10.1002/smj.4250090104

Jayathilake, P. M. B. (2012). Risk management practices in small and medium enterprises: evidence from Sri Lanka. Zenith *International Journal of Multidisciplinary Research, 2*(7), 226–234.

Johnson, M. S., Sivadas, E., & Garbarino, E. (2008). Customer satisfaction, perceived risk and affective commitment: An investigation of directions of influence. *Journal of Services Marketing, 22*(5), 353–362. https://doi.org/10.1108/08876040810889120

Kim, C., Lee, C., & Kang, J. (2018). Determinants of firm's innovation-related external knowledge search strategy: The role of potential absorptive capacity and appropriability regime. *International Journal of Innovation Management, 22*(6), 1850044. https://doi.org/10.1142/S1363919618500445

Kirchberger, M., & Pohl, L. (2016). Technology commercialization: A literature review of success factors and antecedents across different contexts. *Journal of Technology Transfer, 41*(5), 1077–1112. https://doi.org/10.1007/s10961-016-9486-3

Knight, F. H. (1933). *Risk, uncertainty and profit.* London School of Economics and Political Science.

Koen, P. A., Ajamian, G. M., Boyce, S., Clamen, A., Fisher, E., Fountoulakis, S., Johnson, A., Puri, P., & Seibert, R. (2002). Fuzzy front end: Effective methods, tools and techniques. In P. Belliveau, A. Griffin, & S. Somermeyer (Eds.), *The PDMA ToolBook 1 for new product development* (pp. 5–35). John Wiley & Sons.

Kotabe M., & Swan, K.S. (1995). The role of strategic alliances in high-technology new product development. *Strategic Management Journal, 16*(8), 621–636. https://doi.org/10.1002/smj.4250160804

Lanyon, D. (2022, 1 February). Jack Dorsey's block completes $29bn afterpay acquisition. *Altfi.com* https://www.altfi.com/article/8782_jack-dorseys-block-completes-29bn-afterpay-acquisition

Laperche, B., & Liu, Z. (2013). SMEs and knowledge-capital formation in innovation networks: A review of literature. *Journal of Innovation and Entrepreneurship, 2*(1), 1–16. https://doi.org/10.1186/2192-5372-2–21

Lee, V.-H., Leong, L.-Y., Hew, T.-S., & Ooi, K.-B. (2013). Knowledge management: A key determinant in advancing technological innovation? *Journal of Knowledge Management, 17*(6), 848–872. https://doi.org/10.1108/JKM-08-2013–0315

Lumpkin, G. T., & Dess, G. G. (1996). Clarifying the entrepreneurial orientation construct and linking it to performance. *Academy of Management Review, 21*(1), 135–172. https://doi.org/10.5465/amr.1996.9602161568

March, J. G., & Shapira, Z. (1987). Managerial perspectives on risk and risk taking. *Management Science, 33*(11), 1404–1418. https://doi.org/10.1287/mnsc.33.11.1404

Massa, L., Tucci, C. L. & Afuah, A. (2017). A critical assessment of business model research. *Academy of Management Annals, 11*(1), 73–104. https://doi.org/10.5465/annals.2014.0072

Mazzarol, T., & Reboud, S. (2009). *The strategy of small firms: Strategic management and innovation in the small firm.* Edward Elgar.

Mazzarol, T., & Reboud, S. (2020a). *Entrepreneurship and innovation: Theory, practice and context* (4th ed.). Springer-Nature.

Mazzarol, T., & Reboud, S. (2020b). *Small business management: Theory and practice* (4th ed.). Springer-Nature.

Mazzarol, T., & Reboud, S., (Eds.). (2011). *Strategic innovation in small firms: An international analysis of innovation and strategic decision making in small to medium sized enterprises.* Edward Elgar Publishing.

Mazzarol, T., Reboud, S., Clark, D., Moore, M., Malone, P., & Soutar, G. N. (2022). *Commercialisation and innovative strategy in small firms: Learning to manage uncertainty.* Springer-Nature.

Meglio, O., Li Destri, A., M., & Capasso, A. (2017). Fostering dynamic growth in new ventures through venture capital: Conceptualizing venture capital capabilities. *Long Range Planning, 50*(4), 518–530. http://dx.doi.org/10.1016/j.lrp.2016.09.003

Miller, C., & Swaddling, D. C. (2002). Focusing NPD research on customer perceived value. In P. Belliveau, A. Griffin, & S. Somermeyer (Eds.), *The PDMA toolbook 1 for new product development* (pp. 87–114). John Wiley & Sons.

Mitchell, R. K., Busenitz, L., Lant, T., McDougall, P. P., Morse, E. A., & Smith, J. B. (2002). Toward a theory of entrepreneurial cognition: Rethinking the people side of entrepreneurship research. *Entrepreneurship Theory and Practice, 27*(2), 93–104. https://doi.org/10.1111/1540–8520.00001

Olander, H., Hurmelinna-Laukkanen, P., & Mahonen, J. (2009). What's small size got to do with it? Protection of intellectual assets in SMEs. *International Journal of Innovation Management, 13*(3), 349–370. https://doi.org/10.1142/S1363919609002339

Osterwalder, A., Pigneur, Y., Bernarda, G., & Smith, A. (2015). *Value proposition design: How to create products and services customers want.* John Wiley & Sons.

Osterwalder, A., & Pigneur, Y. (2010). *Business model generation: A handbook for visionaries, game changers, and challengers.* John Wiley & Sons. ISBN: 978-0-470-87641–1

Osterwalder, A., Pigneur, Y., & Tucci, C.L. (2005). Clarifying business models: Origins, present, and future of the concept. *Communications of the Association for Information Systems, 2005*(16), 1–25. https://doi.org/10.17705/1CAIS.01601

Ostgaard, T., & Birley, S. (1994). Personal networks and firm competitive strategy - A strategic or coincidental match? *Journal of Business Venturing, 9*(4), 281–306. https://doi.org/10.1016/0883-9026(94)90009–4

Partanen, J., Möller, K., Westerlund, M., Rajala, R., & Rajala, A. (2008). Social capital in the growth of science-and-technology-based SMEs. *Industrial Marketing Management, 37*(5), 513–522. https://doi.org/10.1016/j.indmarman.2007.09.012

Pérez-Luño, A., Valle-Cabrera, R., & Wiklund, J. (2007). Risk, proactivity, and uncertainties as determinants of the decision to imitate or to innovate. *International Journal of Technology Intelligence and Planning, 3*(4), 343–354. https://doi.org/10.1504/IJTIP.2007.016305

Reboud, S., & Séville, M. (2016). De la vulnérabilité à la résilience: développer une capacité stratégique à gérer les risques dans les PME. *Revue Internationale PME, 29*(3–4), 27–46.

Rogers, E. M. (1976). New product adoption and diffusion. *The Journal of Consumer Research, 2*(4), 290–301.

Rogers, E. M. (1995). *Diffusion of innovations.* The Free Press.

Rosenbusch, N., Brinckmann, J., & A. Bausch (2011). Is innovation always beneficial? A meta-analysis of the relationship between innovation and performance in SMEs. *Journal of Business Venturing, 26*(4), 441–457. https://doi.org/10.1016/j.jbusvent.2009.12.002

Rothaermel, F. T., & Deeds, D. L. (2004). Exploration and exploitation alliances in biotechnology: A system of new product development. *Strategic Management Journal, 25*(3), 201–221. https://doi.org/:10.1002/smj.376

Sarasvathy, S. D. (2001). Causation and effectuation: Toward a theoretical shift from economic inevitability to entrepreneurial contingency. *Academy of Management Review, 26*(2), 243–263. http://www.jstor.org/stable/259121

Sedighadell, S., & Kachquie, R. (2013). Managerial factors influencing success of new product development. *International Journal of Innovation Management, 17*(5), 1–23. https://doi.org/10.1142/S1363919613500229

Shane, S. (2000). Prior knowledge and the discovery of entrepreneurial opportunities. *Organization Science, 11*(4), 448–469. https://doi.org/10.1287/orsc.11.4.448.14602

Sharma, L. (2019). A systematic review of the concept of entrepreneurial alertness. *Journal of Entrepreneurship in Emerging Economies, 11*(2), 217–233. https://doi.org/10.1108/JEEE-05-2018-0049

Shepherd, D. A., Williams, T. A., & Patzelt, H. (2015). Thinking about entrepreneurial decision making: Review and research agenda. *Journal of Management, 41*(1), 11–46. https://doi.org/10.1177/0149206314541153

Shepherd, D., & Patzelt, H. (2017). *Trailblazing in entrepreneurship: Creating new paths for understanding the field.* Palgrave Macmillan. https://link.springer.com/book/10.1007/978-3-319-48701-4

Shepherd, D., & Patzelt, H. (2018). *Entrepreneurial cognition: Exploring the mindset of entrepreneurs.* Palgrave Macmillan. https://link.springer.com/book/10.1007/978-3-319-71782-1

Sher, P. J., & Lee, V. C. (2004). Information technology as a facilitator for enhancing dynamic capabilities through knowledge management. *Information & Management, 41*(8), 933–945. https://doi.org/10.1016/j.im.2003.06.004

Teece, D. J. (1996). Firm organization, industrial structure, and technological innovation. *Journal of Economic Behavior and Organization, 31*(2), 193–224. https://doi.org/10.1016/S0167-2681(96)00895-5

Teece, D. J. (2007). Explicating dynamic capabilities: The nature and microfoundations of (sustainable) enterprise performance. *Strategic Management Journal, 28*(13), 1319–1350. https://doi.org/10.1002/smj.640

Teece, D. J. (2010). Business models, business strategy and innovation. *Long Range Planning, 43*(2/3), 172–194. https://doi.org/10.1016/j.lrp.2009.07.003

Teece, D. J. (2012). Dynamic capabilities: Routines versus entrepreneurial action. *Journal of Management Studies, 49*(8), 1395–1401. https://doi.org/10.1111/j.1467-6486.2012.01080.x

Teece, D. J. (2014a). The foundations of enterprise performance: Dynamic and ordinary capabilities in an (economic) theory of firms. *Academy of Management Perspectives, 28*(4), 328–352. http://dx.doi.org/10.5465/amp.2013.0116

Teece, D. J. (2014b). A dynamic capabilities-based entrepreneurial theory of the multinational enterprise. *Journal of International Business Studies, 45*(1), 8–37. https://doi.org/10.1057/jibs.2013.54

Teece, D. J. (2016). Dynamic capabilities and entrepreneurial management in large organizations: Toward a theory of the (entrepreneurial) firm. *European Economic Review, 86*(1), 202–216. http://dx.doi.org/10.1016/j.euroecorev.2015.11.006

Teece, D. J. (2018). Business models and dynamic capabilities. *Long Range Planning, 51*(1), 40–49. http://dx.doi.org/10.1016/j.lrp.2017.06.007

Teece, D. J., Pisano, G., & Shuen, A. (1997). Dynamic capabilities and strategic management. *Strategic Management Journal, 18*(7), 509–533. https://doi.org/10.1002/(SICI)1097-0266(199708)18:7%3C509::AID-SMJ882%3E3.0.CO;2-Z

Timmons, J. (1999). *New venture creation: Entrepreneurship for the 21st century* (5th ed.). McGraw-Hill International Editions

Tsai, K.-H. (2009). Collaborative networks and product innovation performance: Toward a contingency perspective. *Research Policy, 38*(5), 765–778. https://doi.org/10.1016/j.respol.2008.12.012

Tuscan Equity. (2023). *Ned Montarello, chairman and founder of tuscan equity and ThinkSmart.* Tuscan Equity Pty Ltd. https://www.tuscanequity.com/team/

Urbano, D. E., Guerrero, M., Ferreira, J. J., & Fernandes, C. J. (2018, June). New technology entrepreneurship initiatives: Which strategic orientations and environmental conditions matter in the new socio-economic landscape? *The Journal of Technology Transfer, 1*, 1–26. https://doi.org/10.1007/s10961-018-9675-3

Uzkurt, C., Kumar, R., Kimzan, H. S., & Sert, H. (2012). The impact of environmental uncertainty dimensions on organisational innovativeness: An empirical study on SMEs. *International Journal of Innovation Management, 16*(2), 1–23. https://doi.org/10.1142/S1363919611003647

West, J., & Bogers, M. (2014). Leveraging external sources of innovation: A review of research on open innovation. *Journal of Product Innovation Management, 31*(4), 814–831. https://doi.org/10.1111/jpim.12125

Yin, R. K. (2014). *Case study research: Design and methods* (5th ed.). SAGE Publications Inc.

York, J., & Danes, J. (2014). Customer development, innovation and decision-making biases in the lean startup. *Journal of Small Business Strategy, 24*(2), 21–39. https://libjournals.mtsu.edu/index.php/jsbs/article/view/191

Zafar, A., & Kantola, J. (2019). The effect of macro environmental and firm-level factors on open innovations in product development and their impact on firm's performance. *International conference on applied human factors and ergonomics: Advances in human factors, business management and leadership* (pp. 61–71), Springer 961. https://doi.org/10.1007/978-3-030-20154-8_6

Zahra, S., & George, G. (2002). Absorptive capacity: A review, re-conceptualization and extension. *Academy of Management Review, 27*(2), 185–203. https://doi.org/10.2307/4134351

HARNESSING THE POWER OF BRILLIANT LEADERSHIP

Chapter 10

Inspiring the Next Generation of Leaders

Alan T. Belasen and Nicole Pfeffermann

Brilliant leaders have the know-how to handle paradoxes and competing tensions. They invest in digital technology (structures, processes) to integrate the organization optimally while considering learning and development (employees, teams); they use strategic imagination to initiate disruptive innovation (markets, customers) while addressing the impact of their initiatives on customers, partners, and stakeholders (industries, competitors). The conceptual framework in Figure 10.1 captures these competing tensions and paradoxes and uses a panoramic lens to reinforce the significance of the dynamic interplay between these factors. This is where brilliant leaders unleash their inner capacity to effectively navigate disruptive times and lead through complexity in four important areas: strategy innovation, open innovation, cultural innovation, and business innovation.

Strategy innovation is a critical entrepreneurial activity that uncovers innovation opportunities and creates value by using new knowledge and capabilities to commercialize or scale new services and products with the potential to have a major transformational effect on the evolution of markets and industries. It is the cornerstone of forward-looking organizations (Varadarajan, 2018), and a strategic differentiator for achieving competitive advantage. Strategy innovation helps leaders harness the concentrated brainpower of organizational members as a catalyst for sustainable long-term growth and for enhancing brand value and reputation.

Microsoft's is aggressively investing in healthcare AI. The company explains its mission:

> Led by a team of experts in the fields of life sciences, oncology, pathology, technology, machine learning, and healthcare... [we strive] to transform cancer diagnostics. We make it possible not only to provide additional

DOI: 10.4324/9781003495307-15

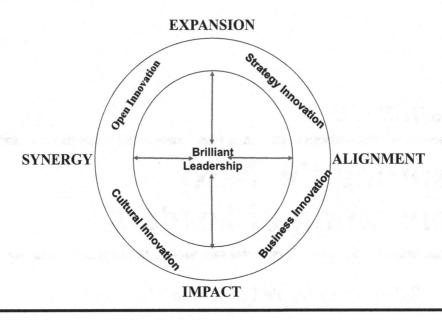

Figure 10.1   The Scope of Brilliant Leadership

information from digital slides to help pathologists perform their diagnostic work efficiently and confidently, but also to go beyond by extracting novel insights from digital slides that can't be seen by the naked eye. These unique tissue signatures have the potential to help guide treatment decisions and enable the development of novel biomarkers from tissues for diagnostic, pharmaceutical and life sciences companies.

(Forbes, 2023)

Other examples include Tesla's electric cars, which provided a more sustainable and environmentally friendly alternative to traditional gas-powered vehicles; Apple, which revolutionized the smartphone industry; Netflix, which transformed the entertainment industry; and Amazon, which disrupted the retail industry by offering an online marketplace where customers can buy and have delivered almost anything they need directly to their homes.

These companies are led by brilliant leaders with strong co-imagination and strategic visioning skills. They use dialogic loops to mobilize support for new ideas, reward learning and adaptation, and champion new explorations. Their leaders are disruptive innovators who master the ability to challenge the status quo, critically look for new opportunities, and create alliances that endorse new ideas, experiment, and scale the innovation to achieve sustained growth and market leadership.

Open innovation aligns with a culture that promotes the exploration of new ideas, joint action through entrepreneurial engagement, and a high tolerance for risk-taking behavior, learning, and adaptation. Brilliant leaders have the know-how and sensitivity skills to communicate to employees the value of learning from failure as an important part of improving and changing organizational practices (Weinzimmer & Esken, 2017). They encourage forward thinking, drive creativity, model collaborative behavior, and reward breakthrough ideas. Fostering an open innovation environment requires transparency, accountability, credibility, and honesty – qualities that influence trustworthiness.

Transparency enables trustworthy leaders to learn from others and make revisions to their existing disaster preparedness plans. Accountability reflects the importance of complying with regulations and communicating important information or pathways to stakeholders. Credibility reinforces important goals and interests and the need to be open to feedback from employees. Honesty enables the trustworthy leader to promote openness and participation in the decision-making process while holding members to high standards of truthfulness.

Trustworthy brilliant leaders acknowledge uncertainty, communicate with compassion, show understanding, and are empathetic. They embrace paradoxical skills to identify integrative solutions to problems and use mixed strategies of messaging, and navigate the seemingly competing tensions and demands in dynamic work environments. These mixed strategies include informal means of communication to promote cooperation and strategic visioning for leveraging resources and capabilities needed to achieve desired results. Messaging that appeals to collective values and the history of their organizational commitment and mission plays a key role in enhancing public trust and stakeholders' acceptance during major disruptions (Belasen & Belasen, 2019). When the communication is clear, empathetic, transparent, and frequent, internal dialogues are more positive, and organizational members show more confidence in their own ability to pursue innovation and, at the same time, trust the ability of trustworthy leaders to avert unnecessary risks (Belasen & Eisenberg, 2023). This is the art of brilliant leadership. Brilliant leaders empower organizational members, promote mutual respect, emphasize moral ethics and integrity, use dialogue communication, embed empathy and authenticity in their leadership style, and model the way by asking the right questions.

Procter & Gamble is an example of a highly progressive company that applies the concept of open communication inside out. Through its "Connect + Develop" program, the company partners with universities, startups, research institutions, and individuals to source innovative ideas and technologies to create new solutions in every aspect of business, from supply chains to products and technologies to in-store and e-commerce experiences.

P&G corporate citizenship framework places employees at the center of attention with shared goals and mutual commitment that value personal contribution, impact, and mastery. The company provides employees with opportunities to develop their skills and capabilities and enhance their abilities in line with P&G's goals and strategies. The company also supports the leadership potential of employees through impactful work, expert mentoring, delegated decision-making authority, and the opportunity to move across brands, businesses, and geographies. This next-generation operating model is a new way of running the organization with integrated digital technologies, operations capabilities, and agile structures. It is a new approach that prioritizes a customer-centric mindset that simultaneously disrupts existing processes, drives value, and improves customer experience and cost (McKinsey & Company, 2023).

Cultural innovation relates to open innovation by instilling the values of creativity, experimentation, high tolerance for ambiguity, and the pursuit of new ideas in agile organizational structures and processes, and capabilities designed to enable employees to quickly respond to changing environments. This agility is achieved through synergistic activities across functions, interprofessional collaboration, and joint action where individuals and teams are empowered to think critically, take risks, and challenge current practices to generate breakthrough solutions and implement innovation. Successful healthcare systems provide good examples.

Collaboration in healthcare involves complementary roles of professionals (e.g., primary physicians, bedside nurses, specialized practitioners, and other team members) who work cooperatively, share the responsibilities for problem-solving, and make the decisions needed to treat patients effectively (Belasen, 2019). In healthcare systems where care teams collaborate, patient outcomes improve by reduced medical errors and preventable complications (Belasen & Belasen, 2018).

Interprofessional collaboration bridges the gaps in communication by delivering pertinent information to the right individuals using mobile technologies to communicate in real time, thus improving the patient experience as well as the hospital's reputation (Belasen et al., 2024). The cornerstone of these interactions is electronic health records (EHR), a real-time, digital platform of patients' records that includes everything clinicians need to know about patients' history.

Hospital CEOs have critical roles in shaping a culture of innovation and in the development and retention of advanced technology. They encourage collaboration between hospitals and communities, develop effective financial strategies during times of crisis, support wellness programs for hospital employees, and drive innovation. With the persistence of COVID-19, hospital CEOs act as chief entrepreneurs who actively engage patients, care teams, staff members, and communities in contributing to and implementing innovation. Resilience is key (Belasen, 2022). Hospital leaders must be advocates who build a culture of resiliency and flexibility into their organizational structures and work on behalf of their staff and patients with higher levels of accountability and transparency. Some of the best 5-star hospitals were found to be led by expert leaders, and physician CEOs, who fit many aspects of the framework of brilliant leadership (Belasen et al., 2023). In fact, 13 of the 21 hospitals on the 2019 *U.S. News & World Report*'s best hospitals list, 62%, were led by brilliant physicians – including the entirety of the top 6.

Transformation Readiness

In addition to defining transformation ambitions, CEOs can also help assess the organization's readiness for change and plan to close the gap on any mismatch between ambitions and readiness. Four core dimensions help determine the organization's overall readiness for transformation.

Leadership. Some CEOs place importance on the leadership team supporting the transformation vision and having a positive attitude and willingness to transform. As such, CEOs should consider their C-suite's motivation and capability of executing the vision, with consideration whether it might be necessary to replace key individuals who are not ready to contribute. CEOs can focus on bringing C-suite leaders on board by being provocative, accessible, and transparent, and by demonstrating personal vulnerability, which may create internal engagement and tolerance for change.

Culture. Bureaucratic, reactive, risk-averse ways of working can be at odds with the collaborative, proactive learning mindset necessary for ambitious transformations. "Communications are as important as the actual transformation of the systems," says Owen Wilson, CEO of REA Group Ltd., a multinational digital advertising company that focuses on property.

A transformation-ready culture may benefit from metrics tied to organizational change. As an example, OhioHealth made a percentage of its leadership compensation contingent on the transformation's progress metrics. "It's not just tying accountabilities," says Stephen Markovich, CEO of OhioHealth. "It's tying the economic reward to the project's success. That way, if the project goes well, we all win."

Structure. If an organization hopes to operate differently, it may need to organize differently. CEOs can help lead the reorganization of teams, assignment of new roles, revision of incentives, strategies to collapse organizational hierarchies or layers to increase agility, and implementation of a new governance structure. CEOs also have an important role to play in securing adequate resources, which may need to be in place early to work out logistics before implementing significant changes.

Capabilities. CEOs may need to equip their organizations with nimbleness and scalability to harness digital technology for a superior capacity for change. It can also be important for organizations to have stability, or the ability to maintain excellence even while pivoting and scaling rapidly, coupled with optionality, or the integration of new capabilities perhaps from third parties to become more nimble, scalable, and stable quickly.

One of the CEO's most crucial roles in leading through disruption could be to stay ahead of the organization and be more ambitious than others about realizing the art of the possible. Says Panote Sirivadhanabhakdi, Group CEO of Singapore-based multinational real estate company Frasers Property, "The end game is making sure I drive a better organization that allows us to evolve even after me" (Deloitte, 2022).

Overall quality scores in physician-run hospitals were also 25% higher than those run by non-physicians. Moreover, while in 2019 only 5% of hospitals in the United States were led by CEOs with medical degrees, 11.3% of the 5-star hospitals on "Hospital Compare," a U.S. government-sponsored program, during 2019 were physician-led. And the *U.S. News & World Report*'s 2022–23 was not different: 65% were physician-led, and 35% of these physician-led hospitals also received 5 stars in the Overall Hospital Quality Star Ratings. Brilliant leaders center on continuous improvement efforts, alignment of AI-driven structures, innovation communication, interfunctional collaboration, framing constructive disruptions, and engaging others in innovation integration.

Business innovation through digital transformations can fundamentally change the business model as it requires new investments in technology and tech-enabled processes. However, in disruptive times, enterprise-wide transformation is quite challenging to achieve or sustain over time as evidence shows that even companies with successful transformations do not always capture the full financial benefits of these efforts (McKinsey & Company, 2021). To reverse this trend, leaders of successful companies shift from merely championing transformation to embracing it by embedding transformation in the cultural fabric of their organization and through their messaging and preparation.

Brilliant leaders have the skills to drive transformation by communicating its significance, and by aligning an organization's vision with the desired changes. They create a sense of urgency and high aspiration in the organization, build a strong alliance in support of the transformation, and model the way through ownership. These leaders engage personally in the transformative steps by working closely with individuals and teams and by building an execution discipline into the culture of their organization (McKinsey & Company, 2019). Brilliant leaders drive digital transformation with follow-through communications and success stories to keep the momentum going. They align brand and reputation, increase the organization's value proposition by optimizing the supply chain, celebrate results to generate energy, and engage stakeholders for valuable insights and feedback to sustain the digital transformation.

Profile Awareness

Brilliant leaders have an authentic personality, have the empathy to engage individuals and teams, facilitate co-creation, inspire, and commit to making significant contributions to their organizations, community, and the environment. Brilliant leaders are aware of their vulnerabilities and have the humility to defer to experts or delegate responsibilities to competent team members. Integrating vulnerabilities into the range of the leader's behavior increases their perceived authenticity and trustworthiness and reflects dependability that not only enhances leadership attributes of self-awareness and relational transparency but also encourages followers' preference to work with leaders who reveal their weaknesses (Jiang et al., 2022).

Self-aware leaders reflect on their personal strengths and weaknesses, are sensitive to how others perceive their words and actions, and act on feedback to take corrective steps to remedy their weaknesses so they can lead more effectively (Roberts et al.,

2005). Self-awareness leads to personal control and growth that help leaders play to their personal strengths in guiding individuals and teams to pursue targeted outcomes.

To foster the alignment between actual behaviors and expectations from others, assessments can be used periodically to determine how well leaders hone their skills and adjust their behaviors over time. Another option is to obtain feedback from relevant constituents (e.g., stakeholders, executives, board members, direct reports) using the same survey to assess the perceived behaviors of leaders. A gap analysis could then reveal focused areas for self-improvement. Ideas and actions for improvement or self-development could be prioritized to reflect inputs from others and eventually lead to a better alignment between the leader's self-perceptions and perceptions by others.

Respondents can answer the survey questions twice – as a manifestation of their "actual" behavior and second, as a reflection of how they would like to be perceived by others ("desired"). The 32-item survey includes a 5-point Likert-type scale response with options ranging from 1 ("I do not demonstrate this behavior") to 5 ("demonstrate this behavior to a great extent") to score the individual items.

Brilliant Leadership: Self-Assessment

The survey is aimed at assessing your self-rating on the brilliant leadership scale. To determine whether you are engaged in these behaviors, reflect on specific instances of past or actual behaviors ("actual").

Rate each item on a scale from 1 to 5 where:

1 – I do not demonstrate this behavior
2 – I demonstrate this behavior to a small degree
3 – I demonstrate this behavior to a moderate degree
4 – I demonstrate this behavior frequently
5 – I demonstrate this behavior to a great extent

To determine whether you prioritize these behaviors in the future, rate yourself again, this time by considering expectations from others that you specifically interact with (e.g., direct reports, people you coach or mentor, your supervisor, and so on) or by reflecting on how you would like to be perceived by others ("desired").

Open Innovation

1. I have the skills to initiate innovation
2. My behaviors are aligned with my values
3. Employees view me as trustworthy
4. I help employees understand the importance of change

5. I reveal my weaknesses to others
6. Others know where I stand on issues
7. I am open to feedback even if it's negative
8. I am interested in the feelings of others

Strategy Innovation

9. I promote entrepreneurial thinking
10. I pursue disruptive innovation
11. I encourage risk-taking and experimentation
12. I influence teams to drive innovation
13. I use crowdsourcing to generate ideas for change
14. I know how to move quickly and bring individuals and teams on board
15. I guide individuals to assume innovation roles in my organization
16. I drive linking technology across the value chain

Business Innovation

17. I know how to scale innovation
18. I am engaged in innovation implementation
19. Our stakeholders perceive us as an innovative organization
20. I promote the use of disruptive technology to penetrate new markets
21. I understand and support digital transformations
22. I value the human factors of brand affinity: cognitive, emotional, linguistic, and action
23. I promote investments in hiring, growing, and retaining talent analytics
24. I know what consumers in our target market think about our brand

Cultural Innovation

25. I embrace collaborative technologies that play an important role across digital transformations
26. I have a high tolerance for ambiguity
27. I identify resources for innovation champions
28. I reward innovative ideas and efforts
29. I engage in disrupting existing norms and conventional thinking
30. I influence my organization to empower change agents
31. I have the know-how to mobilize support for change
32. I have strong project management skills

Examples of current and desired profiles are provided in Figures 10.2–10.5. Figure 10.6 transposes the two profiles to provide a single view of the gaps across the four dimensions of brilliant leadership. The gap between the two profiles signifies opportunities for improvement.

Leaders whose ratings are relatively low on the dimensions of cultural innovation and business innovation (Figures 10.2–10.3) need to resist the temptation to make decisions quickly, even though the urgent pressures of the moment may push them into deciding too quickly. This deficiency is usually marked by a tendency to shoot from the hip, resulting in unilateral decisions without the benefit of input from affected people or all the available information. Higher ratings, however, signify accountability for actions and credibility associated with desirable outcomes, both internally and externally. Feedback from others can help guide leaders about possible remedies and continuous improvement.

A deficiency in strategy innovation (Figure 10.4) occurs when a leader is too inwardly focused, paying attention to operational and financial objectives, as well as to managing internal dynamics. While these are important matters and they cannot be ignored, the temptation is to act with a sense of urgency rather than strategy. Refocusing on purposeful ideas as the basis for strengthening strategic visioning, entrepreneurial thinking, and becoming the architect of change by embracing an innovative mindset can help bridge the gap between the actual and desired profiles.

Deficiency in open innovation (Figure 10.5), however, may prove to be the most difficult to remedy, since it relies on the leaders' emotional intelligence and the ability to use open communication and empathize with others despite facing highly stressful situations (Dilawar et al., 2019). A report by *Deloitte Global Human Capital Trends* (2019) showed that 80% of business and HR leaders worldwide believed they need to promote leadership capabilities with a focus on openness and honesty as great behavioral mitigators for building trust in organizations.

The ratings across the four dimensions of brilliant leadership are displayed in Figure 10.6. These aggregate profiles show a more 'panoramic' view of the differences between actual and desired values and behaviors. Self-improvement could be integrated into a leadership training and development program that more systematically can guide aspiring leaders to pursue qualities of brilliant leadership.

In the next section, we describe a brilliant leadership development framework (BLDF) that links self-discovery and self-development with a developed ability to unlock the power of innovation communication.

Brilliant Leadership Development Framework

Brilliant leaders step out of their comfort zone into an individual growth zone and inspire thought-provoking, interdisciplinary approaches and creative ideas. They are

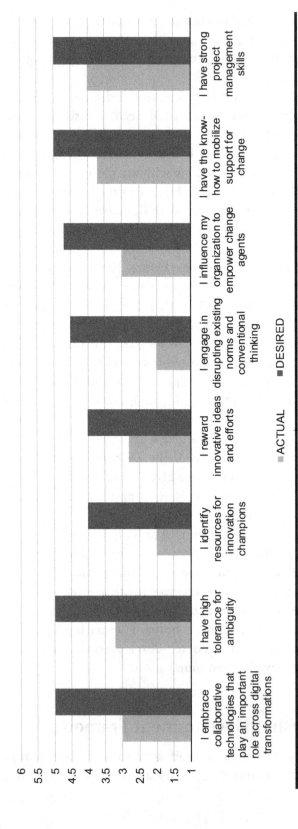

Figure 10.2   Actual and Desired Behaviors: Cultural Innovation

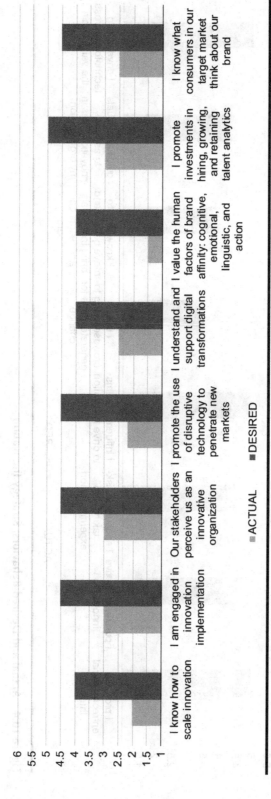

Figure 10.3   Actual and Desired Behaviors: Business Innovation

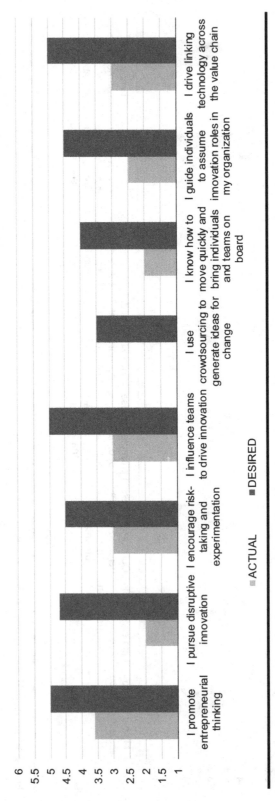

Figure 10.4 Actual and Desired Behaviors: Strategy Innovation

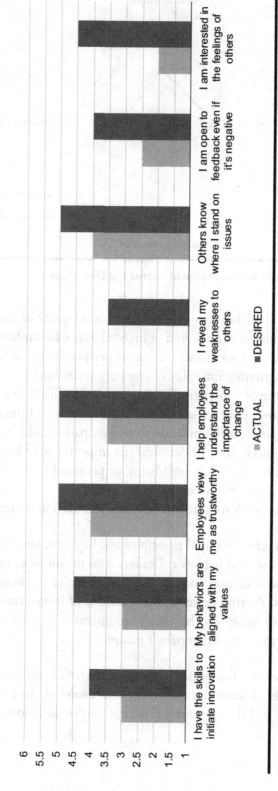

Figure 10.5 Actual and Desired Behaviors: Open Innovation

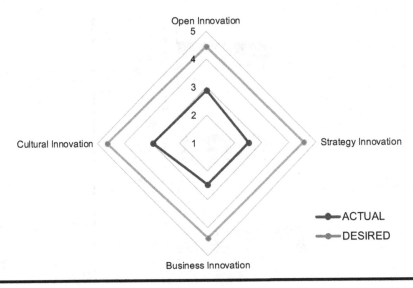

Figure 10.6   Brilliant Leadership: Assessment Across the Dimensions

open to new ideas from collaborative teams and early adopters of change and build a synergistic culture of innovation anchored in high tolerance for ambiguity that rewards growth-related experimentations, draws on diverse perspectives, and have the cognitive ability to integrate the dynamic interplay of competing tensions.

The brilliant leadership development process starts with self-discovery. Self-discovery and self-reflection lead to higher self-awareness and values for a human-centered, conscious organization. Aspiring brilliant leaders value empathy and compassion and lead with their minds and hearts. They understand the importance of higher values, integrity, and respect, and care about the well-being of people. Figure 10.7 delineates the competencies and stages of self-development.

It is important to start with six competencies as a foundation for brilliant leadership:

Ethical – Being ethical refers to moral principles and higher values that guide a leader's thinking, communication, and behavior. Leaders who prioritize ethics in their leadership style can enhance co-creation and co-imagination, solve the bigger problems, and develop visionary ideas. Putting ethics at the forefront of innovation means to recognize the effects of higher values and how they are linked to desired behaviors and to a transformative culture to create a company's future.

Relevant – Being relevant is a fundamental qualification of a brilliant leader. Innovation is a continuous process of learning, adapting, and evolving, and it is important to become more relevant, and thus an integral part of corporate vision.

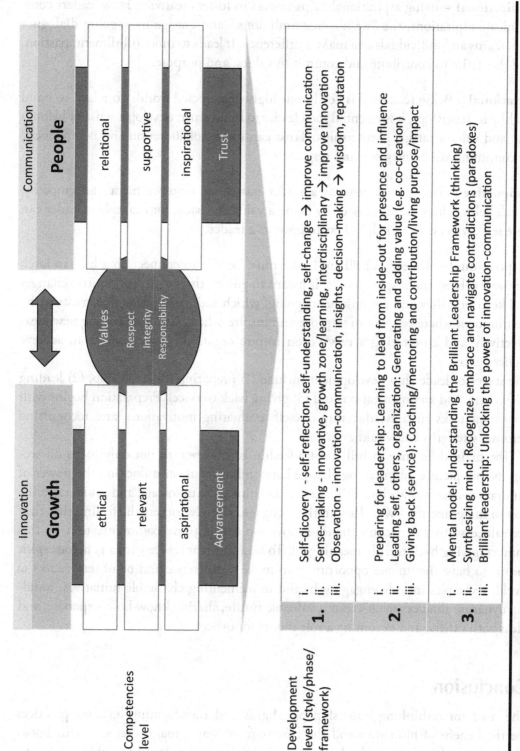

Competencies level	Growth					People			
	Innovation					Communication			
	ethical	relevant	aspirational	Advancement	Values Respect Integrity Responsibility	relational	supportive	inspirational	Trust

Development level (style/phase/ framework)		
1.	i.	Self-dicovery - self-reflection, self-understanding, self-change → improve communication
	ii.	Sense-making - innovative, growth zone/learning, interdisciplinary → improve innovation
	iii.	Observation - innovation-communication, insights, decision-making → wisdom, reputation
2.	i.	Preparing for leadership: Learning to lead from inside-out for presence and influence
	ii.	Leading self, others, organization: Generating and adding value (e.g. co-creation)
	iii.	Giving back (service): Coaching/mentoring and contribution/living purpose/impact
3.	i.	Mental model: Understanding the Brilliant Leadership Framework (thinking)
	ii.	Synthesizing mind: Recognize, embrace and navigate contradictions (paradoxes)
	iii.	Brilliant leadership: Unlocking the power of innovation-communication

Figure 10.7 Brilliant Leadership Development Framework

Aspirational – Being aspirational helps leaders to foster creativity. How leaders communicate aspirations, the "we-inspired-ambitions," and engage in ongoing dialogues with teams and individuals can make a difference. It leads to inner fulfillment, passion, and the desire to contribute and commit to values, and purpose.

Relational – Being relational is key in our highly connected world. To relate, to build healthy relationships, it is essential for a leader to build trust, develop a sense of belonging, and value strategic partnerships. Trust can foster collaboration and is influenced by communication, integrity, and respect.

Supportive – Being supportive as a leader stands for empowerment and empathy, which helps others to feel valued. By being a valuable coach, for example, a leader can raise self-awareness and help others to grow as a leader.

Inspirational – To lead, a brilliant leader must be able to connect on a human level, motivate others, and inspire people. It means to guide others to accept positive changes and keep promises and commitments going, which ultimately leads to a trustworthy environment where people can improve and inspire others. Communicating new ideas effectively and co-creating a new vision inspire organizational members to achieve higher goals.

The stages of leadership development include (1) preparing for leadership, (2) leading self, others, and an organization, and (3) giving back (service). Preparation begins with important tasks such as educating oneself, evaluating motivations, and recognizing personal strengths and weaknesses.

The main difference in brilliant leadership is, however, to not only focus on seeing the big picture and making change happen but focus on unlocking the power of innovation-communication. Brilliant leaders think, communicate, and act in a specific way to underline the "We.' They initiate, engage, and give others the feeling that they are valued so that they can enhance innovation and improve communication. In this context, giving back is truly meaningful. To be a brilliant leader with a generous spirit means to have the unique opportunity to make a difference and be of service to the world. Examples include engaging in and implementing charitable initiatives, building dynamic alliances to co-create a valuable future, sharing know-how, expertise, and ideas with others, and becoming a role model for others.

Conclusion

The need for rethinking leadership paradigms and transforming business practices for the benefit of humanity and the environment was a major theme of this book. The framework of brilliant leadership in this book was developed to guide strategists, game changers, senior executives, and aspiring leaders to navigate the digital era. It was also developed as a diagnostic tool to help coach and develop prospective leaders. Brilliant leaders have an authentic personality, the willingness to engage people/teams, inspire others, facilitate (co-)innovation, commit to making significant contributions to humanity and the environment, and be ethical and relevant. The framework is also consistent with the United Nations Sustainable Development Goals (SDG) of ensuring inclusive and equitable quality education, fostering innovation, and developing a lifelong learning mindset.

Chapter 2 centered on empathy as a critical leadership quality. Empathy takes effort, hard work, and commitment. Authenticity is a core component of brilliant leadership as well. It helps to build trusting relationships based on transparent and open communication. Chapter 3 extended these ideas by focusing on how leaders in human-centric workplaces promote innovation and creativity by influencing individuals and teams through a culture of shared value. Chapter 4 built on these ideas by exploring the concepts of trustworthiness and shared leadership, reviewing the dynamics of co-creation and non-traditional forms of collaborative culture, strategic visioning, and iterative loops essential for navigating the challenges of the digital era and driving purpose-driven innovation.

In Chapter 5, we underscored the topic of shaping a better future. The core principle of innovative value-driven alliances is to contribute to a better world. Brilliant leaders deal with eight fundamental contradictions in alliances' life cycles and their communications. The main value of alliances is in their collective capacity to make a positive change in our society. Anyone can be a leader by taking the initiative and asking others to join in.

Consequently, brilliant leadership is a shared activity—activities that people undertake together to shape a valuable future. Chapter 6 turned the focus on stayers, a valuable resource for an organization to co-create change and successfully innovate in today's world. Stayers possess a wealth of insights, best practices, and lessons learned and often serve as role models or mentors who can be invaluable during times of change.

Chapter 7 introduced the AI-Responsiveness Leadership Framework, which identifies and organizes how leaders' responsiveness and relationship to AI affect their own leadership style and effectiveness, as well as that of others. AI is an inextricable part of brilliant leadership's mental model. Brilliant leaders understand the importance of how generative AI affects the emotions, cognitions, and behaviors of individuals and teams. Chapter 8 extended this line of thinking by showing how the dynamics of disruptive technologies commit brilliant leaders to continuous learning and positioning their organizations at the forefront of digital transformation. A transformative strategy is a prerequisite for the brand's survival. Brilliant leaders should take advantage of digital transformation by introducing innovations that improve branding capabilities and performance.

Chapter 9 focused on innovation and successful commercialization by recognizing the relevance of soft skills to stakeholder engagement and knowledge-based, interactive communication. Brilliant leaders are equipped with a sense of integrity and humility and have effective interpersonal and negotiation skills essential for developing trust and promoting stakeholder engagement. They prioritize social capital building, knowledge management, and dynamic capabilities to succeed in commercialization. Entrepreneurial cognition and business model design skills are also important tenets of brilliant leadership.

If this book can teach you one thing, it is that the value of leading brilliantly is to harness the power of human connection, empathy, and meaningful communication to successfully innovate and directly affect employee engagement, productivity, and co-creation for a better future.

References

Belasen, A. T. (2019). *Dyad leadership and clinical integration: Driving change, aligning strategies.* Health Administration Press.

Belasen, A. T. (2022). *Resilience in Healthcare Leadership: Practical Strategies and Self-Assessment Tools,* New York, NY, Routledge.

Belasen, A. T., & Belasen, A. R. (2019). The strategic value of integrated corporate communication: Functions, social media, stakeholders. *International Journal of Strategic Communication, 13.* https://doi.org/10.1080/1553118X.2019.1661842

Belasen, A. T., Belasen, A. R., & Feng, Z. (2023). The physician CEO advantage and hospital performance during the COVID-19 Pandemic: Capacity utilization and patient satisfaction. *Journal of Organizational Healthcare Management.* https://doi.org/10.1108/JHOM-04-2022-0126

Belasen, A. T., & Eisenberg, B. (2023). Building trust for better crisis communication: Lessons for leadership development, Chapter 7. In N. Pfeffermann & M. Schaller (Eds.), *New leadership communication - inspire your Horizon* (pp. 93–110). Springer. https://doi.org/10.1007/978-3-031-34314-8_7

Belasen, A. T., Eisenberg, B., & Borgos, J. (2024). *Transforming leadership, improving patient experience: Communication strategies for driving patient satisfaction.* Routledge.

Belasen, A. R., & Belasen, A. T. (2018). Doctor-patient communication: A review and a rationale for using an assessment framework. *Journal of Health Organization and Management, 32*(7), 891–907.

Deloitte. (2022). *How the CEO's leadership in digital transformation can tip the scales toward success.* https://www2.deloitte.com/us/en/insights/topics/strategy/leadership-in-digital-transformation.html?id=us:2el:3dp:wsjspon:awa:WSJCIO:2023:WSJFY23

Deloitte Global Human Capital Trends. (2019). https://www2.deloitte.com/za/en/pages/human-capital/articles/2019-deloitte-global-human-capital-trends-.html

Dilawar, S. M., Durrani, D. K., Li, X., & Anjum, M. A. (2019). Decision-making in highly stressful emergencies: The interactive effects of trait emotional intelligence. *Current Psychology, 40,* 1–18.

Forbes. (2023). *Microsoft is aggressively investing in healthcare AI.* https://www.forbes.com/sites/saibala/2023/01/23/microsoft-is-aggressively-investing-in-healthcare-ai/?sh=9a28e823a096

Jiang, L., John, L. K., Boghrati, R., & Kouchaki, M. (2022). Fostering perceptions of authenticity via sensitive self-disclosure. *Journal of Experimental Psychology: Applied, 28*(4), 898–915. https://doi.org/10.1037/xap0000453

McKinsey & Company. (2019). *The wisdom of transformations: How successful CEOs think about change.* https://www.mckinsey.com/capabilities/transformation/our-insights/the-wisdom-of-transformations-how-successful-ceos-think-about-change

McKinsey & Company. (2021). *Losing from day one: Why even successful transformations fall short.* https://www.mckinsey.com/capabilities/people-and-organizational-performance/our-insights/successful-transformations

McKinsey & Company. (2023). *Introducing the next-generation operating model.* https://www.mckinsey.com/~/media/mckinsey/business%20functions/mckinsey%20digital/our%20insights/introducing%20the%20next-generation%20operating%20model/introducing-the-next-gen-operating-model.ashx

Roberts, L., Spreitzer, G. M., Dutton, J. E., Quinn, R. E., Heaphy, E., & Barker, B. (2005). How to play to your strengths. *Harvard Business Review, 83*(1), 75–80.

Varadarajan, R. (2018). Innovation, innovation strategy, and strategic innovation. *Innovation and Strategy, 15*, 143–166. https://doi.org/10.1108/S1548-643520180000015007

Weinzimmer, L. G., & Esken, C. A. (2017). Learning from mistakes: How mistake tolerance positively affects organizational learning and performance. *The Journal of Applied Behavioral Science, 53*(3), 322–348. https://doi.org/10.1177/0021886316688658

Index